THE NAZI RICH LIST

THE NAZI RICH LIST

THE EVIL PROFITEERS OF THE THIRD REICH

JULIAN FLANDERS

This edition published in 2025 by Arcturus Publishing Limited
26/27 Bickels Yard, 151–153 Bermondsey Street,
London SE1 3HA

Copyright © Arcturus Holdings Limited

All rights reserved. No part of this publication may be reproduced, stored in a retrieval system, or transmitted, in any form or by any means, electronic, mechanical, photocopying, recording or otherwise, without prior written permission in accordance with the provisions of the Copyright Act 1956 (as amended). Any person or persons who do any unauthorised act in relation to this publication may be liable to criminal prosecution and civil claims for damages.

AD011234UK

Printed in the UK

Contents

Foreword 7

Chapter 1   From Rags to Riches 11
Chapter 2   Respectability and Disgrace 29
Chapter 3   *Mein Kampf* and the Golden Years of Weimar 47
Chapter 4   Resurrection 65
Chapter 5   The Pendulum Swings 83
Chapter 6   Road to Power 99
Chapter 7   Masters of Germany 117
Chapter 8   The Big Guns Arrive 133
Chapter 9   Blitzkrieg! 151
Chapter 10 Annihilation 169
Chapter 11 A Huge Criminal Gang 187
Chapter 12 The Nazi Rich List 201

Afterword 219

Notes 223

Bibliography 232

Index 235

Foreword

On the evening of Friday 12 September 1919, Adolf Hitler attended a committee meeting of the German Workers' Party (*Deutsche Arbeiterpartei*, DAP) held in a dimly lit room at the Alte Rosenbad tavern in Munich's Herrnstrasse. At the age of 30, still employed by the German Army (Reichswehr) and living in barracks since joining up in 1914, after several years as a down-and-out in Vienna, Hitler had been appointed as a *V-Mann* (*Verbindungsmann*, lit: contact man, informer) whose jobs included fostering nationalist and anti-Bolshevik sentiments among the troops said to have been 'infected' by Bolshevism and Spartacism. The army's Information Department paid him a salary of 20 gold Marks a week, a lower-than-average wage. Earlier in the month, Hitler had been sent in his army role to report on the political leanings of the DAP at a party meeting in the former Sterneckerbräu beer hall. Very few people had even heard of the party but its programme was said to be 'radical, anti-Semitic and nationalistic'[1] and was therefore possibly worth a helping hand. Despite being there as an observer, Hitler could not restrain himself when one of the speakers advocated the separation of Bavaria from Germany. He stood up and gave a 'fiery' speech against separatism and in favour of the unity of all Germans, before walking out of the hall. Hurrying after him came the party's chairman, Anton Drexler, who had been impressed with Hitler's emphatic intervention and gave him a copy of his pamphlet, 'My Political Awakening'.

In his subsequent 'autobiographical' treatise *Mein Kampf*, Hitler recounts waking early the following morning and remembering the 'little book' he had been given the previous night. He began to read and his attention was 'secured [...] the moment I began to read, and I read it with interest to the end. The process here described was similar to that which I had experienced in my own case ten years previously.'[2] A week later, Hitler received a postcard informing him that he had been admitted into the German Workers' Party and was expected at the party committee meeting on 24 September. Although 'astonished' to have been asked to join a party in which he had shown little or no interest, curiosity and the memories that were 'stirred in his mind' by Drexler's pamphlet persuaded him to attend.

There were six attendees in addition to Hitler at the Alte Rosenbad. Minutes of the previous meeting were read out, as were letters received, for which replies were composed. The treasurer's report announced that the party's funds totalled 7 Marks and 50 Pfennigs (recorded in *Mein Kampf* as equivalent 'to 7s 6d in English money at par'[3]), which was kept in a rusty tin cigar box. Hitler was not particularly impressed, describing it as 'all very awful…', '… the worst kind of parish-pump clubbism.'[4] He noted that the party had nothing: no programme, no pamphlet, no membership cards, not even a party stamp, 'nothing but obvious good faith and good intentions'.[5]

Two days later, he joined the party.

*

On Friday 20 April 1945, Adolf Hitler and members of his inner circle toasted his 56th birthday in the relative safety of the *Führerbunker*, 'a sprawling, two-floor complex 50 feet beneath the garden of the Reich Chancellery in Berlin'.[6] But there was little to celebrate. That morning, the city suffered its second-last air raid – a particularly heavy one, as the Allies were aware of the significance of the date. There was a sense of anticipation as the locals came out after the raid for the daily queue for food. The Soviet army was approaching the city from the south and, though still at relatively long range, Berliners could hear the distant thunder of the Russian guns as they opened fire on the city. That afternoon, the Führer made his final public appearance in the Chancellery garden, presenting Iron Crosses to members of the Hitler Youth, some as young as 12 years old, who had shown bravery in the defence of Berlin. The deterioration in Hitler's physical condition was obvious as he made his way down the line of his young fighters. He was unable to present the medals himself and instead '… dragged himself along slowly and laboriously'[7] down the line of expectant youths with a pronounced shuffle and shoulders slumped.

He shook, some say as a result of the onset of Parkinson's disease. He held both hands behind his back, gripping his left arm with his right to prevent its alarming shake. He let it go for a moment or two to cup a cheek or tweak the ear of one of his loyal youngsters or to wipe a drip from the end of his nose before returning to the gloomy bunker.

On 24 April – the day before RAF Lancaster Bombers dropped 1,270 tonnes (1,400 tons) of bombs on Obersalzberg near Berchtesgaden, high in the Bavarian Alps, where chalets and mountain lodges belonging to the Nazi elite, including Hitler's Berghof housing complex, were located and six days before the Führer's suicide in Berlin – Adolf Hitler was probably the richest individual in Europe, with a fortune estimated to be worth around $6.5 billion.

*

Of course, political power does not come cheaply. Especially not back in 1919 for a 30-year-old former tramp with few friends and little money, with no profession and no political experience of any kind. But the German Workers' Party needed funds and Hitler took on the task. He urged the committee to arrange some public meetings but their timid approach drew few people. In October 1919, Hitler placed an advertisement in a local paper for a DAP meeting at Munich's Hofbräukeller during which he would make his first party speech. His words to the 111 people who attended clearly had an effect, as a collection of 300 Marks was taken at the end. Meetings became more frequent and attendances grew. Their first mass meeting took place on 24 February 1920 in the Festsaal, a big hall on the first floor of the Hofbräuhaus in the city centre, with seating for 2,000 people. Preparations were intense: posters and leaflets were printed advertising the event and outlining the party's new 25-point manifesto.

The hall was packed when Hitler began to speak. There was jostling, shouting, a 'hailstorm of interruptions', arguments, and 'violent encounters' between party supporters and those who came to heckle, '… communists or independents…' according to Hitler's account of the event in *Mein Kampf*.[8] But, as he explained the programme, he wrote 'the applause began to drown out the interruptions and the hootings… When I finally came to explain the twenty-five points and laid them [...] before the masses gathered there and asked them to pass their own judgement on each point, one point after another was accepted with increasing enthusiasm. When the last point was reached, I had before me a hall full of people united by a new conviction, a new faith and a new will.'[9] His movement was on the march.

The story of the rise and fall of Hitler and the Nazis has been written about, photographed, filmed, examined, documented, archived and researched in forensic detail for over a hundred years. Some areas of interest have been covered more than others. One aspect that has been under-researched is the financing of National Socialism, of Hitler himself and of the other individuals and companies who made huge amounts of money out of one of the cruellest and most heinous regimes in the history of the modern world. There are a number of reasons for this: first, money moves quietly, particularly cash, which also leaves no tracks and can be laundered; second, discovering information on exact amounts and the identity of the individuals who contributed is difficult and only began to come to light in the 1980s. Add to that the facts that the Nazis were prepared to use illegal means, such as bribery, blackmail and thievery, to access funds before and after they took power and that contributions came from German citizens as well as from other individuals all over Europe and the United States, and the problems become apparent. Of course, after 1933, the National Socialists were both the government and the state and had full access to state funds. This book attempts to tie these strings together and present an account, using facts, supposition and speculation, of who sits where on The Nazi Rich List.

Chapter 1

From Rags to Riches

In just over a decade, the Nazis (as the DAP soon became known) rose from a fringe political movement to a totalitarian dictatorship through opportunism in a fragile post-First World War landscape. Facing national humiliation, economic crisis and political instability, the German people searched the political scene for answers. Following the Wall Street Crash of 1929, the German economy sank into deep depression, unemployment soared and living standards declined. This additional economic failure was blamed on Weimar Republic democracy and the people looked for change. The economic situation continued to decline, and extremism became more popular as the German people desperately sought a solution. Into the void came Nazi messages of hope for 'Bread and Work', 'Blood and Soil' and 'One People, One Empire, One Leader'. Messages of blame were also used against the 'enemies' of Germany, such as Jews and communists, but also capitalists and intellectuals. The messages were extremely effective, and Adolf Hitler was appointed chancellor in 1933.

While working for the army's Information Department, Hitler had been quick to understand that in Germany in 1919, 'political parties were little more than tools for powerful interest groups'.[1] Once he had joined the DAP, he turned his attention to fundraising. It seems likely that the reasons for his joining this 'absurd little group', as he described the party in *Mein Kampf*, were twofold. Firstly, as a fledgling party with little character, it offered him the chance to influence its direction. Secondly, and equally important, he knew the party had a powerful political sponsor behind the scenes: the Thule Society.

Chapter 1

Corporal Hitler (right) was a dispatch runner in the 16th Bavarian Reserve Regiment during the 1914–18 war. He served on the Western Front, taking messages from command staff to the fighting units and winning two Iron Crosses.

The *Thule-Gesellschaft*, to use its German name, was a shadowy group founded in 1918 from the rump of the Germanen-Orden. Part of the *völkisch* (racial and nationalist) movement, its well-heeled members included lawyers, judges, university professors, university lecturers, aristocrats and the like. Ostensibly a study group for German antiquity, it peddled anti-Republican and anti-Semitic propaganda as well as notions of the superiority of the Aryan race. Its membership was for 'only those who could prove their racial purity for at least three generations'. They 'were admitted to the organization whose motto was: "Remember that you are a German! Keep your blood pure!"'[2] Its symbol was the swastika; its outlet was a nationalist newspaper called the *Münchener Beobachter* (the *Munich Observer*), but this was renamed the *Völkischer Beobachter* (the *Racial Observer*) in August 1919. Its most important project was the funding of the *Freikorps Oberland*, a regiment of some 2,000 ex-soldiers with close associations to right-wing groups in Bavaria and often called on to fight against communist units. In early 1919, members of the Thule Society included Karl Harrer and Anton Drexler, both committee members of the DAP. Other connections came too, courtesy of the army, who still employed Hitler, and the Thule Society, which was beginning to take an interest in him.

From the military, Hitler was introduced to Ernst Röhm, officially a captain in the army's District Command in Munich though in reality a man with much wide-ranging political power, including the organization of new *Freikorps* units and the stockpiling of thousands of weapons out of sight of the Allied Control Commission. Röhm, who hated the Weimar government and the 'November criminals' who set it up, took to Hitler immediately and joined the DAP, attending their meetings regularly, bringing new members, many of them ex-servicemen and *Freikorps* volunteers, and settling bills and other expenses using army funds. Other notable members of the Thule Society were Dietrich Eckart, a well-connected dramatist and publicist, Hans Frank, Rudolf Hess and Alfred Rosenberg – the roll call read like a '*Who's Who* of early Nazi sympathizers' according to historian Ian Kershaw.[3]

Chapter 1

ECKART AND ROSENBERG

Despite Röhm's financial support, little actual money changed hands. The party continued to rely on membership subscriptions and collections at meetings, both of which grew slowly but surely. Regular attendees gathered at meetings and at Hitler's Monday evening *Stammtisch* (get-togethers) at the Café Neumaier, in Munich's Petersplatz, where they would chat informally, sharing ideas and opinions on politics and other events. Many of these people were shopkeepers, craftsmen, dentists, furriers, railway men and even a papermaker. Having lived through war, nationalist hatred and revolution, they were desperate. Middle-class virtues of thrift and hard work were no longer valuable; inflation was eating away at their savings. Hitler was developing ideas of a return to social justice, a decent wage and a secure livelihood.[4] These were Hitler's most passionate supporters. Though they were not rich, they would pay for Hitler's food and drink and regularly give something for the party coffers. By the early months of 1920, the party's income came from subscriptions, donations, the sale of booklets, selling a tobacco called '*Anti-Semit*' and cigarette cards featuring a picture of Hitler.

By this time Hitler's speaking skills were very much the party's USP. The drama and the passion with which he put his points across were mesmeric. He was the real thing, an army veteran decorated with Iron Crosses, his arguments made sense, and his words were aimed at his listeners' emotions. A pattern began to emerge for his appearances. He would arrive late, to build a sense of expectation. On taking the stage, he would stand to attention and wait for silence. He would start with a low voice, encouraging people to lean in to listen. As he built the case for the point he was making, his voice would rise in volume and his hand movements and facial expressions would convey that point with passion. He would feed off the energy of the crowd, using repetition, alliteration and soaring rhetoric, speaking with a rhythm like an evangelical preacher. His body would rock from side to side, his arms gesticulating wildly. Sweat would pour off him, his face turning white, his eyes bulging as his voice cracked with emotion. He would rant and rave about the injustices done to Germany, stirring up the audience's emotional hatred of those who were to blame and envy of those who benefitted, often goading them into a state of hysteria. He would then leave the stage and the building, refusing to be photographed. In doing so, he hoped to create an air of mystery about his performance, encouraging others to come and hear his message.

Hitler honed his themes and his skills night after night in Munich's many beer halls and the crowds and collections began to grow more significant. As a result, he began to consider leaving the army to concentrate full-time on his political work. A key part of this seems to have been his acquaintance with two other like-minded individuals, Alfred Rosenberg and Dietrich Eckart. Rosenberg, a Baltic German, had arrived in Munich in 1918 as a refugee. Well-educated and with anti-communist and anti-Semitic views, he sought work as a political writer. Eckart was a leading player in *völkisch* circles and also a writer and publisher of a popular anti-Semitic, Pan-German periodical, *Auf gut Deutsch* (*In Plain German*), for whom Rosenberg began to write. Eckart had joined the DAP before Hitler and was immediately impressed with the party's new recruit. The two got on well, Eckart taking on the role of close adviser to the charismatic young man quickly rising through the party ranks.

Though Eckart was some 20 years older than Hitler, the two had much in common. Both had spent time living as vagrants, Eckart in Berlin and Hitler in Vienna; both blamed the Jews for their misfortunes; and both fiercely opposed the new government of the German Republic. Eckart had already expressed the opinion that Germany needed a strong leader to lift the country out of its misery. He had even listed the qualities that this man would have: he would be someone 'who can stand the sound of a machine gun', 'a former soldier who knows how to talk', 'he needn't be very brainy', but that 'he must be a bachelor, then we'll get the women'.[5] Hitler fitted the bill for him.

For Hitler, too, it was a perfect match. Eckart, well-to-do and influential, had connections. He could see that Hitler needed more social style and manners and to polish up his looks and dress if he was to take on the responsibility of political leadership. He lent him books to improve his written and spoken German, bought him some clothes and took him to dine in some of Munich's better restaurants. Eckart also began to introduce his protégé to his wide circle of wealthy and influential friends, many of whom began to contribute much-needed funds to the DAP. With Eckart's support, Hitler's confidence began to grow.

FRIENDS WITH INFLUENCE

According to William Shirer, in his days as an itinerant vagrant in Vienna and Munich and living on hand-outs from his aunt and by selling a few paintings, Hitler, 'never seemed to care much about money – if he had enough to live on comfortably and if he did not have to toil for it in wages or a salary'.[6] But appearances can be deceiving and, in truth, both money and art were going to play a big part in his future.

Hitler's fundraising efforts began to bear fruit. As well as Eckart, he made other new friends, such as Ernst 'Putzi' Hanfstaengl, Heinrich Hoffmann and others. Soon Hitler's circle of acquaintances began to include influential and rich members of Munich's social elite. He began to enjoy spending time in the upper-class salons of Munich and Berlin. He cultivated a number of 'friendships', particularly with women, who would invite him to their grand homes. He would arrive with his opinions, his pistol and his whip, present a huge bouquet to his hostess, kiss her hand and proceed to hold court, surrounded by beautifully dressed guests sitting on plush sofas in chandelier-lit rooms full of paintings and other *objets d'art*. He enjoyed the flattery and the adulation, letting the *Hitler Mutti* (Hitler Mothers) as they became known, take him in hand and introduce him into their polite society. He also began to enjoy their patronage, as well as their gifts of jewellery, clothes and other art objects, sometimes items of great value. Through his acquaintances, such as the Bruckmanns and Gertrud and Georg von Seidlitz, Hitler expanded his circle of rich and influential contacts.

A week after his speech at Munich's Hofbräuhaus announcing the DAP's new manifesto, Hitler announced that the party was changing its name to the National Socialist German Workers' Party (*Nationalsozialistische Deutsche Arbeiterpartei* or NSDAP), to increase its appeal to the urban-worker classes. Critics immediately nicknamed them 'Nazis', though Hitler and other party members preferred to refer to themselves as National Socialists. Although he was walking a fine line, threatening to discourage 'respectable' support from the upper classes by promoting the interests of the poor, Hitler knew that the fear of a communist revolution would tip the scales in his favour, 'giving both the masses and the German power elite what they wanted at the same time'.[7]

THE KAPP PUTSCH

Political unrest in Germany prompted by the new government's 'capitulation' at Versailles continued in the early months of 1920. In 1919, it had been the turn of the communists to rebel, but the movement was violently suppressed by right-wing *Freikorps*. The terms of the treaty included drastic reductions to the army and the banning of volunteer paramilitary groups. The deadline for these restrictions was 31 March 1920. On 10 March, right-wing militarist General Walther Lüttwitz met President Ebert and Foreign Minister Gustav Noske to demand the dissolution of the National Assembly and new elections. His demands were rejected. On 12 March, a brigade of *Freikorps*, led by Hermann Ehrhardt and supported by some branches of the army, marched into Berlin to occupy the government buildings in the city centre with the goal of overthrowing the republic and doing away with the terms of peace established at Versailles. The coup had been masterminded by Lüttwitz, following his dismissal by Noske for refusing to disband Ehrhardt's brigade. Lüttwitz, ex-General Ludendorff and German Fatherland Party (DVP) member Wolfgang Kapp joined Ehrhardt in Berlin, occupied the government quarter and formed a provisional government in what became known as the Kapp Putsch. Ebert and his cabinet fled to Dresden.

However, with little popular support for the putsch, government bureaucrats simply refused to co-operate. The regular army announced that it would neither fight against the *Freikorps* nor take up arms in favour of Kapp's agenda. A general strike was called by the legitimate government and the unions and left-wing parties all joined, bringing the country to a standstill and preventing Kapp and his fellow putschists from governing. He resigned on 17 March and Lüttwitz followed suit the next day.

Chapter 1

HITLER'S POLITICAL CAREER BEGINS

During the height of the coup, Captain Karl Mayr, of the army's Information Department, decided to send liaison officers to Berlin to inform Kapp about the reaction to the putsch in Munich. He chose Hitler and Dietrich Eckart for the job, but poor weather had delayed the military plane's flight, and they arrived just as Kapp had resigned. However, Eckart ensured the trip was not wasted by introducing Hitler to some more wealthy potential benefactors, including the Bechsteins – piano manufacturer Carl and his wife Helene. Helene was particularly taken with Hitler and took him under her wing. It was his first introduction to Germany's highest social circle. In time, Frau Bechstein began to contribute large sums to the party and to persuade her rich friends to do likewise. Other connections were established, too, with north German right-wing groups, *Freikorps* leaders, nationalist groups such as the veterans' association and the Stahlhelm (Steel Helmets), many of whom were supported and funded by extreme right-wing business interests. Hitler was also introduced to General Ludendorff and Ernst von Borsig, head of a major German locomotive manufacturer.

Further emboldened by his successful trip, Hitler resigned from the army on 1 April to dedicate himself to politics. He moved into a one-room apartment in Thierschstrasse, Munich. His tiny room – furnished only with a bed, a table and chair, and a bookshelf, and decorated with a few of his drawings and paintings – reflected his spartan existence. However, party members' eyebrows were raised when he bought his first car. He was not paid a salary; he ate little unless members of the party took him to dinner; and he often wore the same clothes. The first car was soon disposed of, and he bought another one. He felt that being seen driving to meetings would give him an advantage over Marxist speakers, who travelled on foot or by tram. It did, but it also raised concerns among some in the party as to how Hitler financed himself.

The summer of 1920 was a busy one for Hitler and the party. He spoke at several meetings a week, which attracted audiences of up to 400 people. Collections averaged around 1,200 Marks, of which Hitler would have received a 'speaker's fee' of somewhere between 20 and 30 Marks a week. He introduced

Hitler's speechmaking skills, honed in the beerhalls of Munich, held the keys to winning the hearts and minds of the people who heard him. By the time he addressed the third Nazi Party rally, in Nuremberg in 1927, his message had a greater power than ever before.

the swastika, printed in black in a white circle on a blood-red flag, as the party's symbol. This was not unique to the NSDAP: it was used by a number of far-right groups, such as the German-Racial Defence and Defiance League, as well as the Thule Society. Hitler favoured it, once describing it as 'like a blazing torch'.[8] It certainly fitted in with the raucous atmosphere of the meetings. They were not boring. They were fun, rowdy, noisy, like a football crowd with revivalist fervour. Hitler was developing his style and his themes, rabble-rousing against Jewish merchants who were putting up prices and profiteering. He aimed to unite left and right, against Jews, social democrats and communists, almost as though he was trying to replace class with race.

FORMATION OF THE *STURMABTEILUNG*

Another growing feature of these meetings was violence. Hitler's words and the manner in which he delivered them were designed to stoke up hatred, 'the hatred that was so deeply embedded in himself'.[9] There was nothing much new in what he said; in Munich alone there were over a dozen other right-wing *völkisch* parties, but it was the way he said it that had such an effect. Of course, the crowds that came to hear and see him talk included his supporters and his enemies. With beer being served and emotions being stirred, conflict was a logical conclusion. Hitler was quick to realize the need for security, not only for personal protection but as an additional symbol to arouse the crowd and give his supporters in it 'a sense of power over the weak'.[10] At first, ex-servicemen from the *Freikorps* were employed to deal with hecklers, doling out punches and beatings to those who would not shut up, before throwing them out on to the street.

As the crowds grew bigger, so did the need for more organized security, and a 'hall security' group was formed. This was renamed in 1920 as the 'Gymnastics and Sports Division' of the party, to escape sanction by the Berlin government. Members wore brown uniforms, breeches, jackboots and caps. Their ranks were swelled in August that year when Ehrhardt brought his former *Freikorps* to join up in a deal made with Ernst Röhm. By now, Hitler was dealing with high political stakes. Under the 'protection' of Gustav Ritter von Kahr, leader of the Bavarian government, Ehrhardt, in his role as *Freikorps* commander, had organized assassination squads to carry out political murders of Republican politicians all over Germany, including the 'November criminal' Matthias Erzberger. Röhm, a career soldier who had loved his time in World War I trenches, had joined the Bavarian War Ministry when an injury sustained at Verdun forced him to abandon active service. In his role as a supply officer, Röhm had built up connections both within the army and the paramilitary and nationalist organizations of the Bavarian extreme right. Approving Hitler's idea to develop the hall security squad into a paramilitary organization, Röhm began to use his connections to help, both with funding and access to weaponry and other illegal equipment.

In the autumn of 1921, a group of some 300, now trained as a fighting unit and as political activists, was officially renamed the *Sturmabteilung*, from which the nickname SA derived. Commanded by Johann Klintzich, a veteran of Ehrhardt's *Freikorps* and under suspicion for the murder of Walther Rathenau, the Jewish Reich foreign minister who helped ratify the Treaty of Versailles, their first actions were to disrupt rival political meetings. One such meeting, at the Löwenbräukeller, where his men stormed the stage and prevented a prospective Bavarian federalist speaker from taking the platform by beating him up, saw Hitler arrested, charged and sentenced to three months in prison. Another meeting, at the Hofbräuhaus in November, saw a pitched battle between hundreds of beered-up 'Reds', brought in from local factories for the occasion, and a small force of fewer than 50 'order troops'. Hitler recounts the story with great pride in *Mein Kampf,* describing how he spoke at length as his audience sank their litres of beer. Then, following an arranged signal, '... the hall was filled with a yelling and shrieking mob. […] The dance had hardly begun when my Storm Troops, as they were called from that day onwards, launched their attack. Like wolves they threw themselves on the enemy again and again in parties of eight or ten and began steadily to thrash them out of the hall.'[11]

VÖLKISCHER BEOBACHTER

December 1920 marked a watershed moment for the National Socialist Party with the purchase of the publisher Eher Verlag and of its right-wing, anti-Semitic newspaper the *Völkischer Beobachter.* Controlled by the Thule Society, the paper's circulation was dwindling and its debts were mounting. A rumour spread that it was in danger of falling into Bavarian separatists' hands. Hitler and Anton Drexler, keen on the wider publicity that the newspaper would offer the party, moved quickly to acquire the 120,000 Marks needed for the purchase. Eckart managed to persuade General Ritter von Epp to loan them half the money, no doubt from secret army funds, while Hitler approached another of Eckart's contacts, Dr Gottfried Grandel, a chemical factory owner in Augsburg, for the remainder. Loans and debts were settled by two prominent

Chapter 1

female members of the Thule Society, Käthe Bierbaumer and Dora Kunze, and by 17 December Anton Drexler was the official owner and Dietrich Eckart was the editor of a newspaper with a circulation of 7,000. On Christmas Day, a note in the paper announced that it had become the official newspaper of the Nazi Party.

Eckart brought journalistic experience to the paper and with it the writer and party member Alfred Rosenberg. Rosenberg, who had arrived in Munich at the end of World War I as an anti-Semite with a hatred of Bolshevism, was an intellectual and an ideologue; he had read Houston Stewart Chamberlain, Arthur de Gobineau and Friedrich Nietzsche and attributed the Bolshevik and German revolutions to the Jews, as evidence of an international Jewish plot for world domination. He outlined his theories regularly in articles for the *Beobachter*, on racial theory, Jewish persecution, *Lebensraum* ('living-space') and 'degenerate' art, all of which became key parts of Nazi ideology. Together, Eckart and Rosenberg oversaw an increase in the paper's popularity, and it was expanded from a twice-weekly to a daily publication in 1923. Following Eckart's death from alcoholism in December that year, Rosenberg took over the editorship.

According to Hitler's own account, early in 1921 he had a fortuitous meeting with a former army colleague, Max Amann, on a busy street in Munich. Amann, described by William Shirer as 'a tough, uncouth character', had been Hitler's regimental sergeant-major, but they had not seen each other since the war. Hitler was impressed with his old colleague's energy and obvious intelligence and the fact that he had a good job in a mortgage bank, and suggested that he join the NSDAP as its full-time business manager. Amann was hesitant at the thought of giving up his career path and generous pension but finally bowed in the face of Hitler's powers of persuasion. It seems likely that there was a connection between Amann's membership of the Thule Society, their sanction of the sale of their newspaper to the Nazis and Amann's subsequent appointment as the manager of the party's business and publishing interests. However, Amann was a great success, bringing order to the finances of both. He also took on the role of Hitler's 'money bag', managing his personal finances.

Amann's business activities, which were well-known to include bullying and intimidation, were hugely successful.

EXPANDING CONNECTIONS

Party membership numbers improved following the purchase of the newspaper, with some 3,000 people registered by July 1921, but money was still short. Hitler and Eckart travelled to Berlin that summer on a fundraising mission. It was the perfect time for such a mission, as Germans were outraged at the huge and punitive reparations that had been imposed on them by the Paris Conference at the end of January and there were increasing signs of another communist uprising. But they had other reasons for their journey, too. There had been talk the previous year of a merger between the NSDAP and the DSP (*Deutschsozialistische Partei* or German-Socialist Party). There was reason in this suggestion: the two parties had much in common, and the DSP had a big following, particularly in north Germany, which the Nazis did not. But Hitler was outraged at what he saw as an attack on his leadership and threatened to resign, as a result of which negotiations collapsed. He intended to go in search of support among north German right-wing leaders.

In terms of financial and other connections, the trip was a success. Hitler stayed at the Bechstein villa, met noted nationalist leader Count Reventlow, the *Freikorps* leader Walther Stennes and Count Yorck von Wartenburg. Dr Emil Gansser, an executive of the electrical engineering company Siemens & Halske, arranged for him to speak to an audience of military, political and diplomatic leaders (Junkers) at the National Club, where he 'made a favourable impression'.[12] Perhaps the most influential connection he made was with Admiral Schröder, former commander of the German Marine Corps, who became one of the first high-ranking officers to join the NSDAP. Influential in naval circles, Schröder was also a member of the Thule Society and a useful conduit for representing Hitler's ideas among the Prussian upper classes in Berlin.

The navy, with most of its officers from north Germany, was firmly in favour of a united Germany. The army, however, was split in two with the nationalist High Command based in Berlin taking its orders from the official government, and its Bavarian regiments, with Bavarian officers, answering to the government in Munich where separatist ideas were still popular. A struggle developed for influence over Hitler and his fast-growing movement. On one side was the Bavarian army, led by von Kahr and General von Lossow, who wanted his support against the Marxist Social Democrats in the event of Bavarian independence. On the other were the nationalist Thule Society, the navy and the government in Berlin, who wanted to keep Bavaria in the Reich and felt that Hitler could help that happen. This put him in a favourable position: with influential connections in both the army and the navy it seems likely that he was able to access funds from both.

REVOLT!

The trip to Berlin, however, was interrupted by news from Munich that Dr Otto Dickel of the *völkisch* German Workers' Community (*Deutsche Werkgemeinschaft* or DWG), whose new book had been favourably reviewed in the *Völkischer Beobachter*, had been invited to speak by the NSDAP. In Hitler's absence, Dickel's firebrand speeches had gone down well and reignited the possibility of a merger with his party, which was popular in Augsburg and Nuremberg. Hitler arrived back in Munich just in time to appear at a meeting between representatives of the two parties. His behaviour was appalling: he raged, shouted and sulked before storming out. When he had gone, the NSDAP delegates announced that they would put Dickel's proposed loose confederation between them to the full party committee. When Hitler heard the news, he resigned. This behaviour was to form a pattern in his political life: when he did not get his way, he would lose his temper and threaten to quit.

It was clear that he had enemies in the party, fed up with his demands, histrionics and bullying tactics. Despite this, the party committee decided they could not do without him, agreeing to his conditions for rejoining, which centred on confirming security against future leadership challenges. Encouraged by this turn of events, Hitler made a triumphant sell-out appearance at the 6,000-seater Circus Krone in Munich on 20 July. A few days later an anonymous pamphlet appeared in the city, criticizing his leadership and his 'lust for power'. It also demanded to know where he got his money from and how often he was seen consorting with women. The leaflet, entitled *'Adolf Hitler – Verräter?'* ('Adolf Hitler – Traitor?') was featured on placards around the city and was reprinted in at least two newspapers. But he had built up a head of steam. On 29 July, at a specially convened members' meeting at the Hofbräuhaus, a vote was taken on his reinstatement and passed by 553 votes to one. Hitler was duly installed as first chairman, with 'almost absolute powers', replacing Drexler, who was appointed 'honorary chairman' with none.[13]

HITLER'S GANG

In November 1921, the National Socialist Party moved its headquarters to new offices in Munich's Corneliusstrasse, near the Gärtnerplatz, an address more suited to the rapidly expanding party. Within six months, the party would employ 13 salaried staff. By this time, Hitler's group of supportive acolytes, who met regularly at the Café Heck, was also expanding. Along with Eckart and Rosenberg came Rudolph Hess, also a member of the Thule Society, whom Hitler had met in 1920 and with whom he shared a passion for anti-Semitism. They were often joined by another member of the Thule Society, Hans Frank, a *Freikorps* fighter, and later a doctor and a lawyer. He was obsessed with brutal violence and was converted to Nazism after hearing Hitler speak in January 1920.

Others too brought new, important connections and, most importantly, money. Ernst 'Putzi' Hanfstaengl, a wealthy American socialite art dealer and publisher, was also converted having heard Hitler speak, particularly admiring his anti-communist views. In turn, the socially awkward Hitler was impressed by Hanfstaengl's easy sophistication, his skills playing Wagner on the piano and his endless list of influential friends among Munich's social elite. Soon after they met, Hanfstaengl gave the party an interest-free loan of a thousand dollars, his share of the sale of the family art gallery in New York. The money, paid directly to Max Amann, was enough to finance the conversion of the party's newspaper from a twice-weekly tabloid to a daily broadsheet format, increasing sales and advertising revenue. 'Putzi's' other important contacts were the Bruckmanns, Gertrud von Seidlitz, William Bayard Hale, a Hearst Press journalist who paid handsomely for Hitler's articles, and Wilhelm Funk, who had connections to Germany's biggest businesses.

Help of another kind came from playboy-gambler-businessman and conman Kurt Lüdecke, who spent many years travelling in the USA and Europe before returning to Bavaria and being called up in 1914. After the war, he had started a successful business selling weapons and other military equipment and putting the profits into a French bank and a dollar account in Switzerland to insure his money against the threat of inflation. Concerned that the greatest threat to Germany came from Jewish influence, he was impressed enough by Hitler's speech at the Circus Krone on 11 August 1922 to join the party the following day. Having, as he claimed, 'found myself, my leader, and my cause', Lüdecke offered his services to Hitler.[14] He was taken on to write propaganda materials and help with recruitment at party rallies. With his experience in travelling and his foreign bank accounts, he also agreed to undertake fundraising outside Germany. In addition, he was generous with his money, often paying bills with dollars and French francs, which had retained their value. He even offered to address and finance what he saw as the lack of discipline in the SA, recruiting, training and arming a company of 140 highly disciplined troops.

Perhaps the most successful fundraiser for Hitler at this point was Max Erwin von Scheubner-Richter, who was introduced to the NSDAP leader in November 1920 by fellow Baltic-German Alfred Rosenberg. Having fought for the Imperial government during the First Russian Revolution in 1905 and for Germany during World War I, Scheubner-Richter was firmly nationalist and anti-Bolshevik in outlook. He became a German citizen to further his business career, using his fluent Russian and German business connections to build a virtual monopoly in trade between Germany and White Russia. Having heard Hitler speak he became convinced that 'the prophet of Germany', as he described the party leader, would one day 'destroy Marxism.'[15] Tapping up his upper-class connections, he began to use his diplomatic skills to persuade right-wing Russian émigré industrialists and Bavarian businessmen to donate money to the National Socialist Party. Well-known, well-respected and wealthy in his own right, Scheubner-Richter was able to convince both parties that Hitler's anti-communist, anti-Semitic and pro-rearmament programme would help their causes. Even during a time of economic crisis in Germany, Scheubner-Richter was able to prise large donations from such people as Fritz Thyssen of the Ruhr steelworks and locomotive manufacturer Ernst von Borsig, and Russian oil traders such as Gukasov, Lenison and Baron Köppen, for the National Socialist cause.

This increase in funds came in handy for the party in October 1922 when Julius Streicher, another former soldier impressed with Hitler's progress, offered to bring the Nuremberg branch of Otto Dickel's DWG, together with his newspaper the *Deutscher Volkswille* (the *German Voice of the People*), into the NSDAP. The only catch was that Streicher's organization was bankrupt and owed Dickel some 70,000 Marks. Hitler agreed, paid the debts and bought the newspaper, meaning that the Nazi Party 'virtually doubled in size overnight', greatly increasing its influence in north Germany.[16]

Streicher was a short, squat, brutish thug with a shaved head. He had started his working life as an elementary school teacher, wrote poetry and, like Hitler, fancied himself as an artist. Described by William Shirer as a 'depraved sadist', he was also a notorious 'fornicator' who 'blackmailed even the husbands of women who were his mistresses'.[17] In Nuremberg, his power base, he was known as the 'Uncrowned King of Franconia', 'where his word was law'. Anyone who dared cross him could expect prison or at least torture. In 1923, he started to publish a new weekly tabloid-format, violently anti-Semitic, anti-communist and anti-monarchist newspaper, *Der Stürmer* (*The Stormer*). It was full of vicious, sexually explicit and obscene material, depicting hooked-nose Jewish men committing pornographic acts on innocent Jewish girls. By 1927, its circulation was some 27,000 copies per week, eventually making Streicher a multi-millionaire. It was not an official Nazi publication – indeed, many Nazis were embarrassed by it – but it played a significant part in the spread of Nazi propaganda.

Chapter 2

Respectability and Disgrace

The economic and political situation in Germany in the early 1920s was dire. There were uprisings from left- and right-wing groups, disorder on the streets, and strikes, with unemployment high and wages low. The reparation payments set by the Treaty of Versailles were punitive, particularly with Germany blocked from many export markets, and the government struggled to find the money or materials to pay. At home, inflation began to rise alarmingly. In 1921, there were 4 Marks to the dollar; the following year there were 400. Businesses were going bankrupt, and people's personal savings were rapidly losing their value. Criticism that the government were unable to do anything about the situation swelled the crowds gathering to hear Hitler's rants against the 'November criminals' and the humiliation of the Versailles Treaty.

In the autumn of 1922, the German government asked the Allies for a moratorium on their reparation payments. French Premier Poincaré refused. In January 1923, with Germany also falling behind on its payments of coal and wood, French and Belgian troops marched into the Ruhr to ensure coal deliveries and at the same time cut most of Germany's coal and steel production. With few soldiers to assemble in its defence, the German government called for a general strike and, in addition, for a campaign of 'passive resistance' against the invaders, which, in the event, did include violent clashes between workers and soldiers. Worried that the government's campaign would prove popular, Hitler began a new propaganda campaign during a speech at the Circus Krone two days after the occupation. He was outraged at the occupation and at the government's weak response and named them as the enemy within, leaving the country defenceless and allowing the French to subject Germany to total enslavement, 'like a colony'.[1] But he needn't have worried. In order to finance their campaign, the government printed more money, which caused inflation and prices to rise further and faster. The Mark immediately fell to 10,000 to the dollar and then 50,000. Panic ensued, with people literally running to the shops to buy food before prices went up again.

Squeezed middle-class families were hardest hit, many having to sell their houses to settle their debts. Between putting them up for sale and completion, a house worth $20,000 might be bought for the equivalent of $1,000. Speculators and those institutions with money were able to make millions as bills, loans and debts were paid off with money worth a fraction of its previous value. The government took advantage, letting the Mark tumble further to free the state of its public debts, including war debts. Others with vested interests, such as the big industrialists, landlords and the army, were also benefitting from those in financial ruin. Industry was able to pay its debts in worthless currency.[2] Hitler raged at the government, warning the people that their 'misery will increase', and that banknotes would have no value beyond the paper on which they were printed. The government's defence was to say that inflation was an economic process over which it had no control. But Hitler had seen it for what it was: 'the method chosen by the German financial elite to escape their obligation and push off the burden onto the middle class'. He accused the government of being 'a robbers' state' made up of 'rogues and swindlers'.[3] He had exposed the fraud; people's confidence in the government was crumbling and they began to trust him. As the value of German currency went down, the people looked elsewhere for help, and Hitler's popularity grew further.

HITLER'S WOMEN

While the expanding size of the party brought with it increasing financial worries, Hitler had a growing reputation as the right man to lead Germany out of trouble. The workers and the middle classes had already lost their money, and many believed that he could help get it back. The upper classes, now worried about their wealth, also turned to him for help, granting him access to the boardrooms of conservative businesses in Munich, Berlin and elsewhere. With purses loosened, money, often in stable foreign currencies, and expensive gifts that could be sold on or used as security on loans, were more forthcoming. An article in the 3 April 1923 edition of the *Munich Post* noted that society women were particularly keen to help the firebrand politician, with Frau Bechstein, Elsa Bruckmann and Winifred Wagner – the English-born wife of Siegfried Wagner, son of Hitler's favourite composer Richard Wagner – often mentioned.

Perhaps the biggest donations came from Frau Gertrud von Seidlitz, a Baltic German with strong ties to Finland, where she had shares in a number of paper mills. As a result of the Finnish Civil War between the Whites, led by the civil government, and the communist Reds in 1918, she is said to have been firmly anti-communist. Possibly introduced to Hitler by Hanfstaengl, she secured a loan from Finnish sources guaranteed by her shares for enough money to enable the party to purchase the rotary press capable of printing the broadsheet version of the *Völkischer Beobachter*. In addition, she persuaded others in Germany and abroad to donate funds.

BRINGING RESPECTABILITY TO THE PARTY

Of course, money was essential for the continued growth of the NSDAP, but equally important was influence, especially with the upper classes and, in particular, with the aristocracy. In his early days with the DAP, Hitler established a friendship with a Belgian nobleman, the Prince of Arenberg, who once insisted on driving him in his Benz car towards Switzerland on one of his early fundraising trips. They became friends. Hitler listened to his new friend's stories of his years in Africa with the Belgian army, which informed him with ideas of colonial policy, often more successful when operating racist policies. He learned that despite the state of his car, which was decrepit and slow, Arenberg was a multi-millionaire. There are no records of him donating money to the party, but Hitler hinted that he was not so stingy about everything.

Chapter 2

Hitler had more success cultivating friendships and getting donations among the aristocratic German émigrés from the Baltic states. Following the Kapp Putsch (see p. 17), in which he was involved, a former Russian army officer named General Vasily Biskupsky was taken to hear Hitler speak by Scheubner-Richter. Impressed by what he heard, the two combined their skills as fundraisers for the Nazi and anti-communist cause. With close connections to the White Russian émigrés who were concentrated in Bavaria, including the Grand Duke Cyril Romanov, first cousin to Czar Nicholas II and therefore the rightful heir to the Russian crown, connections were top-level. The Nazis and the White Russians had much in common: they were right-wing, radical, anti-communist and anti-Semitic. The Duke's family lived in Coburg and many of those in his circle were avid Nazi supporters. These began to contribute racist-nationalist articles to the *Völkischer Beobachter*, as their causes were so alike. Cyril's wife Victoria was also much taken with the Nazi cause and began to contribute funds and attend meetings and parades. She soon began to contribute some of her valuables, too. In addition, and perhaps more significantly, Biskupsky's connections with Russia's grand dukes and generals made Hitler more acceptable in the eyes of upper-class Germans.

Hitler made two other important connections in the early 1920s. In his book *Hitler's Fortune*, Swedish historian Cris Whetton suggests that the Munich publisher, Julius F. Lehmann – a member of the Fatherland Party and the Thule Society and a publisher of many naval publications – was also secretly channelling funds from the navy to Hitler and the NSDAP on the orders of Admiral Schröder. The other significant figure appeared on the scene in November 1922 when the former war hero, Hermann Göring, attended one of Hitler's speeches and was immediately smitten with him. The following day he sought out Hitler and offered his services. Hitler was delighted to accept. Göring's fame as a fighter ace in the Richthofen Squadron during World War I brought respectability to the party. He was also from an aristocratic family and had money and rich, powerful friends. It is said that Göring and his beautiful Swedish wife, Countess

Carin von Kantzow, played an important role in persuading their friend General Ludendorff that Hitler's views 'deserved serious consideration'. A few months later, Hitler appointed Göring as head of the brown-shirted *Sturmabteilung* in place of Ernst Röhm. Hitler was impressed, recalling later, 'He's the only one of its heads who ran the SA properly. I gave him a dishevelled rabble. In a very short time, he had organised a division of eleven thousand men.'[4]

FOREIGN CURRENCIES

Because of the rampant inflation, visitors and those with access to foreign currency could buy German Marks for next to nothing and live like kings. In consequence, 'inflation profiteers' from Switzerland, Holland, Czechoslovakia, Italy and Austria made regular visits to Germany to take advantage of the situation, which meant that there was plenty of hard currency available. Even small donations in these currencies and from Germans and other Nazi supporters living abroad were valuable. Swiss francs were particularly attractive to the party. During the summer of 1923, Hitler travelled to Zurich in the company of long-standing supporter Dr Emil Gansser. He is said to have returned 'with a steamer trunk stuffed with Swiss francs and American dollars.'[5] In addition, Dr Gansser is said to have obtained a gift of 33,000 Swiss francs from various other right-wing Protestant benefactors. Money came from France, too, most notably 90,000 gold Marks, a currency that had retained its value during the period of inflation. The money was presented to Captain Karl Mayr, and some found its way into the NSDAP coffers. In addition, Hitler earned speaker's fees and funds arrived from collections at German nationalist events in Czechoslovakia and Austria. These were modest amounts, perhaps, but they were worth a lot more when taken back to Munich. Indeed, it is said that the *Völkischer Beobachter*'s new offices were paid for by Hitler from a wallet 'stuffed full of Czech money'.[6]

In Germany, large donations from big business were still hard to come by. However, concern over the developing problem with inflation was slowly opening doors to the Munich business community.[7]

From 1920–30, the 6,000 capacity Circus Krone was the Nazi Party's main venue for rallies and hosted Hitler's grandstand appearances in Munich. Pictured here in 1929 are Hitler, Franz Pfeffer von Salomon, Rudolf Hess and loyal supporter Elsa Bruckmann (foreground).

QUID PRO QUO

As Germany's economic and political crisis got worse in the later months of 1922 and in early 1923, Hitler's influence grew stronger. His entourage began to talk up his leadership qualities, particularly after Mussolini's March on Rome (see p. 43–4). An article published in the *Völkischer Beobachter* in December 1922 described Hitler as a special kind of leader. Ian Kershaw identifies a growing change in his self-perception, too, filling his speeches with talk of leadership and of 'a strong man who would rescue Germany'.[8] His increasing prominence brought him into contact with other Bavarian, nationalist right-wing groups, such as the Bund Bayern und Reich, a *Freikorps* unit led by Dr Otto Pittinger. On 16 August, Hitler spoke in Munich alongside other nationalist leaders, from the Bund Bayern, the Bund Oberland and the Reichsflagge, at a mass-protest rally with the slogan 'For Germany – Against Berlin'. A further rally was planned for the following week amid rumours of a coup. As a result of the rumours, which were true as a putsch had been planned by Pittinger and the commander of his troops Ernst Röhm and supported by Hitler, the meeting was banned. The coup fizzled out, leaving its supporters in the lurch. Hitler was furious. 'No more Pittingers, no more Fatherland Societies!... these gentlemen – these counts and generals – they won't do anything. I shall. I *alone*.'[9] Hitler had learned the wisdom of taking care of his choice of allies.

He learned another lesson about the value of independence in early 1923 when trying to raise funds for new and larger Nazi Party headquarters. In his search, he turned to Richard Frank, a wealthy coffee merchant and generous contributor to party funds. Frank suggested that they went to see Dr Kuhlo, director of the Association of Bavarian Industrialists, where they discussed Hitler's future economic policies. This introduction led to several speaking engagements in front of audiences of Munich businessmen. While little in the way of funds were forthcoming, Hitler's ideas were received favourably, and a number of supportive articles appeared in the city's conservative newspapers. Dr Kuhlo proposed a scheme that, on receipt of the deposit (in Swiss francs – a condition of the current owners) he would form a syndicate to buy the Hotel Eden, located near Munich's main railway station, as the party's new HQ. According to the lawyer Heinrich Heim, Hitler reported that: 'When all was ready, the syndicate met, with Kuhlo in the chair. The latter rose to his feet and announced that the hotel would be put at the Party's disposal for a modest fee. He suggested, in passing, that perhaps the Party might suppress the article in its programme concerning Freemasonry. I got up and said good-bye to these kindly philanthropists. I'd fallen unawares into a nest of Freemasons!'[10] The deal did not go through as Hitler was no longer prepared to compromise and particularly with those who sought to exert influence on his policies.

Chapter 2

Stormtroopers and Hitler Youth assemble in Coburg in October 1921 to participate in Deutscher Tag with the intention to show the local population that there was an alternative to socialism and communism in Upper Franconia.

BREAKTHROUGH

Following the occupation of the Ruhr and the Weimar Republic's campaign of passive resistance, Hitler's anti-government propaganda campaign was stepped up. He had been encouraged by the success of the party's participation in *Deutscher Tag* (German Day) in Coburg in October 1922, where Hitler and some 800 of his stormtroopers caused uproar and mayhem fighting local socialist workers and trade unionists with sticks and rubber truncheons. Support from local police ensured that the Nazis won the day, proving that the party had made its mark in Upper Franconia. Early the following year, preparations were being made for the NSDAP's first Reich Party Rally, scheduled for 27–29 January in Munich. Fearful of the threat of violence and amid rumours of a putsch, on 26 January the Bavarian government declared the rally banned. Hitler was furious and declared that it would go ahead anyway.

Ernst Röhm, however, more concerned with confronting the French in the Ruhr, had other ideas. He persuaded General von Lossow, the army commander in Bavaria, to support Hitler's right to hold the rally, as long as he guaranteed it would be peaceful and that there would be no putsch. With further support from Upper Bavarian President Kahr and the police, the rally was allowed to go ahead. It was a propaganda triumph for Hitler. On the first day, he spoke briefly at several meetings, travelling by car to 12 venues across the city. Each venue was in a fever of mass excitement. Political and economic tensions were palpable in Munich at the time and seemed to have been leading up to this day. Huge crowds, booming music, flags, song, uniforms, short speeches from subordinate leaders and suddenly… shielded by bodyguards, there he was, acknowledging a hero's welcome. Ian Kershaw described it as, 'The leadership cult, consciously devised to sustain maximum cohesion within the party, was taking off.'[11] The following day there was a flag-display by some 6,000 stormtroopers, and on the final day there was a general membership meeting at the Circus Krone hall – setting the forms and rituals of Reich Party rallies to come.

POWER OF THE REICHSWEHR

The Treaty of Versailles in 1919 had limited the size of the German Army to 100,000 soldiers. But during the turbulent years of the revolution and the early 1920s there was a lot of other military activity in Germany, much of it taking place out of sight of the prying eyes of the Military Inter-Allied Commission of Control. The *Freikorps*, though officially disbanded in 1920, comprised battle-hardened First World War veterans and was still an effective fighting force. There was also the Black Reichswehr, the Stahlhelm and others. These groups tended to be politically right-wing, anti-communist, anti-Jewish, anti-Slavic and nationalist. They were often engaged in 'national defence' operations on behalf of the German government. However, acting autonomously against the restrictions of Versailles and with the aim of German rearmament, the Reichswehr – the army's new name from 1 January 1921 – grew in numbers and in power and was careful to maintain its independence from the government.

Chapter 2

By then in the hands of General Hans von Seeckt, the army began to become a state within a state, with an increasing influence on foreign and domestic policies, 'until a point was reached when the Republic's continued existence depended on the will of the officer corps'.[12] This would turn out to be a fatal mistake for the Republic.

Hitler, Röhm and Lossow were to meet again shortly after the party rally in January. Hitler had been approached by 'a certain Councillor Schäffer' offering to sell him 'a store of weapons'.[13] Normally leaving such matters to others, Hitler decided to accept the proposal and travelled to the town of Dachau, outside Munich, with his party colleague Hermann Göring, for the arranged rendezvous. There they met Schäffer's wife and a gang of men with 'gallows-birds' faces to complete the deal. Once done, they were taken to a disused airfield in Schleissheim and presented with what Hitler remembered as 'thousands of rifles, mess-tins, haversacks, a pile of useless junk'. 'But,' he continued, 'after it had been repaired, there was enough to equip a regiment'.[14] Hitler immediately handed the cache of weapons over to Lossow for safekeeping.

While political events in the early months of 1923 seemed to indicate the mobilization of forces against the occupation of the Ruhr – indeed, the various paramilitary organizations in the Working Committee had also handed over their weapons to the Reichswehr specifically for that purpose – nothing actually happened. Hitler and others grew impatient. Tensions rose.

Inflaming the tensions further, economic life in Germany ground to a virtual halt. Inflation was out of control and farmers began to refuse to sell their produce for worthless paper money. In 1922, a loaf of bread had cost 3 Marks; in May the following year it had risen to 1,200 Marks; in July it was 100,000 Marks; and by October a loaf cost 670 million Marks. Egg prices followed the same pattern: a dozen eggs cost 3 Marks in 1921, 500 Marks in January 1923 and 30 million Marks in September. 'The country is on the brink of a hellish abyss,' said Hitler and the people responded, swelling the numbers of Nazi party membership and its sympathizers.[15] There were strikes in cities across Germany, often turning to riots stoked up by communist agitators.

The situation was set to explode and a May Day confrontation in Munich between the socialist left, who had already planned their traditional parade, and the nationalist right seemed likely. Hitler planned a counter-demonstration and an armed attack on the 'Reds'. With tensions rising and the prospect of violence increasing, the authorities banned the parade and downgraded it to a limited demonstration in one of the city's squares. Even so, rumours of a socialist putsch led to calls for 'defence' by the paramilitaries. Hitler went to see Lossow and demanded 'his' weapons back for the purpose. Lossow refused. Hitler had overestimated his influence and withdrew in a rage. In the end, the rally passed off without any trouble. The incident was seen by many commentators as a major loss of face for Hitler. He himself had learned a valuable lesson: that he had little power without the support of the army.

HITLER IN HIGH CIRCLES

In February, Röhm, independently of Hitler, announced that he had founded a Working Community of the Patriotic Fighting Associations, which included the main paramilitary organizations in Bavaria. He then asked Hitler to be the group's political leader. Hitler unwillingly accepted the role. He was worried that he would lose control of the SA, as the new force was to be trained by the Reichswehr. However, subsequent moves would change his attitude. At a mass meeting of some 100,000 people in Nuremberg in September held in celebration of Germany's defeat of the French at Sedan in 1870, a new, tighter and stronger group was announced. The *Deutsche Kampfbund* (German Fighting Union) comprised the National Socialists, the Bund Oberland, the Bund Blücher, the Reichsflagge and the Wikingbund. As one of its three leaders, Hitler stood on the reviewing platform alongside General Ludendorff, Prince Ludwig Ferdinand of Bavaria and Oberstleutnant Kriebel, the new organization's military leader. They watched a two-hour march-past of the military formations before various speeches were made. Hitler used the opportunity to continue his propaganda offensive against the government, stating that 'the objectives of the new Kampfbund were the overthrow of the Republic and the tearing up of the Treaty of Versailles'.[16] Hitler was now moving in high circles indeed; already in regular contact with Lossow, he had also been introduced to von Seeckt and had now shared a stage with General Ludendorff. Hitler was not slow in understanding how to use his new connections for propaganda and arranged that a short film be made showing him and Ludendorff talking together as equals.

It was about this time that Hitler met the photographer Heinrich Hoffmann at Hermann Esser's wedding. Hitler was negotiating fees that an American news syndicate had offered him for his photograph. He wanted more money and called on Hoffmann for help. Hoffmann, described by historian Alan Bullock as 'a vulgar, jolly, earth Bavarian with a weakness for drinking parties and hearty jokes, understood little about politics'.[17] The two became friends, often dining at Hoffmann's home where Frau Hoffmann would prepare Hitler's favourite spaghetti with tomato sauce. Up to this point Hitler was unwilling to have his photograph taken, said to be because he had a 'pathological fear for his life'. But when badly taken photos of him on the street began to appear in the press, he asked Hoffmann to become his 'official' photographer. He readily agreed and for some time became the one man allowed to take and sell official portraits of Herr Hitler. Hoffmann's photographs did much to help Hitler's early popularity.

STATE OF EMERGENCY

On 26 September 1923, the differences between the powers that be in Bavaria and the German Republic in Berlin boiled over again. The staunch conservative Chancellor Stresemann, who had replaced Wilhelm Cuno the previous month, called off the passive resistance campaign in the Ruhr and announced the resumption of reparation payments to the Allies. The government's reasoning was that a period of stability and co-operation would allow the German economy to recover. The response in nationalist Bavaria was immediate, with both nationalists and communists condemning the move in the strongest terms. Inflation remained unstoppable; money had become worthless; and the people were starving. Although this opposition was expected, the chancellor had proclaimed a State of Emergency on the same day as his announcement of a policy change in the Ruhr. However, threats of uprisings by communists in Saxony, Thuringia and Hamburg and, more importantly, by factions of the Reichswehr itself in Bavaria and the north, were of serious concern for Commander of the German Army, General von Seeckt. Fears in Berlin were that Bavaria might secede from the Reich, while von Seeckt knew that there were pockets of sympathy in his forces for both the separatists and the communists.

Fortunately for Stresemann, von Seeckt chose to stand behind the Republic, not because he was a Republican but because he knew it was necessary for the preservation of the Reichswehr. In early October, he moved against Black Reichswehr troops who had seized three forts east of Berlin and arrested their leader, Major Buchrucker. He then turned his attention to the communist insurgents. Hitler and the Kampfbund army leagues stood by, eager to find the right moment to take advantage of the explosive situation.

MAKING WAVES ABROAD

Hitler seemed to thrive in chaos, and the situation in Germany in 1923 ensured that his fame was spreading abroad. Foreign governments, particularly the US, began to ask for information about him. The American embassy in Berlin dispatched an assistant military attaché, Captain Truman-Smith, to Munich to make discreet enquiries. His report, sent to the US Secretary of State in December 1922, noted, 'He [Hitler] is obtaining a great deal of money from the manufacturers just as Mussolini did [...] he is collecting funds and equipment and all is going well.'[18] Around the same time, Putzi Hanfstaengl introduced Hitler to William Bayard Hale, once the chief correspondent of the US-based Hearst newspapers, who began to pay him for interviews and articles, as did British newspapers such as the *Daily Mail*. However, in an interview in October that year with the paper's Berlin correspondent Rothay Reynolds, Hitler and Reynolds spoke more about Mussolini than Hitler. An article appeared in the *New York Times* in November 1922 claiming that a portrait of the well-known anti-Semite Henry Ford hung on the wall of Hitler's private office. In another interview with Hitler, in the *Chicago Tribune* in March 1923, remarking on a

Chapter 2

Though natural political and military allies, the relationship between Mussolini and Hitler was complex and ambiguous. Hitler admired the Fascist takeover in Italy and used a similar playbook himself. However, when both in power, their rivalry, spite and small-mindedness soured Italio-German relations.

possible presidential run by Ford, he said, 'I wish I could send some of my shock troops to Chicago [...] to help with the elections. We look on Heinrich Ford as the leader of the growing fascist movement in America. Germans admire particularly his anti-Jewish polity, which is the Bavarian fascist platform.'[19]

Historians often point out that it is no surprise that Hitler and Mussolini were often mentioned in the same breath. The 1920s were difficult years for countries that had lost the war; the Treaty of Versailles had redrawn Europe's borders and ushered in a period of migration while the Wall Street Crash at the end of the decade had a major impact on the economies of many European countries. Added to the ongoing fear of communism after the Russian Revolution, xenophobia was resulting from mass migration. There followed, in Italy and in Germany, a destabilization of politics, which became increasingly more authoritarian. Many countries in Europe, including Britain, France, and some in Scandinavia and Eastern Europe, saw the emergence of major right-wing ultra-conservative movements stating that they could make their country great again after the humiliations of World War I. Like Mussolini and Hitler, a number of populist revolutionary leaders claimed that they represented the 'real people', were anti-capitalist and anti-communist, and represented a 'third way' through 'unity, discipline and class cooperation'.[20]

But it was only in Italy and Germany that this ideology was successful. Historian Elisabetta Wolff explains that in countries such as France and Britain power was already in the hands of strong right-wing political parties and therefore had no need to seek help from the fascist movements. In Italy, Mussolini's fascists were invited into an alliance with the ruling liberal conservatives, while in Germany opposition to the Weimar Republic was always strong. Despite their widespread use of violence and coercion against their political opponents as a legitimate means of achieving their goals, both movements also came to power legally through the ballot box.[21]

In his early years as leader of the NSDAP, Hitler was a great admirer of Mussolini. The Nazi leader was particularly fascinated with Mussolini's 'March on Rome' – a threatened and feared protest that should have seen thousands of fascists and fascist supporters stride into the Italian capital on 28 October

1922. In the event, pouring rain and disruption of the rail system meant that only 5,000 fascists assembled and they were not allowed to enter the city. Mussolini arrived in Rome from Milan by train the following day. However, the threat was enough to ensure Mussolini's appointment as prime minister. In 1923, Hitler wrote to his Italian counterpart about the March on Rome; the putsch that followed was Hitler's attempt at replicating it.

THE BEER HALL PUTSCH

Meanwhile, under the dictatorial triumvirate of State Commissioner Kahr, General von Lossow, Commander of the Reichswehr in Bavaria, and head of the state police Colonel Hans von Seisser, Bavaria remained defiant of Berlin. They refused to obey orders. Berlin announced that the Bavarian rebellion would be put down by force and the triumvirate's determination weakened. The moment had come. Despite knowing that he did not have the support he needed from the army or the police, Hitler understood that there was no turning back and that he had to act immediately. The Berlin government had to be removed.

Plans were drawn up for a putsch, which they hoped would be supported by the triumvirate in response to the offices they would be offered in Hitler's new government. Hitler and his co-conspirators, Kriebel (military head of the Kampfbund), Scheubner-Richter, Weber (head of the Bund Oberland), Theodor von der Pfordten (a regional court judge), Göring and General Ludendorff (so claimed later by Hitler), along with others, had various options. Hitler's hand was somewhat forced, however, when rumours emerged that Kahr was planning to declare Bavarian independence during a speech at the Bürgerbräukeller on the evening of 8 November.

Late on the evening of 7 November, the conspirators spread the word to the SA leaders and others: 'Tomorrow at 8 o'clock it's happening.'[22] Hundreds of armed SA brownshirts surrounded the beer hall on Munich's Rosenheimer Strasse. At around 8.30pm, as State Commissioner Kahr, along with von Seisser and General von Lossow, was on the stage holding forth to a crowd of 3,000 local businessmen, Hitler and some of his men burst into the hall, setting up a machine gun in the main doorway. Uproar followed. Kahr broke off his speech as Hitler approached the stage. Standing on a chair, Hitler fired a shot into the ceiling, quieting the crowd. 'The National Revolution has begun!' he shouted. 'The Bavarian and Reich governments have been removed and a provisional national government formed. The barracks of the Reichswehr and police are occupied. The army and the police are marching on the city under the swastika banner!'[23] Hitler then departed the stage, leaving Göring to calm the crowd. Next, he forced Kahr, Lossow and Seisser into a back room, where he coerced them at gunpoint into supporting his *coup d'état* against Berlin. At first they refused but then changed their minds following the arrival of General Ludendorff. Apparently triumphant, they returned to the hall, and each made a short speech outlining the make-up of their new national government.

On being told that there was trouble in the streets between the SA and some regular troops, Hitler left, putting Ludendorff in charge at the Bürgerbräukeller. The situation outside was not good: other conspirators had been tasked with taking over government buildings and communication centres in the city but had largely failed in their attempts. Planning had been poor and only Ernst Röhm had succeeded, taking over the headquarters of the Reichswehr in Ludwigstrasse. Meanwhile, Ludendorff had let Kahr, Lossow and Seisser leave the beer hall on their 'word of honour', and they immediately alerted law enforcement to the situation and ordered them to suppress the putsch.

Overnight, the situation was one of huge confusion. Hitler said nothing and knew little more. Some, like Röhm, had been told the coup had succeeded and had spread the word, prompting SA troop movements into the city and the appearance of billboards proclaiming Hitler as Reich Chancellor. Others knew that Hitler's attempt to take control of the state had already failed. Sometime in the early hours of 9 November, the putschists realized their predicament. As a frozen dawn broke, the SA troops, having received no orders, began to drift away. At around midday, on Ludendorff's suggestion, Hitler agreed to take the bull by the horns and march to Marienplatz, picking up Röhm and his troops on the way and stirring up popular support for the putsch. With Hitler, Ludendorff and Scheubner-Richter leading the way, some 2,500 members of the Kampfbund set off from the beer hall.

Chapter 2

When the marchers reached the Feldherrnhalle on Odeonsplatz, the police opened fire. Four policemen, 16 putschists and one innocent bystander were killed in the ensuing shoot-out. Ludendorff carried on marching through the firing and into the ranks of police; Scheubner-Richter was killed; and Hermann Göring was shot in the groin. Hitler, who dislocated his shoulder falling to the ground, fled the scene. His exit plan was to have his friend Dr Walter Schultze waiting in his yellow Fiat parked nearby with its engine running. After hiding for a few days in Putzi Hanfstaengl's home in Uffing, south of Munich, the police surrounded the house, found him in the attic dressed in white pyjamas and a blue bathrobe with his arm in a sling, and arrested him on 11 November.

Chapter 3

Mein Kampf and the Golden Years of Weimar

Hitler had appeared alongside General Erich Ludendorff on the speakers' podium at the Deutsche Tag Rally in Nuremberg at the beginning of September 1923. It had been a great moment for the ex-corporal to stand side by side with a man whose reputation as a war hero had earned him an exalted position in nationalist circles. Ludendorff himself had little money but was well connected in all walks of German life and known as a man with good judgement – a man you could trust. The two had met on a number of occasions and many people, including naval officer and journalist Count Ernst Reventlow and the Görings, urged the general to take the young politician seriously. They shared similar political beliefs, such as nationalism and anti-communism, and were set against the Jews, the Versailles Treaty and Bavarian separatism. At the rally, Ludendorff, who had little political sense, gave the appearance of endorsing the provincial politician with whom he shared the stage.

This was enough for Hitler's purposes. Although Ludendorff was acting on his own behalf, with an eye on the leadership of the nationalist counter-revolution, Hitler wanted that role for himself. However, he was happy to exploit the general's connections in industry and other businesses, many of whom came to him asking how they could support anti-communist forces, giving him money to divide between right-wing groups as he saw fit. It is assumed that donations given by the industrialist Hugo Stinnes to Ludendorff found their way to the NSDAP and created the financial base for the Beer Hall Putsch. Donations to the party came too from Fritz Thyssen, heir of the Thyssen steel empire and chairman of the board of the giant United Steel Works. Encouraged by Ludendorff to go and hear Hitler speak, Thyssen began to finance the party. In October, he gave the general 100,000 gold Marks to distribute between the Nazis and the Bund Oberland. Other German industrialists were also keen to hand out donations to right-wing parties in the fight against communism. For example, locomotive manufacturer Ernst von Borsig, who was president of the German Employers' Federation, made regular payments to *Freikorps* units and to the NSDAP as a form of insurance payments against the communist threat. But, according to some journalists and historians, Hitler had another major asset in funding coming from the founder of the world's most famous car maker, Henry Ford.

HENRY FORD, ANTI-SEMITE

In the first few decades of the 20th century, Henry Ford was famous. When he spoke, people stopped to listen. This ability to gain a national audience with his words made him a very dangerous person. Ford was a famous anti-Semite. In 1918, he bought a local newspaper: the *Dearborn Independent*, named after the Detroit suburb in which it was founded. A weekly paper subtitled the 'Ford International Weekly' and given away free at Ford car outlets, it became a vehicle for his own personal views: 'anti-profiteer, antimonopoly, anti-reactionary', anti-liquor and anti-Semitic.[1] In May 1920, he published the first of 91 articles under the title 'The International Jew: The World's Problem'. Together, they promoted the idea that Jews were behind many of the world's troubles, had invented the stock market and the gold standard to corrupt the world and were planning to form an 'international super-capitalist government'. Ford was a pacifist and had opposed World War I. He believed that Jews were responsible for starting the war, indeed all wars, in order to profit from them. He also blamed Jews for a decline in American culture, values, products, music and entertainment by focusing only on price. 'They cheapened it,' he said, 'to make more money.'[2]

Despite the outcry from Jews and others across America, Ford's views spread quickly. By 1925, the newspaper's circulation had risen to 900,000, second only to the *New York Daily News*. His views echoed the fears and assumptions of many Americans who had witnessed the arrival of millions of Jews to the USA, which reached its peak in the 1920s. Ford's newspaper articles set up a kind of paranoia: that the Jews were responsible for all of America and the world's ills, workers' strikes, financial problems, failing harvests and so on, making them a symbol of a world that was being manipulated and controlled. These were backed up when the *Independent* reprinted text from *The Protocols of the Elders of Zion*, a forged document, originally written in Russia, that 'claimed the existence of an international Jewish conspiracy – that a group of Jews got together and basically planned the fate of the world'.[3]

Starting in 1920, Ford's articles were republished in a four-volume book set entitled *The International Jew*. Distributed widely, in the USA and elsewhere, the books were also translated into 16 different languages, including German. It was published in Germany in 1921 by the *völkisch* publisher Hammer, who claimed that by 1927 there were 90,000 German-language copies in circulation. For Hitler and other Nazis, this was manna from heaven. At his trial in Nuremberg in 1946, Baldur von Schirach, former leader of the Hitler Youth, said, 'The decisive anti-Semitic book which I read at that time and the book which influenced my comrades was Henry Ford's book, *The International Jew*; I read it and became anti-Semitic. In those days this book made such a deep impression on my friends and myself because we saw in Henry Ford the representative of success, also the exponent of a progressive social policy. In the poverty-stricken and wretched Germany of the time, youth looked toward America, and apart from the great benefactor, Herbert Hoover, it was Henry Ford who to us represented America.'[4] Hitler too was quick to credit Ford with his belief in racial anti-Semitism, agreeing with his assertion that 'the Jewish question is not a religious question [...] it is one of race and nationality.'[5] Hitler's conclusion that Jews 'were not Germans with a special religion, but an entirely different race' became one of the building blocks of Nazism.[6]

FINANCIAL CONNECTIONS WITH FORD

It seems natural, then, that the famous anti-Semitic, anti-communist car manufacturer Henry Ford and the upcoming German politician with similar views would be interested in each other. Of course they were, according to reports in various American and British newspapers in the early 1920s. There were business interests to consider. As well as hitting German trade restrictions, the Versailles Treaty impacted foreign investment in Germany, by companies such as Ford Motors. By 1920, economists were admitting that foreign investors needed a prosperous Germany in order to help themselves. Hoping that this sensible view would bear fruit and restrictions on trade would be lifted, in 1921 Ford sent an executive to Germany to find a site for a Ford factory.

At the same time, suggest historians James and Suzanne Pool in their book *Who Financed Hitler*, payments were made – indirectly, of course – by Henry Ford to the Nazi Party in support of its anti-Semitic campaign. There were articles about this too in the *Manchester Guardian*, the *New York Times* and the *Berliner Tageblatt*. Actual evidence is hard to find because the payments were not made public, but the Pools outline a number of possible ways in which money may have been channelled. The best way for money to travel was through third parties. For example, Boris Brasol, a White Russian émigré with Czarist and anti-Semitic leanings, worked for the Russian army and for US intelligence. In 1920, he was given a job at Ford's newspaper in Dearborn. He was heavily involved in the paper, promoting and publishing the *Protocols* and, according to its one-time editor Edwin Pipp, 'helped fan the flame of prejudice against the Jews in Ford's mind.'[7] Although Hitler denied receiving funds from Ford, Brasol is said to have made frequent trips to Germany with money for the 'Russian monarchist cause'; it seems highly likely that this money found its way into other pockets. Other potential money 'mules' for the White Russians were Kurt Lüdecke and General Biskupsky, who both travelled widely in the USA and in Europe, stressing the advantages that would come to the émigrés if the anti-Bolshevik, anti-Semitic Hitler came to power. It is rumoured that Lüdecke received funds from Ford via the *Dearborn Independent*'s editor Bill Cameron. The Pools also claim that one of Mr Ford's agents, Lars Jacobsen, met Dietrich Eckart during a trip to 'sell tractors'. An article in the *New York Times* later that year revealed the real reason for the trip: Jacobsen was there to express Ford's interest in the Hitler movement and money 'apparently' soon began to flow into the NSDAP coffers.

An even more direct contributor was Ernest G. Liebold, Henry Ford's personal secretary, a committed anti-Semite who held Nazi sympathies. According to Ford's biographers Allan Nevins and Frank Hill, Liebold possessed a 'cold, ruthless intensity'. Edwin Pipp remembers that along with Brasol, Liebold heavily influenced Henry Ford's attitudes towards Jews, saying, 'The door to Ford's mind was open to anything Liebold wanted to shove in it [...] in one way and another, the feeling [of anti-Semitism] oozed into his system until it became part of his living self.'[8] Recent research has revealed further connections between Liebold and Brasol in that they both acted as spies before World War I. As a German, Liebold 'owed his allegiance to the Kaiser.'[9] In 1921, he re-established contacts with the dethroned German royal family. It was Liebold who sent Jacobsen to see Dietrich Eckart, thus establishing a direct link between the former German royal family, the Nazi Party and the Ford Motor Company. The royal family – great admirers of Hitler, who still held out hope that he would restore the monarchy should he take power – maintained close ties with the Nazis. With Liebold claiming that he kept 'as much as one million dollars of Ford's personal money in his office safe at any one time – what he called "the kitty"' – it would have been easy to transfer money across the Atlantic through one of his family contacts with no questions asked.[10]

Although there is little but speculative evidence of any real connections between Fordism and Nazism, there is one piece of evidence in a letter between Ernest Liebold and Fritz Hailer, the German consul in Detroit. The two were close friends and Hailer kept Liebold updated on events in Germany at the time. Dated 7 April 1938, the letter reads, 'Dear Mr Liebold. Acknowledging your check in the sum of $10.00 for the German "Winter Relief Fund" and thank you very much for your contribution. Your name was inserted on the contribution list.'[11] Although Hitler denied receiving money from Henry Ford, in light of the huge amount of money that German Ford made from its vehicle production factories in Cologne and Berlin during the war years – estimated at more than $2.5 million (over $43 million today) – it may be that this $10 was only the thin end of the wedge.

HITLER'S TRIAL

Following his arrest, Hitler was taken to Landsberg prison, a stone-walled facility some 80 km (50 miles) west of Munich. Labelled Prisoner No. 45, he was put into Cell 7. Despite the seriousness of his crime – he was charged with high treason – he was placed in 'fortress confinement', and was able to wear his own clothes, visit cellmates, entertain visitors and walk around in the prison grounds for up to five hours a day. Despite this leniency, he was downcast, admitting to the prison psychologist, 'I've had enough. I'm finished. If I had a revolver, I would take it.'[12] Refusing to talk to investigators, he went on a week-long hunger strike.

The crisis in Munich fizzled out and in due course the NSDAP and the SA were banned, Hitler's name disappeared from view and the danger from the extreme right lost its immediacy. Without the support of the army, the paramilitary and patriotic organizations were dissolved or had their weapons confiscated. For the Nazi leadership, several of whom met in secret in Salzburg to discuss party finances a week after the disastrous putsch, the outlook was bleak. Hermann Esser, Gerhard Rossbach, Hoffmann and Putzi Hanfstaengl discussed the possibilities of printing counterfeit banknotes or even robbing banks to acquire funds but eventually agreed merely to send the party fundraiser Kurt Lüdecke to the USA to raise money.

It did not take long for Hitler to recover from his depression. A few days' thought gave him a new perspective on his position. It was clear that right-wing sentiments had not disappeared in Bavaria and neither had its criticism of the Berlin government. Hitler knew that his knowledge of the complicity of the Bavarian government and police from Kahr, von Lossow and Seisser, the help he received from the Reichswehr in his plans for his 'March on Berlin', and the failed *coup d'état* to overthrow the Weimar government would give him great leverage in his upcoming trial. And so it proved when the trial, originally set for the Reich Court in Leipzig, was moved by the Bavarian authorities

(Left to right) Hitler and fellow putschists Emil Maurice (on the mandolin), Herman Kriebel, Rudolf Hess and Friedrich Weber pose in the comfortable, well-appointed light and airy common room of Landsberg prison.

to a People's Court in Munich. The judge, Georg Neithardt, a well-known nationalist, was appointed by Bavarian Justice Minister Franz Gürtner, an old friend of Hitler's. In terms of justice, the trial, beginning on 26 February 1924, was a stitch-up. As Richard Evans suggests, 'It seems likely that they offered Hitler leniency in return for his agreement to carry the can.'[13] In terms of Hitler's future, it gave him 'the opportunity to sell his extremist ideas to a receptive German public.'[14]

According to historian David King, Hitler was able to use the trial as an opportunity 'to redefine himself as this national hero. [The putsch] caused headlines over the international press, and Hitler's name became known thereafter. He could not have bought the kind of publicity he got at the trial even if he wanted to.'[15] During proceedings Hitler was allowed to speak freely, and did so without interruption, blaming Jews and Marxists for Germany's decline and claiming that the putsch could not be treasonable, as it was his attempt at restoring the nation to its former glory. During his final words, he said to judge Neithardt, 'You may pronounce us guilty a thousand times but the goddess who presides over the eternal court of history will with a smile tear in pieces the charge of the public prosecutor and the verdict of this court. For she acquits us.'[16] The judge did not acquit them and Hitler and several co-conspirators were found guilty of high treason. Ludendorff, of course, was acquitted. However, despite the seriousness of a crime usually punishable by death, Hitler was given a sentence of five years in prison, and the Nazi Party and the Youth League were disbanded and outlawed on Weimar government orders. In addition, the party's newspaper – the *Völkischer Beobachter* – was also banned. However, Max Amann somehow accessed funds, held off creditors, set up another company and kept Eher Verlag going, publishing a daily news sheet in the paper's stead.

PRISON

Some nine months later, on 20 December 1924, Hitler was released on parole. During his 264 days in captivity, according to historian William Shirer, he was 'treated as an honoured guest, with a room of his own and a splendid view'.[17] Dressed in his lederhosen, he would sit in his wicker chair and read the newspapers or a book and chat with his fellow prisoners. Guests were permitted and plentiful, bringing gifts of flowers, chocolates, wine, cakes and more books. Letters and parcels, particularly from women, came from all over Germany. According to Putzi Hanfstaengl, 'Frau Bruckmann had been one of the most generous donors.'[18] On 20 April Hitler was allowed 40 guests to celebrate his 35th birthday – an event, he was delighted to read in the newspapers, that was celebrated in the Bürgerbräukeller by some 3,000 National Socialists. He was even able to negotiate with a car dealer in Munich on the purchase of a new Benz. During any of the hours he spent alone, he had time to collect his

Bought by the Nazis in December 1920, the Völkischer Beobachter *newspaper formed part of the party's official face for 24 years. An statement in this edition (25 December 1920) announced its new ownership.*

thoughts, and to reframe his political opinions and the lessons he had learned from the failed putsch. That summer, he cut down on the number of visitors, summoned the admiring Rudolph Hess and began to dictate his 'manifesto for world domination', which would be published in the autumn of 1925.[19]

Just as Hitler was drawing together his thoughts for the book, which had the rather clumsy working title *Four and a Half Years of Struggle Against Lies, Stupidity and Cowardice*, so the right-wing *völkisch* movement, now deprived of its 'leader', broke up into squabbling factions, unable to agree on the way forward. Alfred Rosenberg, Hitler's choice of party leader in his absence, set up a new party – the *Grossdeutsche Volksgemeinschaft* (GVG, Greater German National Community) – in place of the banned NSDAP, but was soon ousted from its leadership by Hermann Esser and the fervent anti-Semite Julius Streicher. The dull, bookish editor of the *Völkischer Beobachter* was a poor choice for the job, though many believe that Hitler chose him because he would pose no threat to his leadership. Gregor Strasser, who had much influence in north Germany and had participated in Hitler's failed putsch, joined a rival party, the *Deutschvölkische Freiheitspartei* (DVFP), itself an offshoot of the *Deutschnationale Volkspartei* (DNVP). Many of the people involved had supported Hitler's attempt at overthrowing the Weimar government, but in his absence were jostling for influence and power. Such squabbling, however, led to disastrous results in the Reichstag elections in December 1924, shortly before Hitler's release.

MEIN KAMPF

According to Ian Kershaw, it seems likely that Hitler was persuaded to write what was basically his autobiography by Max Amann, who ran the Eher Verlag, the party's publishing house, in order to take advantage of the publicity engendered by Hitler's trial. Amann was disappointed with the first draft he received and a number of people, such as Amann himself, Hess, Hanfstaengl and other sympathetic journalists, were brought in as editors. In essence, the text published was considerably improved from the original manuscript but was still an incoherent and turgid mix of 'autobiographical reminiscences and garbled political declamations.'[20] However, those who made it through to the end of the 400 pages were left in no doubt about the kind of Germany Hitler would create if he came to power.

It is helpful to realize that as Hitler dictated his thoughts to his underlings, he was in the process of remaking himself. With plenty of time for reflection and for reading, he told the NSDAP's legal adviser Hans Frank, 'I recognized the correctness of my view.'[21] He recounted incidents from his life, his youth, his time as a soldier, his hatred of the Treaty of Versailles and the reparations that Germany had to pay. However, it is clear that much of this autobiographical information had little truth in it and, in essence, it was more like pieces of propaganda, twisting historical facts to achieve a desired effect. He confirmed his worldview of history as a racial struggle between the Aryans and the Jews. 'The racial problem,' he wrote, 'furnishes the key not only to the understanding of human history but also to the understanding of every kind of human culture.'[22] Hitler now claimed that 'Juda is the world plague.' He used the inhumanity shown by the Bolshevik Jews in killing and starving 30 million people during the Russian Revolution as a reason for the Nazi mission of destroying what he called 'Jewish Bolshevism' to justify the removal of Jews from Germany and his intended acquisition of 'living-space' in Eastern Europe for the German people. For Hitler, the state was not an economic entity but a racial one. His belief was that racial purity was absolutely necessary for a revitalized Germany. According to Ian Kershaw, *Mein Kampf* points out that in Hitler's worldview, his 'authority [...] derived from the certainty of his own convictions [...] Everything could be couched in terms of black and white, victory or total destruction. There were no alternatives.'[23]

But there was a new theme in his thinking ... on the matter of leadership. Hitler writes on his vision of the People's State that he will form, that there will be a parliament but that there will be 'no decisions made by the majority vote, but only responsible persons [...] Every man in a position of responsibility will have councillors at his side, but the decision is made by one individual person alone.'[24] By now he had realized that *he* was that 'one individual person alone'. The fact that the National Socialist movement had fallen apart during his incarceration, that his rhetoric during the trial had produced such a positive reaction and the adulation that he received from the nationalist right following the failed putsch convinced him that 'he was the man to turn these views into reality'.[25] For Ian Kershaw, Hitler's self-belief had been elevated 'beyond measure. His almost mystical faith in himself as walking with destiny, with a "mission" to rescue Germany', dated back to his last months in Landsberg prison.[26]

When preparing the book for publication, Max Amann is said to have come up with the title *Mein Kampf*. Published on 18 July 1925, priced at RM12 (some three times the price of most books published in Germany during that time), the book was not an immediate success. Despite Amann's claims to the contrary, it sold 9,473 copies that year and fewer in each of the subsequent three years. A second book appeared in December 1926, written after Hitler's release from prison, focused more extensively on the ideology and organization of National Socialism, the nature of the *völkisch* state and ideas on foreign policy. When published together, the book was some 700 pages in length. Royalties from the sale of the book (10 per cent rising to 15 per cent) were Hitler's chief source of income during these years and drew in a reasonable amount. There was money too from the sales of the *Völkischer Beobachter*, when it reappeared on the newsstands in February 1925 following the lifting of the ban. By 1929, the paper was selling some 20,000 copies each day. In fact, the paper was so popular that in 1926 the *Illustrierter Beobachter*, an illustrated journal put together by Amann and Hoffmann, was launched. However, his earnings in 1925 were dwarfed by his income from the book from 1930 and beyond. The reason for the increased sales of all these publications was the efforts of two busy men, Hitler and Max Amman, who happened to be the main beneficiaries of all these products.

STRESEMANN AND THE DAWES PLAN

Over in Berlin, the Weimar Republic, which had crafted a new democratic constitution, was led by a president, a chancellor and a parliament (the Reichstag), to replace its pre-war Imperial system. It had staggered through

Mein Kampf and the Golden Years of Weimar

The hyperinflation crisis in Germany in 1923 was one of the worst in history. The government's only response was to print more paper money with higher denominations – in November, the treasury reported that there were over 400 million trillion Deutsch Marks in circulation.

four years of economic and political turmoil, mainly as a result of the terms of the Versailles Treaty but also because it adopted proportional representation, which led to a massive increase in the number of parties, making a majority almost impossible and even a coalition difficult to achieve. With the Kapp Putsch in 1920, the staggering cost of reparations, the occupation of the Ruhr in 1923, a general strike, the devaluation of the Deutsche Mark, the subsequent rapid rise in the cost of living and the hyperinflation that brought economic disaster to millions of Germans, Weimar was increasingly unpopular.

Faced with this crisis, Gustav Stresemann was elected as chancellor in September 1923. Founder member of the *Deutscher Volkspartei* (German People's Party, DVP), he managed to form a coalition of Social Democrats and the Centre Party and brought in a policy of fulfilment – attempting to fulfil the terms of the Treaty of Versailles, including the reparation payments – while lobbying for better terms. Despite the cries of betrayal and the scorn of the nationalists, Stresemann's policy was successful: striking workers in the Ruhr returned to work and Germany's international relations began to improve. Stresemann appointed a banker, Hjalmar Schacht, to deal with the hyperinflation. Since the imposition of reparations, the German economy, hampered by land losses and other restrictions imposed by the treaty, struggled to raise sufficient money. Following the occupation of the Ruhr, the government had little choice but to print more banknotes, monetizing its debts for paying wages and so on. The resulting inflation was so great that the currency collapsed in November. Schacht, who had replaced Rudolf Havenstein as president of the newly established Reichsbank, stopped issuing new money and instead issued a new currency – the Rentenmark, with its value tied to the price of gold and backed by mortgage bonds. It was decided that 1 trillion Marks (1,000,000,000,000) would equal 1 Rentenmark. On the same day, through foreign exchange market interventions, the Reichsbank stabilized the value of the Mark against the US dollar. As 1 trillion Marks was equal to 1 Rentenmark, the exchange rate was 4.2 Rentenmark for 1 US dollar – the same exchange rate that had existed between the Mark and the US dollar in 1914. The plan was a leap of faith, and the desperate German people had that faith, believing that the plan would work. By December, the period of hyperinflation in Germany was over and the currency stabilized. The following year, the Rentenmark was renamed the Reichsmark (RM).

In 1924, Stresemann's efforts to improve international relations and secure better terms for reparations bore fruit. After discussions with France, Britain and the USA about a way out of the crisis, the Inter-Allied Reparations Commission agreed to revisit the terms of Versailles and set up the Dawes Committee to compile a report. The committee, led by US representative Charles Dawes and consisting of two expert financiers from each of Belgium, France, Britain, Italy and the USA, produced a report setting out a new schedule of terms. Under the new Dawes Plan, reparations – set initially at somewhere around 132 billion gold Marks – were reduced to 50 million Marks per year for five years, and then 125 million Marks a year following that. Although no end date was set, it was agreed that if the German economy underperformed, it would pay less in reparations. It also recommended that the German National Bank be reorganized. The report also ordered France and Belgium to end their occupation of the Ruhr and agree not to invade Germany if it defaulted on its payments again. Most significantly, it agreed that Germany should receive an international loan of $200 million, which would be financed in the main by the USA.

Although the plan ended the hyperinflation, its effects on millions of Germans were huge. The economy functioned again – farmers produced food, factories produced goods and mines produced coal, but people's savings were gone forever. With the Deutsche Mark gone, so had the lifetime plans of the average citizen. As brides-to-be were expected to bring some money to their marriage, many weddings were cancelled. Widows, dependent on insurance, had no income. Pensions, which had taken a lifetime to accrue, were worthless. American writer Pearl Buck, who was in Germany at the time, later wrote: 'The cities were still there, the houses not yet bombed and in ruins, but the victims were millions of people. They had lost their fortunes… [and] did not understand how it happened and who the foe was who defeated them … they had lost their self-assurance… [and] the old values of morals, of ethics, or decency.'[27]

GOLDEN YEARS

Hitler left prison intent on reorganizing the Nazi Party to continue with his work but with only vague plans as to how he was going to achieve the 'greatness' of his ambitions on the road to power. He found a different Germany, with an improving economy, a stable currency and a drop in unemployment rates. Starting in mid-1924, Germany had entered a period of prosperity, which shored up the appeal of the more moderate political parties.

For William Shirer, newly arrived in Europe from the USA, 'a wonderful ferment was working in Germany' and everywhere with the accent on youth. Writing, drama, music and fine arts were full of new talents and new currents. Prussian austerity seemed to be long gone and 'Most Germans one met – politicians, writers, editors, artists, professors, students, businessmen, labour

Chapter 3

Although initially met with a mixed reception when released in 1927, Metropolis, the first-ever feature length science fiction film, is now widely regarded as one of the greatest and most influential films ever made.

Mein Kampf and the Golden Years of Weimar

Another classic film, Nosferatu *was released in 1922 and immediately struck a chord with German audiences. Critics attribute this to the wartime experiences – bloodletting and death on the battlefields and rats in the trenches – of those who made and starred in the film and its audience.*

leaders struck you as being young, democratic, liberal, even pacifist.'[28] On the streets and in bars and homes there was little talk of Hitler, except as the butt of jokes around the famous 'Beer Hall Putsch' as it had become known.

Often described by historians as the 'golden years' between 1924 and 1929, Germany experienced a kind of artistic and social revolution. Its major cities, such as Frankfurt, Cologne and, in particular, Berlin, expanded with new arrivals in search of work, and a vibrant new urban life developed. In an atmosphere of increased social and economic freedom, nightlife and its associated hedonism thrived, with cabarets and bars packed with both gay and straight revellers. In 1919, the Weimar Constitution had extended the right to vote to all men and women over the age of 20 and this sense of sexual liberation was extended further during these years with increases in women's and even Jews' rights. A new system of welfare, to protect the young, the unemployed and the disadvantaged, was brought in, and housing projects were introduced using government investment, tax breaks, land grants and low-interest loans. Homelessness was reduced and wages in the industrial sector began to rise.

In turn, cultural output – often funded by grants from the government – exploded: in cinema, with the release of films such as *The Cabinet of Dr. Caligari* (1920), *Nosferatu* (1922) and Fritz Lang's *Metropolis* (1927); with plays by the likes of Bertolt Brecht; with paintings by Expressionists such as Otto Dix and George Grosz; and in other fields, such as music and dance. There were advances too in design from the Bauhaus school, Dada and Der Ring, which was established by ten architects in Berlin in 1923–4. There were also great authors living in Berlin at the time, such as Franz Kafka, Vladimir Nabokov, W.H. Auden, Virginia Woolf and Graham Greene. These years also saw advances in science and philosophy.

In reality, not everyone shared in this 'golden age'. The bankrupted middle classes in particular failed to benefit from any new government policies and white-collar workers did not see the same wage rises as those in the industrial sector. Farmers too continued to struggle. Faced with competing with cheaper imported food, they were forced to modernize. But investment in new technologies to improve productivity was expensive. Some borrowed and struggled with repayments; others didn't, could not compete and went to the wall. Others living in rural areas, where the influence of the church was still strong and traditional values remained in place, were actually disgusted by the 'tide of filth' they heard about in the cities. Stories of nudity, homosexuality, birth control and Americanism in general were fearfully labelled 'cultural communism'. Hitler, initially hampered by the conditions of his parole, had found a new Germany in which he had little influence. However, intent on reorganizing the party, raising more funds and finding his way to power through the ballot box rather than through violence, he had also noted other fertile areas of support: among the working-class, Protestant and rural populations.

Stresemann's credit-financed economy may have saved Germany's political reputation, particularly when it was invited to join the League of Nations in 1926, but the Dawes Plan left the nation heavily dependent on the fragile state of the world economy, leaving Germany overly reliant on US loans, planting the roots of another economic collapse in 1929.

Chapter 4

Resurrection

Hitler was released from Landsberg prison on 20 December 1924. He was collected by his friend and personal photographer Heinrich Hoffmann. Of course, Hoffmann wanted to record the moment for posterity and publicity, but the prison guards did not allow him to take pictures of the prison. Instead, they drove to the Bayertor (Bavarian Gate), the southern entrance to the old town of Landsberg, where Hitler posed next to Hoffmann's Mercedes and in front of the impressive late-Gothic arch, giving the impression of him leaving his 'fortress' prison.

They then drove back to Munich and Hitler was welcomed home to his small, second-floor apartment at 41 Thierschstrasse where his landlords, the Reicherts and his dog Wolf, greeted him warmly. He had much work to do: unite the warring *völkisch* factions, reorganize the party, convince everyone that 'he' was the one to lead them to power via democratic rules, and finance the whole undertaking. His first move was to approach Heinrich Held, the Governor of Bavaria, and ask for the bans on his party and its newspaper to be lifted. Hitler went cap in hand, expressing his remorse, renouncing his party's violent past and promising not to stage another putsch. Held accepted Hitler's word and removed the bans, saying, 'The wild beast is checked... We can afford to loosen the chain.'[1]

Hitler's first speech was quickly arranged for 27 February 1925 at the Bürgerbräukeller, venue of Gustav Kahr's speech on the night of the infamous putsch. In an editorial in the *Beobachter* published a week before the meeting, Hitler had sent a message to his rivals in the party. Factionalism was to end; there would be no shared leadership and no joint decision-making. Everyone had to rejoin the party and in doing so pledge their unconditional obedience to him.

On the night of Hitler's comeback, expectations among Nazi supporters were high and the venue was packed. There had been a few issues over who would attend, with Ludendorff, Gregor Strasser, Ernst Röhm and Alfred Rosenberg staying away. Anton Drexler was asked to open the evening but did not agree to it, so Max Amann stepped in. After a raucous welcome from the 3,000 people in the bar, Hitler spoke with his usual style and roused the crowd further, setting out the terms of his leadership and how the fight against Jewish Marxism was to continue, with violence if necessary: 'Either the enemy walks over our dead bodies or we over theirs.'[2] His two-hour speech ended with throaty roars and 'heils' from the audience. He then brought on to the stage various members of the warring factions who were in attendance: Gottfried Feder, Wilhelm Frick, Rudolph Buttmann, Hermann Esser, Julius Streicher and Artur Dinger, who shook hands and pledged their commitment to the cause in front of the cheering crowd. It was an uplifting return for Hitler, who was full of optimism for the future, even promising that if he had not met his supporters' expectations within a year, then he would resign. A week later, on hearing news of Hitler's speech, the Bavarian authorities once again banned him from public speaking, a move copied a little later by most other German states.

HITLER REASSERTS HIS POWER

Despite the new ban, events were moving fast for Hitler and the party. His reorganization was big news in Germany; his original supporters continued to be vocal and pay their dues; he continued to receive support from the Wagners, the Bechsteins, the Bruckmanns and Putzi Hanfstaengl. Other information on less public financial support, such as that of Henry Ford (see pp. 48–52) had been aired during Hitler's trial. Later still, the post Second World War US Kilgore Committee reported that, 'By 1919 Krupp [a German arms manufacturer] was already giving financial aid to one of the reactionary political groups which sowed the seed of the present Nazi ideology [...] By

1924 other prominent industrialists and financiers, among them Fritz Thyssen, Albert Voegler, Emil Kirdorf and Kurt von Schröder, were secretly giving substantial sums to the Nazis.'[3] Other industrialists, too, such as Albert Pietsch, are said to have contributed to the cause. Even so, new recruits and new major contributors were hard to come by.

Hitler's new style of unconditional leadership had been well received in Bavaria and, significantly, in other states such as Westphalia, the Rhineland, Hanover and Pomerania, but popularity in northern Germany, where the movement was strong but doubts remained as to what direction the 'new' party was taking, had so far eluded him personally. The day after Hitler's comeback speech in Munich, Friedrich Ebert, President of the Weimar Republic, died. Knowing that he would fail, Hitler persuaded General Ludendorff to stand in his place. His candidacy was a disaster: he polled 1 per cent of the vote, a result that effectively ended his leadership of the *völkisch* right. Hitler's calculated move had worked, and his rivals were losing ground. In northern Germany, however, Gregor Strasser was ploughing his own left-wing, National Socialist furrow. Although in general the two had similar aims and Strasser remained a Hitler loyalist, a split had opened up between the two branches of the Nazi movement during the 'vacuum' while Hitler had been in Landsberg prison.

On his release, Hitler had to concentrate on re-exerting his power in Bavaria, where Esser and Streicher, in particular, were throwing their weight around. There was resentment in north Germany, who felt they were being ignored – a matter that got worse when Hitler announced that because of his newly imposed ban, he would not get involved in party matters while he wrote the second volume of *Mein Kampf.* Internal difficulties continued throughout 1925 with the Munich headquarters attempting to impose itself on the whole movement and those in other states claiming to favour other policies in their particular area.

In essence, according to historian Louis Snyder, the northern Nazis thought of themselves as 'urban, socialist with a revolutionary trend', whereas district leaders in the south supported 'rural, racialist and populist ideas'.[4] In truth there was also something of a religious divide between the mainly Protestant northerners and the Catholics in Bavaria. For James and Suzanne Pool, one major bone of contention was what to do with the properties that had once belonged to the royal dynasties who had ruled the German states before 1918. In his search for potential new donors from 'wealthy individuals, the aristocrats and big business' and including a payment of RM1,500 he received each month from 'the divorced Duchess of Sachsen-Anhalt', Hitler, of course, was in favour of returning the properties to those families, though he did not broadcast the fact.[5] Strasser, by now the second most powerful leader in the Nazi Party, and one of his leading activists, Joseph Goebbels, were dead set against the idea. Another major difference lay in Hitler's edict, decided without consultation, that the party would henceforward participate in elections and parliamentary activities. This did not go down well in the north, where the party was dominated by former *Freikorps* who still had contempt for parliamentary government. There were, of course, other splinter groups and other differences contributing to the Nazis' internal conflicts, which, as we have seen, contributed to the poor results achieved by the *völkisch* movement in the Reichstag elections of December 1924.

NORTH VS SOUTH

Matters came to a head during the summer of 1925. Strasser, along with Goebbels and others, decided to face up to the policies emanating from the party's central office in Munich by forming a working committee to produce a document outlining their own leftist vision of radical 'national socialism'. On 22 November, Strasser called a meeting of the party Gauleiters (Nazi district governors) of northern Germany in Hanover, at which the document would be discussed. Opinions would be shared through the organization's journal, the *NS-Briefe*. At the meeting, delegates firmly rejected the idea that participation in elections was a legitimate political weapon, that in answer to the question 'Nationalist and socialist – what comes first?' the answer was obviously 'socialist' and that 'national-bolshevism' in Russia was of interest to them. The meeting went well enough for Strasser to hope that his document would eventually be the basis of a new party programme to replace Hitler's original 25-point plan.

Resurrection

Following his humiliation at Bamberg, Joseph Goebbels's opportunism and political nous led him to change sides from Gregor Strasser to Hitler. He was immediately appointed Gauleiter of Berlin. He rose quickly through the ranks to become its chief propagandist and the second most important person in the National Socialist Party.

Knowing that the gauntlet had been thrown down by Strasser, Hitler announced a party leadership conference on 14 February 1926 at Bamberg in northern Bavaria. It was clear to all that this meeting was to be a showdown, and Hitler had pulled out all the stops. The small medieval town was packed with stormtroopers and other party supporters. Delegates from northern Germany were greeted at the station by a band of brownshirts. The streets were lined with SA troops standing to attention below hundreds of swastika banners. They arrived at the meeting hall to be greeted by cheering crowds. They were impressed. Although there was no particular agenda for the meeting, of the northern delegates only Strasser was prepared to stand up and outline the committee's demands. In reply, Hitler's two-hour speech hit all the right notes, arguing skilfully against the expropriation of royal estates and houses – and as the party now stood by the rule of law it had to return property to its rightful owners, since not to do so would be to push the party down the road towards communism, and because there was no mention of Jewish property owners having their houses taken away. He spoke on foreign policy and outlined his plans to acquire land by colonization in the east. He then argued point by point with Strasser's programme as against his own, asking whether a change from one to the other would be a 'betrayal' of those who had died in the November putsch. He ended his speech by asking the delegates, 'Shall we create chaos or shall we "worm" our way to power? Will the party rule the masses, or the masses rule the party?'[6]

At the end of his speech, Hitler received backing from both southern and northern supporters. Strasser realized that there was no room for compromise and that if he was to insist on his proposals then he would have to break from the party. Although he and Goebbels were shocked at their humiliation, Strasser knew that without Hitler his movement would fail. A few weeks later, Strasser withdrew his proposals and called for the return of copies of his draft policy document. In return, Hitler agreed to dismiss Hermann Esser, his head of propaganda in Munich, whose bullying behaviour towards Strasser's organization had seriously exacerbated the split.

TIGHTENING HIS GRIP

Although it took a few weeks to become clear, Hitler had done himself a world of favours at Bamberg, some intended, others by chance. In March, Strasser was seriously hurt in a car crash and was off the scene for several weeks. In April, Hitler invited Goebbels to Munich to make a speech. At a meeting the following day, with Goebbels and two other leaders of the northern branch – Franz Pfeffer and Karl Kaufmann – they discussed recent events. Hitler admonished them for their part in the north–south split, lectured them on his own policies and offered his forgiveness if they pledged their allegiance to his leadership. They agreed and were rewarded further: Goebbels was appointed Gauleiter of Berlin; Pfeiffer was made head of the brownshirt paramilitaries; Kaufmann was made Gauleiter of Rhine-Ruhr. In addition, Gregor Strasser, whom Hitler had visited at home during his recovery, was appointed Reich Propaganda Leader of the Party. In terms of the party's and his own personal finances, Hitler's dismissal of the left-wingers' support of expropriation of royal palaces helped him dodge a bullet by enabling him to hang on to his wealthy donors: the Bruckmanns and the Bechsteins.

Other party rules were tightened. Hitler made it clear that religious questions had no place in the National Socialist movement. He also reasserted the centrality of his 25-point party programme. Orders were issued to the effect that all pamphlets issued by local party organizations had to be approved by headquarters. The chairman of the party (Hitler) was above the other board members and answerable only to the annual general meeting; any dissenting members and local branches could be excluded at the discretion of the chairman for 'opposing the aspirations of the association'.[7] Finally, the chairman alone was able to nominate all chairmen of the party's committees, apart from finance, which was already in the hands of Hitler's loyal party treasurer, Franz Schwarz.

At the beginning of July 1926, the Nazis held their second Party Congress (the 'Refounding Congress'). Taking place in Weimar, Thuringia – one of the federal states in which the party was not banned – it was an intended triumph for Hitler. There was little time for discussion; instead, the rally concentrated on 'speeches, ritual and marching'. Some 8,000 people attended and watched mass marches by SA stormtroopers. There were also the first public appearances of the *Schutzstaffel* (SS), which had been founded the previous year, and the renamed youth section of the party, the *Hitlerjugend* (Hitler Youth). Also present was the 'Blood Banner', the flag that led the putsch march towards the Feldherrnhalle in Munich in front of which the troops each swore a personal oath to Hitler. Though the rally was smaller than the one that had occurred in the run-up to the putsch, the Nazi Party was better organized, united and in the hands of a powerful leader.

Chapter 4

PARTY REORGANIZATION

During the later months of 1926 and in 1927, Hitler all but disappeared from public view. He spoke occasionally at 'private' gatherings, and enjoyed being entertained in the 'better circles' provided by the Bruckmanns. He took a few weekends, a number of holidays and eventually rented a house on the Obersalzberg, with its beautiful mountain scenery, which became his summer retreat and where he began work on the second volume of *Mein Kampf*. He put on a bit of weight and even flirted, often in rather strange circumstances, with a number of unsuitable women. Unsurprisingly, these relationships usually came to nothing.

The party reorganization continued with a realignment of party regions to coincide with the boundaries of the Weimar Republic, illustrating the Nazis' commitment to the electoral system. New, younger recruits were joining the party, who were free from the influence of Pan-Germanism and the *Freikorps* paramilitaries and had probably never even heard of the Thule Society. The leadership group was also young: Hitler was only 40 in 1929 and the others, such as Göring, Hess and Strasser, were all in their 30s. Since his appointment as Gauleiter of Berlin, a city in which the Nazis had only a few hundred members, Joseph Goebbels was making a name for himself. Confronting the more popular Social Democrat (SPD) and Communist (KPD) parties head-on, he used his considerable oratory skills to speak, in halls usually used by his opponents, in a manner intended to provoke. Brawls would often follow, in which he used the brown-shirted SA. Made up of the unemployed, the underemployed, apprentices and high-school students, Goebbels regarded the task of the *Sturmabteilung* as the 'conquest of the streets' with Jews and Marxists as their targets. Despite his small stature and his limp – he was born with a club foot and had not been able to fight in World War I – Goebbels became the 'top soldier' in Berlin's mini civil war. 'Our Dr Goebbels' as he was known by the party members, was much loved. He spent time with his supporters, 'comforted the severely wounded and attended the funerals of the dead.'[8] Despite the party's ban in Berlin in May 1927, its popularity grew, and Goebbels was elected to the Reichstag in 1928.

Hitler had been impressed with Goebbels despite his opposition and criticism at Bamberg. Goebbels' actions as Gauleiter in Berlin, where he was so effective and successful, informed Hitler that by playing off one member against another, the 'most ruthless, the most dynamic and the most efficient would rise to positions of power within the movement', giving it the necessary vitality, energy and constant forward motion.[9] Given that in-fighting among senior members of the party was rife during the party's entire existence, it was a policy that he was encouraged to use throughout his leadership of the Third Reich.

'THE ROAD TO RESURGENCE'

Of course, the party had lost supporters since the failed putsch and Hitler's spell in Landsberg prison but it had recovered somewhat with membership standing at 75,000 at the end of 1927. The Reichstag elections in May 1928 were disappointing, although the party got 12 deputies into the legislature, including Goebbels, Feder, Göring and Strasser. Recognizing the hold that the Social Democrat and the Communist parties had in urban centres, they decided to target rural, conservative and often Protestant communities, where farmers and their workers were suffering. Having borrowed money from the government – lent to help them fight inflation – and now with rising prices that tariffs could not deal with, bankruptcies and foreclosures were on the rise, again. Support for the Nazis, who began to spread the gospel of 'Blood and Soil' with the peasants at the heart of German society, grew quickly. By October 1928, membership numbers had swelled to 100,000 and then to 150,000 the following year.

With more members came more subscriptions, more donations, more sales of the party newspapers and more money. However, the party was in debt much of the time and Party Treasurer Schwartz had to balance the books as best he could. Hitler was comparatively well-off, earning money from his speeches, his articles and from sales of *Mein Kampf*. He was also still supported by the rich, upper-class families in thrall to him. But even so, eyebrows were raised when he spent 20,000 Marks on a Mercedes soon after leaving prison. He claimed that he had bought the car using a bank loan but that did not stop the speculation in Munich, especially when it was discovered that he could also afford a chauffeur. His tax returns, however, revealed nothing untoward and listed his income as deriving simply from his writings.

It seems most likely that money was being raised in other ways, too, especially after the discovery in 1966 of a pamphlet entitled 'The Road to Resurgence'. It had been written by Hitler in 1927 at the request of the 80-year-old Emil Kirdorf, a successful businessman in the coal industry. He was highly critical of Social Democrat policies, including its social welfare programmes, and of the power of the trade unions. He had little time for the problems and suffering of his workers, arguing against the Weimar government's plan to reduce working hours and introduce unemployment insurance.

Kirdorf heard Hitler speak at an NSDAP meeting in Essen in the spring of 1927 and liked what he heard. On 4 July that year, Kirdorf and Hitler were introduced to each other at a meeting arranged by a mutual acquaintance, Elsa Bruckmann. Over the course of a long conversation Kirdorf – a noted anti-Semite – was impressed, agreeing with Hitler on most important matters. He was, however, worried about the expropriation of industry and the Jewish question that Hitler demanded in *Mein Kampf*, as he felt these would not play well with other German industrialists, many of whom were not anti-Semitic and used Jewish money in their business dealings. Kirdorf therefore asked Hitler to write something more suitable, which he could distribute quietly among Germany's major industrialists and businessmen. He agreed to finance the project, which was then printed by Hugo Bruckmann's publishing company and handed out to an exclusive audience by way of an invitation to private gatherings with 'leading industrial personalities'. The fact that the existence of the pamphlet was 'kept secret' until 1966 illustrates how dangerous the opinions expressed in it were to Hitler's popularity with both conservatives and Marxists.

The pamphlet was skilfully written, summing up the German economic position and explaining how his party would move things away from Marxism and the restrictions of Versailles, in favour of the formation of a national community free of class contrasts. He also recommended expansion eastwards into new *Lebensraum* in order to regain Germany's 'great-power status' and the necessity of rebuilding its military might. Kirdorf was particularly impressed with Hitler's assertion that he would win the working classes back from the Marxist trade unions, and joined the party in the summer of 1927.

No one really knows how successful Hitler's speeches to the industrialist were in financial terms because no records exist, though rumours suggest that between 1926 and 1928 Kirdorf gave over RM100,000 to Hitler. However, the development of the party during those years and on into the early 1930s was increasingly well funded. It is highly likely, therefore, that Kirdorf was influential in opening the right doors for the Nazis even if only by 'taking every opportunity to make him acceptable to German industry'.[10]

'WHAT A FOOL I HAVE BEEN'

Perhaps the biggest fish caught on Hitler's financial fishing rod was that of Fritz Thyssen, heir to the Thyssen mining and steel-making empire based in the Ruhr city of Essen. Suspicious of the Jews and the communists because of the post-war German revolution, from his business dealings and because of the class hostility he experienced during the occupation of the Ruhr, during which he personally organized the campaign of passive resistance against the French and the Belgians, he came to respect Hitler's views. In 1923, Thyssen had given General Ludendorff 100,000 gold Marks to donate to the Nazis and the Bund Oberland. But personal contact between Thyssen and Hitler had to wait another few years.

According to James and Suzanne Pool, a funding crisis arose around Hitler's wish to purchase a new party headquarters in the autumn of 1928. Rudolph Hess asked Emil Kirdorf for the money, but he was unable to raise enough and suggested that Hess try Thyssen. Hitler had identified a 28-room mansion – the Palais Barlow on Brienner Strasse, between Karolinenplatz and Königsplatz in Munich – as a suitable building for his purposes. The 805,864 gold Marks required to purchase it was raised through a combination of 'donations, a special levy of at least two Reichsmarks from each party member, entrance

Chapter 4

fees from party events, and loans from the industrial magnates Friedrich Flick [a partner in Thyssen's United Steel Works] and Fritz Thyssen', which were expected to be repaid, at least in part.[11] The house was soon renamed the 'Brown House' because of the party's brown uniforms. At the time, Thyssen said that his contribution was RM250,000 but with refurbishment costs said to have been around RM800,000 and with evidence to suggest that the Nazis paid back very little, Thyssen's contribution had probably been five times that amount. Once again, Hitler had got his way. The party moved into the building on 1 January 1931, its stately presence helping give the Nazi Party an 'image of respectability'.[12]

For a time, links between Thyssen and the party grew closer. Hitler, Rudolph Hess and, in particular, Hermann Göring, were often invited to one of the

The Brown House included offices for Hitler, Rudolf Hess, Herman Göring, Joseph Goebbels and Heinrich Himmler and served as a centre of operations for the Nazi party from 1931 to 1937. In the basement was a prison where political prisoners were incarcerated and tortured if necessary.

industrialist's castles on the Rhine for elaborate dinners, fine wines and walks through the corridors past fine Old Masters paintings. Money for political and personal expenses regularly came their way too. In his book, *I Paid Hitler*, published in 1941, Thyssen wrote, 'I have personally given altogether one million marks to the National Socialist Party.'[13] It was only when they took power in 1933 that Thyssen realized what a fool he'd been in supporting Hitler.

Although both Kirdorf and Thyssen had obvious reasons for supporting Hitler – Kirdorf because he wanted the trade unions done away with and Thyssen because of his fears of communism, with which he associated Jews – they had another reason in common, one they shared with other heavy industrialists and businessmen in Germany and elsewhere. Their industries – steel, iron, coal, chemicals, textiles – had been involved in war materials until 1918, and had much of their business forbidden by the terms of Versailles. By now, they were in dire straits and on the verge of bankruptcy. Hitler's promises to make Germany 'great again' offered them one last hope.

REVELATIONS OF HISTORY

There were, of course, other businesses on the make too. The Dawes Plan (see p. 58–61) had seen enormous amounts of American dollars flowing into the German economy. The Plan, described by Carroll Quigley as 'largely a J.P. Morgan production',[14] floated a series of foreign loans on the US markets – official sources say $200 million; others say as much as $800 million – and the proceeds, minus fees and commission, were sent to the German government to pay reparations of their war debts to France and Britain. In turn, these countries could service their war debts to the USA. On the face of it, things were on the up. Money began to flow between the USA, Germany and the Allies as the German economy recovered. Reconciliation was now possible; a wartime reconciliation pact was under discussion at Locarno and seemed likely to bring Germany into the League of Nations. For the first time since their defeat in World War I, the German people began to feel normal.

As already explained, the financial arrangements of the Dawes Plan were overseen by a committee of experts: US representatives included banker, lawyer and politician Charles Dawes and J.P. Morgan's Owen Young, and for Germany, Hjalmar Schacht, president of the Reichsbank, and prominent industrialist Albert Vögler, both of whom would become key players in the rise of Hitler's Germany. Although in technical terms nothing illegal was going on, as the Kilgore Committee discovered in 1946, the situation was not exactly what it seemed. The money, ostensibly to be used to rebuild German industrial output, found its way into the pockets of the chemical and pharmaceutical company I.G. Farben and the Vereinigte Stahlwerke (United Steel Works), both of which would supply money and support for Hitler in 1933 and produce the German war materials for use in World War II.

Of course, it did not end there. The Dawes Plan was intended only as a temporary measure and in 1928 a new plan was needed to stave off Germany's growing debts. The Young Plan, devised by Owen D. Young, was intended to settle the reparations issue once and for all. It reduced the reparations total even further, to 121 billion gold Marks payable over 58 years. It also floated another huge loan, said to be in the region of $300 billion, and established a Bank for International Settlements (BIC) to facilitate arrangements.

Historians, such as Anthony Sutton and Carroll Quigley, now believe that the BIC was actually an organization that put the world's money supply in the hands of the New York Federal Reserve, the Bank of England, the Reichsbank and the Banque de France. Carroll Quigley described it as 'nothing less than [...] a world system of financial control, in private hands, able to dominate the political system of each country and the economy of the world as a whole'.[15] Of course, the bankers were not at war with each other; they were simply after the most profitable customers for their loans. In the late 1920s and 1930s these were the German cartels mentioned above, which produced pig iron, pipes and tubes, steel plates, explosives, gasoline, coal and other chemicals, and were now joined by AEG (German General Electric), General Motors, the Ford Motor Company, Dow Chemical, DuPont, Bendix Aviation and others – many of whom set up subsidiaries in Germany. These companies, built mainly on US loans – from the J.P. Morgan-controlled Rockefeller Chase Bank and the Warburg Manhattan Bank – and sometimes utilizing US technology, played a central part in bringing the Nazis to power and preparing Germany for war from an economic and industrial point of view.[16] Although the loans and the technical assistance being given to German companies was reported in the American press in the 1930s and explained by the post-war Kilgore Committee as 'accidental' and 'short-sighted' because of what was to come, the scale of help given and the fact that American financiers sat on the boards of two of the main German cartels points to deliberate collusion for the sake of profit. James Stewart Martin concluded that the 'loans for reconstruction did more to promote World War Two than to establish peace after World War One'.[17]

While the evidence does not mean that all American businesses helped fund the Nazis, it does not preclude the possibility that loans were forthcoming from European sources too. It does show, however, that some of the world's financial elite, including Wall Street, were 'intimately involved in the development of Nazi Germany'.[18]

THE WALL STREET CRASH

With the ink barely dry on the Young Plan agreement, on the morning of Thursday 24 October 1929, the New York Stock Market collapsed and share prices plummeted. Other shareowners began panic-selling, and prices dropped further. The Dow Jones, which shows the average share price of major companies, peaked at 381.2 on the eve of the crash and had fallen to 198 by November. The investment bubble, which had started in the USA in the early 1920s, had seen companies grow so rapidly that they were producing too much, leading to a fall in sales, prices and profits. In September, prices were at an all-time high and people began to speculate that the market would decline. They had been proved correct. The effects were felt not only in the USA but throughout the world, marking the beginning of the Great Depression that would last until 1936. Germany, which was almost totally reliant on loans from American financiers, was hit particularly hard. The foreign loans, on which its economy had come to depend, were called in and German banks, no longer able to obtain credit, struggled to find the money to pay them back and several of them folded. German industries lost access to US markets because the

Chapter 4

In 1933, some 40 per cent of the working population of Germany were unemployed, thousands found themselves without a place to live. Anxiety and fear gripped the masses as bankruptcies, suicides and malnourishment skyrocketed. In desperation, many turned to Hitler for help.

Resurrection

USA raised tariffs to protect its own companies. By 1932, German industrial output had dropped by almost 50 per cent. Some company factories reduced production; others closed completely. The result was spiralling unemployment: 1.5 million in 1929, 3 million the following year and 6 million in 1933.

Instead of increasing its spending, Chancellor Heinrich Brüning had decided to increase taxes and cut wages to reduce the budget deficit and avoid inflation. The measures failed and public discontent grew, meaning that the only beneficiary of the Weimar response was Adolf Hitler.

Chapter 5

The Pendulum Swings

Three weeks before the Stock Market Crash, on 3 October 1929, Foreign Minister Gustav Stresemann, who had done so much to restore Germany's political and economic stability, died. The two events combined to put an end to the 'golden years' of Weimar and plunge Germany into economic catastrophe once more. Hitler, who had little interest in economics, was quick to recognize the opportunities that the depression had suddenly presented to him. William Shirer quotes Hitler from an article he wrote in the Nazi press: 'Never in my life have I been so well disposed and inwardly contented as in these days. For hard reality has opened the eyes of millions of Germans to the unprecedented swindles, lies and betrayals of the Marxist deceivers of the people.'[1]

Former soldier Heinrich Brüning took over as chancellor in March 1930 thanks to a wave of support from the Reichswehr. With foreign loans no longer available, he came up with a financial plan to deal with rising unemployment by restricting benefits. But the idea was deeply unpopular across the political spectrum in which the German social welfare system was a source of great pride. He asked President Hindenburg to use the emergency powers of Article 48 of the Constitution to approve his bill by decree, but the chamber responded with a demand for its withdrawal. Faced with an impasse, in July Brüning, in a pointless attempt to increase his majority, requested the dissolution of the Reichstag and new elections were called for 14 September. Hitler knew that this was an opportunity.

ELECTION SUCCESS

The newly organized Nazi Party machine immediately clicked into gear.

Chapter 5

Hitler toured the cities and rural areas of the country making speech after speech pointing out the weaknesses and failures of the Weimar government. Organized by Joseph Goebbels, the campaign was a major success. Hitler attended meetings and torchlit parades and the towns in which he spoke were plastered with pro-Nazi posters. Millions of special-edition Nazi newspapers heralded each of the events, which also included film shows, rallies, brass bands and propaganda parades. The people wanted to know what had gone wrong and who was to blame, and Hitler provided them with convincing answers. The Versailles Treaty imposed by the Allies, and by the French in particular, was to blame. The Republic was no less guilty with its corrupt politicians, and dodgy financial dealings like the Dawes and Young Plans, which had destroyed the economy. He also slammed the Marxists, whose class hatred kept the country divided, and the Jews who were growing rich on the chaos.

Hitler's appearances were carefully staged, with crowds kept waiting in a hall festooned by Nazi banners and swastikas to set the tone. A band of brownshirts would then march in playing military music, before the dramatic arrival of the speaker himself. His words, starting in low tones at first and then raised to fever pitch in his unique and dramatic style, played on his audiences' emotions, raising in them indignation, anger and hope. Promising to make Germany strong again, he would reject the terms of Versailles, refuse to pay reparations, expand the army, root out corruption, deal with the trade unions and make sure that every German had a job and bread. He promised to deal with the Marxist threat and the Jews. Making his points with simple populist phrases, which he repeated over and over for emphasis, he appealed to the millions of unemployed who were desperate for jobs, money and food – many of them hit by newly imposed restrictions on their unemployment payments. He appealed to the shopkeepers and the farmers who needed customers. He appealed to the youths who wanted a future. Perhaps most importantly, his messages appealed to many leaders in business and in the army through his patriotism and his nationalism.

There was little detail in his plans for the future; the heart of his message was harking back to the Germany of Bismarck, saying, 'What counts is the will and if our will is strong enough we can do anything. We must renew the old German virtues of discipline, industry, and self-reliance. Not so long ago Germany was prosperous, and respected by all.'[2] What he was offering, however, was an alternative to the indignities imposed by Weimar, and his message had gone down well with the people. Despite the fact that the campaign was waged without any particular programme, except for 'an absolute belief that he was the future "saviour" of Germany',[3] on voting day, the Nazis received 6,409,600 votes, 19 per cent of the total, which meant 107 seats in the Reichstag. Their share of the vote had increased particularly in the Protestant countryside of northern and eastern Germany, in Schleswig-Holstein, East Prussia, Pomerania, Hanover and Mecklenburg. They had won support from the middle classes and working classes, from teachers, civil servants, office workers, clerks, small shopkeepers and farmers. The party had gone from the smallest to the second largest political party in Germany with only the Social Democrats ahead of them but with the Communist Party polling 4,592,000. It was the turning of the tide.

STILL CHASING BIG BUSINESS

The Nazi Party's campaign had been forceful and clever. As a party with many young supporters, activists – including by this time members of the Hitler Youth – had great physical energy and enthusiasm for the contest, putting up posters on walls all over the cities and towns, arranging and participating in marches and rallies, leafleting and knocking on doors. Despite the fact that few campaign workers were salaried and paid their own expenses, the costs of the campaign were huge. With the party as hard up as usual, treasurer Franz Schwarz had to use all his expertise to find the money and was ably assisted by Goebbels, who made sure that funds were not wasted by expertly tailoring Hitler's speeches, his fellow speakers, advertising, posters and leaflets to give the right messages at meetings in specific constituencies. In turn, Schwarz worked his magic.

Much of the money was raised at rallies and mass meetings. A typical event would start with a march by men from the SA, accompanied by a band. The meeting would take place in a large hall or a marquee or a sports hall, which would feature films, plays, sideshows and entertainment for children. There would be an admission fee of 1 or 2 Marks, and collection boxes would be passed around once the event got underway. A police report on a rally in Essen in 1920, at which Hitler spoke, recorded that an estimated crowd of 10,000 were in attendance and that there was a total take of RM12,000. During the campaign in 1930, the Nazis held some 6,000 mass meetings in six weeks across Germany. Hitler concentrated on Berlin and Essen while other speakers, such as Alfred Rosenberg, or Rudolf Hess and others, also took the stage. Hitler, of course, took his share of the money, estimated at anywhere from RM200 to RM1,200 for a typical public meeting. In his tax return that year, Hitler's income was reported as RM48,472, of which RM45,472 came from royalties on his now strong-selling book *Mein Kampf.*

In addition to these revenue streams, Schwarz juggled the books, delaying salaries and bill payments. He also mortgaged party cars and other valuables and obtained credit for printing expenses, hire of halls and so on. The party received little financial help from big business at the time, apart from Emil Kirdorf and Fritz Thyssen. For years after the war, the history books were filled with stories of how big business had catapulted Hitler to power. Rumours of financial support from people such as Henry Ford, Krupp, Hugo Stinnes, the Ruhrlade (a shadowy interest group comprising 12 of the most influential industrialists in the Ruhr who raised and spent money in the interest of the area's coal and iron industries) and locomotive maker Ernst von Borsig were common but little evidence of major support was ever offered and payments were certainly not documented. This rumour-mongering was helped in a big way because it was in no one's interest that anyone else knew about any such transactions, as bad press would follow. Even if money was given to the party by businesses, it was rarely in substantial amounts. Although some businessmen clearly approved of Hitler's policies, as Cris Whetton points out in *Hitler's Fortune*, his party was thought of as anti-business and businesses were therefore reluctant to support it. Stated clearly in Hitler's 'unalterable' 25-point Plan of 24 February 1920, the NSDAP demanded, 'nationalisation of all businesses [...] that the profits from wholesale business shall be shared out' and the 'immediate communalisation of wholesale business premises, and their lease at a cheap rate to small traders.'[4] Such sentiments made it seem unlikely that the party would ever amount to anything.

In terms of Hitler himself, the Bechsteins, who had contributed substantial amounts of money to support the *Völkischer Beobachter* in its early days and given generously to his personal funds in the mid-1920s, suffered from press reports of their association with him. As a result, their company sales had suffered, and their income was severely reduced. The Bruckmanns fared better, kept Hitler in funds and guaranteed the rent on his new eight-room luxury apartment at Number 16 Prinzregentenplatz in the fashionable Bogenhausen district of Munich, which he moved into after the election in 1929.

Following the publication of historian Henry Ashby Turner's book *German Big Business and the Rise of Hitler* in 1985, however, many historians have changed their views on the influence of big business on Hitler's road to power. Using a wealth of archival documentation, Turner argues that party funding did indeed come from membership fees, rally collections and sales of party publications along with contributions from the owners of small companies. Alarmed at some of Hitler's anti-capitalist ideas, big business preferred to look to the centrist parties for help.

HITLER'S SELF-BELIEF

Had the election not been successful, the party would have gone bankrupt. Of course, it was a huge success. Many of its new supporters were male, young – born in the first decade of the 20th century – and had experienced war, revolution, unemployment and economic crisis. They turned to Hitler and the NSDAP with their promises of *'Freiheit und Brot'* ('Freedom and Bread') as something 'new and different'. Hitler was particularly popular with students, as Ian Kershaw recalls in his biography: 'In November 1928 [Hitler] had received a rapturous reception from 2,500 students at Munich University.'[5] The audience had already been addressed by the leader of the Nationalsozialistischer Deutscher Studentenbund (NSDStB or Nazi Students'

Chapter 5

Federation), Baldur von Schirach. His work for the party is credited with a huge increase in Nazi votes in the student union elections that year. His efforts would be rewarded in 1931 when he was given the leadership of the Hitler Youth.

The Nazis' election success saw the party and its leader taken seriously as a political force in Germany and abroad for the first time. For Hitler himself, it confirmed the belief that *he* and he alone was the man to lead the party forward. For ten years or so the party had been ignored by the press; now they found themselves on the front pages. During his spell in Landsberg prison Hitler had become convinced that he was a leader, that he was the chosen one, his self-belief elevated beyond measure with an almost messianic conviction that he would lead Germany back to greatness. It seems probable that the party's surprising electoral success in 1930 had a similar effect – one day dismissed as a joke for his crude speeches and tacky rallies, the next day headline news as the leader of the country's second most popular political party. His dream of power was taking shape.

Behind the scenes, though, the man himself was hard to find. His colleagues witnessed the astonishing power of his public appearances at the party's mass rallies, how he could raise the crowds to ecstatic delirium in the certainty that he would lead them to guaranteed victory. But offstage he was, by turns, remote, uncommunicative, unreliable, charming and furiously angry. He was also a work-shy egomaniac with deep insecurities, preferring to criticize others' ideas and express his own in vague terms and expect others to come back to him with ready-made policies. His working style at this point was no different from the early days of the DAP. The reality was that he contributed little to the running and working of the party and his officials had scant idea of what they were supposed to be doing, resulting in chaos and in-fighting as they all either competed for his attention or to avoid his attention depending on his mood that day. He didn't drink, he didn't smoke, he discussed important matters with, as Ian Kershaw explains, '… small – and changing – groups or individuals. That way, Hitler remained in full control.'[6] He believed in himself, that he was always right. He was rigid in his thinking and not prepared to tolerate criticism or to discuss

The Pendulum Swings

Joseph Goebbels and Hermann Göring were both were deeply ambitious, narcissistic and manipulative, sharing a lust for power, praise and distinction. However, in time Göring began to focus more on enjoying the trappings of his elevated position, while Goebbels continued to push the Nazi cause.

alternative solutions. However, he never failed to register who his potential critics were and bear grudges against them. He avoided discussing subjects about which he knew nothing and was unable to take awkward decisions, preferring instead to do nothing.

He did, however, possess a vision, a 'sixth sense in politics' according to leader of the SA Franz Pfeffer von Salomon, a kind of 'genius' and the charisma to persuade millions of Germans that he was right.[7] He also possessed a prophetic talent for political rhetoric, saying the right things at the right time to the right people. He could be a delightful and charming dinner guest, entertaining his friends at the Café Heck. He loved the ladies, indulging in much hand-kissing and flattery, as well as children and animals. His administrative staff, to whom he was invariably courteous, loved him, despite the difficulties they encountered when working with him.

Yet he had few close friends. His inner circle, made up of Julius Schaub, one of Hitler's adjutants, his photographer Heinrich Hoffmann and Joseph (Sepp) Dietrich, one of his bodyguards, were probably his closest confidants with whom he would discuss even secret matters openly. Only then were decisions passed on to those who needed to know. He addressed the other Nazi leaders by their surnames alone, even Goebbels, Göring and Himmler.[8]

STRONG, DECISIVE AND DYNAMIC

As the depression bit deeper, the unemployment figures rose at an alarming pace. By 1932, one in three workers was registered as unemployed. With less money in people's pockets, there was less to spend on food, so unemployment spread to rural areas too. The unemployment system, which had been introduced in 1927, was based on a special insurance and financed by companies, local authorities and the central government. It was designed to offer temporary relief to some 800,000 people. However, in 1932 the unemployment figure stood at 6 million! With tax revenue falling, benefits had to be cut ... and were then stopped altogether.

The situation on the streets of German towns and cities began to deteriorate. With little to do, gangs of men and boys began to gather around on street corners and parks. The atmosphere was menacing, particularly at night. There was violence, often provoked by the communists, whose national membership had been swollen by the unemployed and stood at 360,000 by 1932. Their hatred of the Social Democrats, which dated back to the German revolution of 1918–19, meant that they rejected the faux democracy peddled by what they thought of as the 'fascist' Weimar government. Happy to see lawlessness on the streets, they organized rent strikes and no-go areas in the cities in which transgressors would be beaten up. There were fights too between the communists and the Nazis, whose leaders were busy ordering the SA brownshirts and the Hitler Youth to dole out brutal violence in the poor parts of the big cities, driving the Reds back to their tenement buildings in the slums. There were regular fights in Berlin's East End during the second half of 1929 between the SA and the Communist Red Front Fighters. Goebbels, Gauleiter of the city, was determined to 'smash the Reds' and for nights on end gangs would emerge from their taverns and cafes and engage in vicious battles resulting in serious injuries and deaths.

For a time, the possibility of a communist takeover was a realistic fear for middle-class Germans, who must have wondered who they would choose to replace it if the government fell: would it be Hitler or the communists? At this point, the sympathies of the police and the general population seemed to be on the side of what they saw as 'the strong, decisive, dynamic Nazis'.[9]

In the boardrooms too there was spreading alarm at the situation and, in the light of Hitler's spectacular success in the 1930 election, big business began to take him seriously, some of them putting out feelers in the hope of influencing any forthcoming Nazi economic policies. In January 1931, Emil von Strauss, a director of the Deutsche Bank und Disconto-Gesellschaft, introduced former president of the Reichsbank Hjalmar Schacht to Hermann Göring, who subsequently introduced him to Hitler. The two got on well. Despite the meeting being secret, Schacht's tacit approval of Hitler's views became known in business circles and did much to suggest that he was worth supporting. While there is no documentary evidence, it is rumoured that Strauss told Otto Wagener, head of the Nazis' Economic Policy Office, that he donated money to Hitler through Göring and that there was more, if needed. He also funded an Essen-based Nazi journal to see it through financial difficulties.

Hitler poses with his official photographer Heinrich Hoffmann. The two became friends and travelled together extensively. Hoffmann's cleverly crafted images played a key part in the making of the Hitler legend and made them both rich.

There are similar rumoured connections between Hitler and Friedrich Flick, owner of the Gelsenkirchen iron and steel conglomerate. At a postwar investigation, Flick admitted that he had given some RM50,000 to Nazi organizations such as the SA and Robert Lay's pro-Nazi newspaper the *Westdeutscher Beobachter*, which was published in Cologne. In addition, Flick also donated RM20,000 during the elections in November 1932.

There were reports of donations to the party from the Ruhrlade; from the so-called Keppler Circle, representing manufacturers, minor bankers and merchants; and from the Wagemann Circle, which included representatives of I.G. Farben and other chemical manufacturers, who all offered funds in return for influence. However, though the NSDAP needed the money, Hitler would not compromise. Even if money did indeed pass from big business to Hitler's party in the first few years of the 1930s, it was not in significant amounts.

THE YEAR OF CRISIS

In 1931, as the economic situation in Germany got worse, Hitler was also faced with political and personal crises. With Brüning's government seemingly unable to stabilize conditions and halt rising unemployment, other interested parties came up with their own suggestions: for the employers it was lower wages; for the trade unions it was lower prices. Matters were made worse when the USA increased the duty on imported goods by more than 20 per cent. A mooted customs union with Austria was met with outrage by France, who wanted to keep the German economy in check. As a result, France withdrew its loans to both countries, causing banks to crash. The clamour for strong leadership grew louder.

Hitler, meanwhile, was faced with several crises of his own over the direction the party was taking. In April 1930, Otto Strasser, more radical than his brother Gregor, openly criticized Hitler's cosying up to wealthy industrialists and the upper classes, re-exposing the simmering dispute around the place of socialism in National Socialism. Strasser, who ran a publishing house, used his newspaper, the *Kämpfer Verlag*, to publicize the argument. Hitler was embarrassed and aware that this problem might worry the party's financial

The Pendulum Swings

Close friends when they first met in 1919, Röhm was a military man through-and-through with a disdain for civilian life. They marched together in the Beer Hall Putsch, the failure of which resulted in Röhm's dismissal from the army.

supporters. In response, Goebbels expelled a number of socialist members, and, in July, Otto Strasser jumped before he was pushed. After writing an article in his newspaper entitled, 'Socialists Leave the Nazi Party', he was promptly banned from the NSDAP. In April 1931, Hitler survived a rebellion by the Berlin and East Prussian SA led by Walter Stennes. Frustrated by the party's slow progress, Stennes travelled to Munich to meet Hitler. The meeting was refused. Relations between civilian party workers and the 'party soldiers' were already bad and had been made considerably worse by a perceived lack of recognition of the part played by the SA in the election victory. A revolt seemed likely. Hitler and Goebbels moved quickly to resolve the situation, support for Stennes fell away and SA leader Franz Pfeffer von Salomon resigned. As a result, Hitler took over the supreme leadership of both the SA and the SS, with Otto Wagener in charge of the day-to-day running of the SA and the returning Ernst Röhm as chief of staff.

Röhm began reorganizing the SA immediately. A recruitment drive in 1931 saw its membership rise from 88,000 to 260,000. Many of the new recruits in rural areas came from 'respectable' farming families who were attracted by the Nazis as an alternative to shooting clubs and enjoyed the marching and the music of their parades – there were not many communists in these areas to go after. In the cities, however, the SA that Röhm was rebuilding had real paramilitary characteristics and was rapidly becoming a formidable force.

On his return to the Nazi fold in 1927, Hermann Göring had coveted the job of leader of the SA, a post he had already held in the party's early days. But in 1928 he was elected to the Reichstag and Hitler decided to use his PR skills to woo political and economic support from the German upper classes, to which he had access because of his aristocratic Swedish wife Carin. Based in Berlin, Göring's successful conquests included Prince August Wilhelm of Prussia, Fritz Thyssen and Hjalmar Schacht. In 1930, following his re-election to the Reichstag, Hitler rewarded Göring by appointing him the party's chief political spokesman.

On 18 September 1931, Geli Raubal – the 23-year-old daughter of Hitler's half-sister Angela and his housemate at the apartment on Prinzregentenplatz –

was found dead in her room with his Walther revolver on the couch nearby. Her mother kept house for Hitler at Haus Wachenfeld, a holiday villa on the Obersalzberg (see p. 204), and had taken her daughters Geli and Friedl along with her. Hitler developed a relationship with Geli and, despite the fact that he was 19 years her senior, fell in love with her and invited her to live with him in his new apartment in Munich. The relationship between the bubbly blonde-haired beauty and the sharp-featured, older, more serious, black-haired, moustachioed politician was the talk of the town. He was clearly in love with Geli; her feelings are 'just a matter of conjecture' according to William Shirer.[10] She

The death of Hitler's half-niece and romantic obsession Geli Raubal, found on the couch with a bullet in her chest and Hitler's gun by her side in his Munich apartment, has remained a mystery for over 75 years.

was vivacious, a head-turner, and attracted male attention wherever she went. By all accounts, Hitler was overbearing and hung on to her like a lovelorn teenager. Matters became difficult, each suspecting the other of having affairs, he with Winifred Wagner and she with Emil Maurice, one of Hitler's bodyguards. Apparently, his jealousy boiled over and she announced that she was leaving to live in Vienna. He forbade her to go during a row overheard by neighbours. Hitler set off later that day for a meeting in Hamburg.

The following morning, her body was found. Police removed it immediately via the back stairs and, after a hasty post-mortem, announced that there was no doubt that the 'shot had been self-inflicted'.[11] The body was then shipped off to Vienna for burial. As soon as the news broke in the newspapers, the headlines and the rumours began. It was a major scandal. Stories were rife: that she had been shot by Hitler, shot by Himmler because she had threatened to expose her involvement in a secret money pipeline, that she was pregnant with Hitler's child, that she was going to expose Hitler's unorthodox sexual demands. Almost a hundred years later, no credible evidence as to what really happened has ever turned up.

Hitler was devasted, became depressed and was reported to be close to taking his own life. Whether it was Geli's death or fears that the lurid press reports would ruin his political career, no one knows. Hans Frank used legal means to quieten the press and Hitler spent an evening weeping at Geli's graveside in Vienna. After the funeral, Hitler seemed to have recovered, and the crisis was over.

THE TURNING POINT

Since his time in Landsberg prison, Hitler had been convinced that in order to attain power, he needed the help of the law, the police and the army. It was partly with this in mind that he had given leadership of the SA to Ernst Röhm rather than Göring, as Röhm was a great friend of General Kurt von Schleicher, a man of increasing importance in German politics who had persuaded President Hindenburg to appoint Brüning as chancellor. In 1927, faced with the growing threat of the SA, which it regarded as its rival, the army had forbidden the recruitment of Nazis into its ranks, as well as from its supply depots and arms storage facilities. In September 1930, three young lieutenants were arrested for spreading Nazi propaganda in their regiments, trying to encourage the idea that should there be a Nazi revolt, then their fellow officers would not fire on the rebels. The three were charged with high treason, with the trial set to take place a week after the elections.

The story of the trial, of course, was not that the three officers were found guilty and received light sentences, but that of Hitler's appearance as a witness for the defence. Fully aware that Nazi sentiments in the army were growing, he took advantage of this platform to explain to the Reichswehr that the Nazis posed no threat to the army, and that his plan was to seize power without the 'revolt' threatened by the accused but rather by constitutional means. Once in power, he said, 'Out of the present Reichswehr a great army of the German people shall arise.'[12] For him, the real enemies were the 'November criminals'. His closing speech was applauded by those in the courtroom.

The election results in 1930 showed that the Nazis had convinced millions of Germans that they were the party of the future, ready to lead the country away from the futile, failing democracy of Weimar. For army officers and soldiers, National Socialism appealed not only because of the party's nationalism, but also because of Hitler's promises to restore the army to its former glory. For the likes of Schleicher, the matter was a little more nuanced. The Nazis were the obvious choice to bring much-needed stability to Germany. He was worried that discontent was spreading and that he may need to involve the army to deal with rising anger in the streets. But above that, he hoped that by giving his support to the Nazis now, then when and if they came to power, they would return the favour. Other generals too were reassured, and Schleicher began to make overtures by removing the ban on Nazi recruitment.

THE PENDULUM SWINGS

Meanwhile, Göring persisted with his work raising funds from industrialists and aristocrats, on whom the election results also had a dramatic effect. The 'Austrian upstart',[13] as Hitler had once been known, was now to be taken seriously. In the same way that Schleicher was looking for influence in return for his support, so did an increasing number of industrialists. In 1931, Walther Funk, 'a greasy, shifty-eyed, paunchy little man whose face always reminded this writer of a frog',[14] gave up his job as a financial journalist to join the Nazis. He was urged to join by a number of his industrialist friends from the Rhineland in the hope that he might be able to influence the party's industrial policies. Hitler, as always desperate for money to support his rapidly expanding party's interests, turned his attention to the industrialists. Coal and steel interests, in the shape of Kirdorf, Thyssen and Voegler, of United Steel Works were still involved, but in his testimony to the Nuremberg trials at the end of the war, Funk named others who did not want to miss out if Hitler was to come to power. Among the many industries and company directors he mentioned, the most significant were Georg von Schnitzler, a director at the giant chemical

Chapter 5

cartel I.G. Farben; the two Augusts – Rosterg and Diehn – leading players in the potash industry; Wilhelm Cuno of the Hamburg-America shipping line, Germany's largest shipping concern; and the Continental rubber company and steel magnate Otto Wolff. Connections with several leading German banks were skilfully negotiated by Dr Schacht, who resigned as president of the Reichsbank and joined the NSDAP. His connections and influence ensured that money was forthcoming from the Deutsche Bank, the Dresdner Bank, the Commerz- und Privatbank Aktiengesellschaft as well as the Allianz insurance company.

Hermann Göring's work among the German upper classes did not go unnoticed, particularly in his ability to explain away their worries about the street violence perpetrated by the SA brownshirts. He would host regular parties at his luxurious bachelor's flat in Berlin (his wife was by then very ill, and had returned home to Sweden). In attendance would be prominent members of Berlin's high society, including princes, princesses, 'barons' of the business world and important officers from the army. At the door of the reception room would be a box marked 'donations for the party'. It was customary to give generously.

Although these connections are provable, even if only through personal testimonies, autobiographies and by word of mouth rather than with documentary evidence, the Nazi Party must have had substantial amounts of money to spend during the years that Hitler was preparing for power. By the end of 1931, the pendulum was swinging one way: Hitler's way.

Chapter 6

Road to Power

Since his appointment in 1930, Chancellor Brüning had operated independently of parliament because he did not have a majority in the Reichstag. Instead, he used Article 48 of the constitution, which gave emergency powers to the Reich president to pass bills. Brüning, chosen and appointed by President Hindenburg for his financial expertise, proposed a policy of deflation with drastic cuts in state expenditure including contributions to unemployment insurance, and benefits for the sick, invalids and pensioners. He also announced an internal devaluation by which prices, salaries and rents were reduced by 20 per cent. The bill was opposed by the Reichstag. Hindenburg passed it by decree, but it was rejected a second time. Brüning asked Hindenburg to dissolve the Reichstag, and the 14 September 1931 election was called, changing the political landscape in Germany with the massive rise in the popularity of the Nazis.

Brüning's policies, though slow and steady, did little to help the unemployment figures and there was a growing frustration with Weimar democracy. As the crisis continued, people on all sides were looking to Hitler for answers; everyone wanted a piece of him. The conservative Nationalist Party (DVNP), led by Alfred Hugenberg, wanted his support for a plebiscite to dissolve the Prussian Diet – regarded as a symbol of German democracy and therefore hated by the extremist parties, both left and right. Although 98 per cent of those who voted were in favour of dissolution, the turnout was low and the referendum failed. In late 1931, General von Schleicher – who had leadership ambitions of his own – turned to Hitler too, inviting him to meet Hindenburg to discuss the future of the Brüning government. But the meeting was not a success. By all accounts Hitler, who had no wish to support the government, talked too much and Hindenburg was bored. However, being asked by the president for his opinions had the effect of inflating Hitler's self-importance – a feeling he carried over into his next appointment.

THE HARZBURG RALLY
The day after the meeting, Hitler travelled to Bad Harzburg, a spa town in central Germany, for a huge, patriotic, right-wing rally organized by Hugenberg to demonstrate their unity in the fight against the governments of Germany and of Prussia. Representatives from the National Socialists, the Stahlhelm, the Reichslandbund, the Pan-German League and other right-wing conservative movements were all present. Also present were members of various royal families, the industrialist Fritz Thyssen, some parliamentarians, members of the armed forces, including General Hans von Seeckt, and bankers, such as former Reichsbank president Hjalmar Schacht.

Hugenberg opened the meeting with a speech declaring that what he called the 'national opposition' was ready to overthrow the presidential cabinet of Chancellor Heinrich Brüning, take office and save the country from Bolshevism, unemployment, hunger and economic bankruptcy caused by his policies. He announced the formation of the Harzburg Front, which would utilize the power, influence and money of those attending the rally to persuade President Hindenburg to remove Brüning from office. Hitler spoke too, but with little enthusiasm. His heart was not in it. There had been internal arguments within the NSDAP about attending in the first place, particularly from the left wing of the party, who remained suspicious of any form of collaboration. A further split in the party was revealed following the discovery by the police of documents in Hesse, near Frankfurt, which suggested that the SA was planning a violent putsch, 'followed by food rationing, the abolition of money, compulsory labour for all and the death penalty for disobeying the authorities.'[1] Hitler denied any knowledge of the plan, which was dismissed as a local matter. However, suspicions remained. Hitler was also cautious because he believed that Hugenberg had only invited the Nazis to the rally to use Hitler's popularity for his own ends in the forthcoming presidential elections – Hindenburg's seven-year term was coming to an end in the spring of 1932. Looking to the future, Hitler also suspected that Hugenberg would be his adversary should Hindenburg require someone to replace Brüning as chancellor. The Nazi leader preferred to establish his credentials by arranging a mass march-past of thousands of SA troops, jackboots pounding and swastikas fluttering above their heads.

There were speeches from other leaders too, but they had little new to say. However, the headlines were taken by Hjalmar Schacht's speech, which condemned the Young Plan and Brüning's policies and accused the government of covering up the real problems of the state treasury. He listed the endless catalogue of financial demands on Germany: foreign debt payments that could not be met in time, the illiquidity of financial institutions and the state, and unaffordable public finances. The government was outraged and denied that it was keeping financial secrets from the people. But mud sticks, unemployment figures were rising, and the economy continued to bump along the bottom, further weakening the government's reputation.

The rally ended in disappointment for Hugenberg. The Harzburg Front, though comprising an impressive list of wealthy financial backers, did not include many of Germany's leading industrialists and business leaders, nor did it have the support of Hitler and the NSDAP. In reality, 'the spirit of right-wing unity to which he [Hugenberg] had hoped to give birth had been stillborn'.[2] Despite his best efforts, the rally revealed the deep divisions that existed in the right-wing movement at the exact moment that their chance of seizing power was at its best.

ECONOMIC ADVICE

Nevertheless, the rally had given Hitler food for thought and he stepped up his efforts to win support among the industrialists and big businesses that had not been represented at the Harzburg rally. Although evidence and dates are hard to come by, there are a number of names and events that are held up as marking the start of Hitler's most successful fundraising efforts to that

Chapter 6

At Hartzburg, Hitler noted the lack of common ground among participants apart from enmity to the government. He had no plan, but he knew he needed money for a tilt at power so engaged financial experts such as (left to right) Wilhelm Keppler, Hjalmar Schacht and Walther Funk to help him win support from big business.

point. In early 1932, Hitler was invited by Fritz Thyssen to address some 650 of Germany's wealthiest businessmen at the Düsseldorf Industry Club. Over two hours he explained to the assembled magnates that they had nothing to fear from the Nazis, and that they would crush the trade unions and assert state control over the workers in co-operation with the industrial owners. He attacked communism and socialism. The effect of his words on his concerned audience was profound, judging by the sum collected at the end of the meeting, with Heinrich Hoffmann recalling, 'His appeal met with immediate response. Sixty-five thousand marks made a good foundation; the first step towards the assumption of power had been taken.'[3] Naturally, the left-wing press used news of the meeting to claim that Hitler was a capitalist puppet.

With the need for money to finance his campaign for the upcoming presidential election now paramount to fund a number of propaganda tours, Hitler appointed several business advisors. Most important of these were Wilhelm Keppler, Hjalmar Schacht and Walther Funk. He asked Keppler, a small-time chemical manufacturer, to form a group of experts from different sectors of the economy to advise Hitler on winning the support of big business. The so-called Keppler Circle had 12 members including bankers, such as Kurt von Schröder and Friedrich Reinhard, and industrialists like

Albert Vögler and August Rosterg. While the circle failed to come up with a concrete programme for Hitler's needs, it enabled him to maintain contacts with influential economists and would play a significant part in the events that led to Hitler's appointment as chancellor in January 1933.

Another economic advice group, the Wagemann Circle, formed in 1932, although this one comprised members who wanted to influence Nazi economic policies. Walther Funk was engaged to liaise between the Circle and Hitler himself. Led by government and state economist Professor Ernst Wagemann, the group also included a number of employees from the pharmaceutical company I.G. Farben. It is recorded that Funk requested financial support from the company. There is evidence that money was paid to Funk himself and to the NSDAP at this point, but there are no records of payments to Hitler before 1933.

Despite the lack of evidence of major payments to Hitler from German big business, the Nazis had money – and lots of it at the beginning of 1932. Although Hitler had not actually decided to run for president – indeed at this point he was not even eligible to run, as he was not a German citizen – he knew that his party was on the threshold of power and that funding was essential. It seems most likely that money was collected from the sources already outlined here but that the sums donated were much larger than rumoured at the time. Perhaps the collections at meetings with businessmen at the Haus Elephant hotel in Weimar, the Düsseldorf Industry Club and so on yielded greater sums than were admitted. Perhaps Fritz Thyssen's open support for Hitler around the time of the Düsseldorf speech did, as the industrialist claimed in his book, *I Paid Hitler*, make 'a deep impression on the assembled industrialists, and in consequence of this a large number of contributions flowed from the resources of heavy-industry into the treasury of the National Socialist Party'.[4] Then there are rumours of funds arriving from the USA. In his book *Wall Street and the Rise of Hitler*, Anthony Sutton mentions the so-called 'Kaiserhof Meeting', held in Berlin in May 1932 and attended by members of I.G. Farben, American I.G. Farben, Louis Kiep of the Hamburg-America shipping line and August Diehn, director of the German potash syndicate at which more than RM500,000 was raised and deposited into Rudolf Hess's account at Deutsche Bank. There are also unsubstantiated rumours that Max Warburg, a director at I.G. Farben and the Warburg Bank, was present that day. Added to this was the money coming from regular supporters, such as Friedrich Frick, Emil Kirdorf and others in the coal industry. Donations came too from Alfred Hugenberg, in payment for Nazi support for the Young Plan plebiscite, from the Ruhrlade at the request of Walther Funk and from the banker Emil Georg von Strauss, who is said to have given money via his friend Hermann Göring in support of the Essen-based Nazi journal *National Zeitung*.

HITLER STANDS FOR OFFICE

On 25 February 1932, Adolf Hitler finally became a German citizen, therefore allowing him to stand for election should he choose to. The following day, he announced his candidacy for the presidential elections to be held in March and April. With the Reichstag effectively powerless because of Brüning's continued use of Article 48, the campaign was fought on the streets, in which the depression had bitten deeply. At this point, almost one worker in three was unemployed, meaning that upwards of 13 million people were either without work or in a home without income, as benefits were reduced and sometimes cut completely. Many of those in work were paid at reduced rates or for reduced hours. The situation on German city streets was hopeless, desperate and menacing, with violence in the air. Paramilitaries representing parties across the political spectrum roamed the streets, protecting their own areas and venturing into other territories to fight. On the right were the SA, now boasting 400,000 members. The Stahlhelm were also a political force, representing the more moderate German People's Party, and were not in favour of Hitler as president. In the centre was the Social Democratic Reichsbanner. On the left was the Communist Party, regarded as the party of the unemployed. Led by trade unionists, workers' athletic clubs and their Red Front Fighters League, the party numbered over 360,000 and was growing election by election. Against this backdrop, the contest for the presidency emerged as the stable point in a fluid and volatile political situation.

Hindenburg, now 84, was not keen to stand in another election but Brüning insisted, convinced that if he did not remain president, then Hitler would be voted in. Brüning tried to persuade the other parties to extend Hindenburg's term of office, but they did not agree to the plan. So, Hindenburg reluctantly agreed to stand, opposed by Hitler and Theodor Duesterberg, a candidate put up by the Stahlhelm. In the run-up to the first ballot, the Nazis launched a massive campaign with marches, posters and rallies along with plenty of street brawls and violence. In essence, it was a vote for or against National Socialism, and the Nazis came up short. Hindenburg won 49.6 per cent, not enough for an overall majority; Hitler won 30 per cent and Duesterberg won 6.8 per cent.

For the second ballot, Hindenburg and Hitler were joined by Communist leader Ernst Thälmann. The Nazi campaign continued with even more energy, Hitler travelling across the country by plane, giving 46 speeches – sometimes as many as five a day – to hundreds of thousands of people. In his post-war recollections, NSDAP press chief Otto Dietrich made it clear how the party funded this part of their campaign, explaining that: 'Hitler's great propaganda tours of 1932 financed themselves exclusively through the entrance fees for giant rallies, at which seats in the front rows often went for fantastic prices.'[5] It was worth every pfennig, as Hitler boosted his share of the vote to 37 per cent with over 13 million votes in his favour. Hindenburg won with 53 per cent, with Thälmann coming in at 10 per cent. Hitler had not won but his votes were on the increase, particularly among the middle classes and the rural population, who were increasingly disillusioned with the Weimar Republic. However, following Hindenburg's victory Brüning had yielded to political pressure and imposed a national ban on the SA and SS, blaming them for inciting political violence in the election run-up.

HOLDING HITLER AT BAY

Despite the ban, political turmoil continued later in April in various state elections. Hitler again made flying visits to Prussia, Bavaria and Württemberg, in all of which the Nazis were victorious. In Saxony-Anhalt their 40.9 per cent of the vote gave them the right to form the state government; Nazi momentum

Chapter 6

seemed unstoppable. General von Schleicher, now acting directly for Hindenburg, began some political scheming. Worried by the electoral results, he planned to placate the Nazis by securing Brüning's resignation, in whom he falsely claimed the army had no confidence, and offering Hitler a place in a presidential cabinet under a more right-wing chancellor, namely Franz von Papen. He persuaded the 'old man' to agree with his plan by informing him that Hitler would not stand in the way of a new chancellor as long as the ban on the SA and the SS was lifted and new elections were ordered. On 29 May, Hindenburg summoned Brüning and asked for his resignation. Hindenburg then met with Hitler and outlined the agreement: Hindenburg would choose his presidential cabinet, the SA ban would be lifted, the Reichstag would be dissolved, and new elections would be held in July. Hitler agreed.

Replacing Brüning with von Papen was not a good or popular decision. Although Brüning had failed to halt unemployment and lacked the personal charisma needed to claim the popularity of the masses, he had plans to reflate

 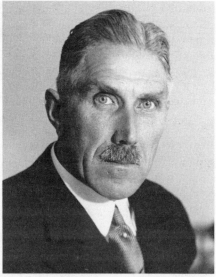

At the centre of political intrigue in 1932 was General Kurt von Schleicher (left) who had dreams of leading Germany. He persuaded Hindenburg to get rid of Chancellor Brüning and replace him with the aristocratic but hapless Franz von Papen (right) who resigned in November and replaced by von Schleicher himself.

the economy and was on the point of negotiating the abolition of reparations. He was also a man of integrity and a patriotic German. Von Papen's credentials were less impressive. He was an ultra-conservative aristocrat, with friends in high places but little political insight. His cabinet, taken from a list already prepared by Schleicher, were businessmen and landowners and it was soon known as 'the cabinet of barons'. Its power was based solely on the support of President Hindenburg and the army.

At this point, the momentum was with the National Socialists. However, Schleicher, now joined by von Papen and his cabinet, had no plans to hand the reins of power to Hitler. Their intention, backed by the rich German industrialists who hoped for an improvement in the international economic situation, was to see the country through a difficult period by 'including' Hitler in their plans but holding him at bay. To assert his new power, von Papen delayed lifting the ban on the SA, much to Hitler's fury. Fearing he had gone too far, von Papen then lifted the ban on 15 June, opening the floodgates on a summer of political violence, often during events organized for the election campaign. There was anarchy in cities and towns across the country as supporters of all four 'armies' fought with clubs, brass knuckles, knives and revolvers. Fighting between the SA and the communists was the most violent, with 86 deaths recorded during the month of July. One of the worst incidents came on 17 July at a Nazi recruitment rally in Altona, a Red suburb of Hamburg in Prussia. As the Nazis paraded through the streets, they were shot at from windows and rooftops. In the ensuing gun battle, 19 people were killed and 285 wounded. Amid clamour from all other parties, von Papen banned all parades until after the election. In order to placate Hitler, while at the same time wooing nationalists to vote for him rather than Hitler and therefore increase his own personal power, von Papen declared a state of emergency in Prussia on the grounds that the Altona riot proved that the Prussian government could not ensure law and order or contain the communist threat. Prussian ministers refused to accept von Papen's accusations and sought an injunction from the Supreme Court. Instead of a legal ruling, a detachment of soldiers arrived from Berlin and made the necessary arrests. Von Papen was appointed as Reichskommissar and Prussia was integrated within the Reich. As Prussia had long been regarded as the bulwark of the Weimar system, its very existence was now under threat.

THE NAZI PROPAGANDA MACHINE STEPS UP

Once again, the Nazi propaganda machine swung into action, concentrating on those at the end of rope after two years of the worst economic depression in history. By now, this included well over 6 million unemployed and the youngsters they had brought into this world. Hitler's air tour allowed him to speak in some 50 towns and cities, culminating in a spectacular mass meeting at the Grunewald Stadium in Berlin on the evening of 27 July. The city was decked out with flags, banners and posters that shouted out slogans, and the streets on the way to the stadium were patrolled by uniformed SA. This was a major event, with more than 100,000 people in the stadium, another huge crowd at a nearby racetrack where loudspeakers were set up, and millions at home ready to listen to Hitler's speech on their radios. It was a theatrical and political triumph.

From the size of the crowds that assembled to hear Hitler speak during the third national election campaign in Germany in 1932, including an estimated 280,000 in two venues on 27 July – Brandenburg and Grunewald Stadium in Berlin (pictured here) – it was evident that the Nazis were gaining significant ground.

Thanks to the efforts of Hitler Youth leader, Baldur von Schirach, the party were turning heads among young people of all classes and social backgrounds. Communist ranks were also swelling, particularly when von Papen announced his plans for 'economic reconstruction', which consisted of little more than lowering wages. There was rebellion in the air from both the left and the right as the German people headed to the polls again on 31 July.

While the results of the federal elections were a resounding success for the National Socialists, who won 13,745,000 votes and 230 seats in the Reichstag – meaning they were by now the largest party in Germany – the absolute majority Hitler craved was not achieved. The Social Democrats won 133 seats, the Communists 89 and so on down. The 6 million new Nazi voters comprised of middle-class traditional Social Democrat voters and young people with little hope for the future. The results persuaded Schleicher and von Papen to offer Hitler a place in the cabinet, but he demanded full powers, a request that was immediately refused. The stand-off continued in September when the Reichstag met. Knowing that he had no chance of governing with such deadlock, von Papen immediately dissolved the Reichstag again and called for more elections. During the autumn, it seemed that no one wanted power in Germany: neither the Reichstag, the Communist Party nor the Nazis seemed prepared to take power. A period of political manoeuvring ensued. Schleicher and von Papen knew that the Nazis were short of money and hoped that a fifth major political campaign would see them go bankrupt.

SCHLEICHER STRIKES

The federal elections on 6 November did nothing to help break the deadlock. The National Socialists were still the biggest party with 196 seats, down 34 since July, with the Social Democrats in second with 121 seats, down 12, and the Communists were in third with 100 seats, up 11, bolstered by extremist voters annoyed that Hitler had not seized power in August. At the end of November, the political situation remained the same, but Hitler was in a weaker position to negotiate than before. Once again, Schleicher moved first and called for von Papen's resignation. Von Papen, thinking that this

Chapter 6

In the early 1920s the Strasser brothers, Gregor (above) and Otto (facing page) along with Joseph Goebbels, were leading members of the Nazi Party in northern Germany (continues opposite).

would be a temporary resignation, agreed. Hindenburg summoned Hitler and offered him two choices: the chancellorship if he could get a workable majority in the Reichstag or the vice-chancellorship under von Papen in a presidential cabinet that ruled by emergency decree. Hitler rejected both offers.

On 1 December, von Papen, fully expecting to be reappointed chancellor, met with Hindenburg and Schleicher, to present his new plan to declare a state of emergency and govern by decree. Hindenburg listened with interest, but Schleicher did not. His plan was to take the chancellorship himself, with the support of the left-wing National Socialist deputies, some 60 in number, led by Gregor Strasser, and the backing of the centre parties. He interrupted von Papen and explained to Hindenburg that von Papen's policies were unconstitutional and 'would place the government in a difficult position in case of [a possible] civil war'[6] and that the Reichswehr did not support von Papen, nor did it have the capacity to fight on several fronts at the same time. The old man had no choice. Von Papen was dismissed, and the following day Schleicher became chancellor.

His 57 days in office started well. A clever man, he realized that the time was right to take advantage of the National Socialists' problems. Moreover, the economy was improving, and he was focused on unemployment, stopping wage and benefit cuts and launching a programme of taking over 3,240 sq km (800,000 acres) of Junker estates and giving them to 25,000 peasant families. He also announced cuts in the price of coal, meat and other essentials. For the moment, the German people slept easier, hoping that their long-awaited 'strong man' had arrived.

110

But things did not go Schleicher's way. His political scheming had made him enemies. Despite his policies to help working men and the trade unions, they did not trust him, nor did the industrialists because of his overtures to the trade unions. The landowners were horrified by his idea of what they called 'agrarian Bolshevism'. A record winter harvest resulted in insufficient demand, with the unemployed unable to buy goods, and led to crashing prices. His plan to split the National Socialists by offering the vice-chancellorship to Gregor Strasser was a spectacular failure. Strasser and a number of his left-wing followers were worried that the party had missed its chance and lost its way since the election results, and that Hitler was to blame. Alarm bells were now ringing on the party finances, which were a cause of serious concern. At a meeting at the Kaiserhof on 5 December, Strasser urged Hitler to take what power he could by joining a coalition

Although anti-Semitic and nationalist, they developed their own idea of 'left-wing' Nazism that put emphasis on economic socialism. While Goebbels jumped ship, disagreements led the brothers into conflict with Hitler: which saw Otto leave the party in 1930 and Gregor's execution four years later.

with Schleicher. Hitler refused but kept negotiations with Schleicher going by sending Göring to see him.

A huge row ensued, with Hitler accusing Strasser of treachery. Strasser denied any disloyalty and accused Hitler of the destruction of National Socialism. The meeting ended in chaos with Strasser storming out. Before he left for Italy the following day, Strasser wrote a letter of resignation to Hitler and an article for the newspapers, which was to appear the following day. It was as though a bomb had gone off at the Kaiserhof when the news hit. 'We are all dejected and depressed,' Goebbels recorded in his diary.[7] According to William Shirer, 'Now, on the threshold of power, his [Hitler's] principal follower had deserted him and threatened to smash all he had built up in seven years.'[8] Hitler was deeply wounded, some say suicidal. It was the most serious crisis that the party had faced since the failure of the Beer Hall Putsch in 1923.

POLITICAL SCHEMING

But all was not lost. News of the events of the previous night was soon forgotten and the National Socialists were still the biggest party in the Reichstag. Everyone wanted a piece of them. Hitler recovered quickly from the shock and acted decisively. With Strasser out of the picture, his friends were kicked out of the party and Hitler assumed leadership of the members with Dr Ley, the Gauleiter of Cologne, as his chief of staff. It was business as usual. On 10 December, von Papen, still smarting from his political disappointment, approached Baron Kurt von Schröder, a partner in the banking firm J.S. Stein of Cologne, and asked him to arrange a secret meeting with Hitler at his home on 4 January (see also p.146). He too was worried that voters were abandoning the National Socialists and moving towards the Communist Party. It is suggested that during the meeting the two thrashed out some sort of agreement that they would form a Nationalist/Nazi coalition, with the two of them as joint chancellors and perhaps with the help of Alfred Hugenberg, to replace Schleicher's government. Of course, Schleicher had got wind of the meeting, and the newspapers had stories and photos from the event the following day. But Hitler was emboldened by it – not just because he was reassured of his political position, but because funds were suddenly forthcoming. With strong connections to the USA, von Schröder had been in touch with Walther Funk to ascertain Hitler's views on the international banking business. Funk had been reassuring. As big business donations to the party had completely dried up, either due to the party's radical ideas, their anti-capitalist messages or their lack of a coherent economic policy, following the meeting it is claimed that von Schröder formed a syndicate, which included a number of industrialists and major bankers, to pay off or at least guarantee the NSDAP debts. Given that the Nazis were said to have spent up to RM200,000 per week during the election campaigns, that debt must have been huge. Of course, this was not done to put the National Socialists in power, 'but to save them from bankruptcy so that they could be used later'.[9]

Schleicher and von Papen continued their political scheming. But Schleicher's grip on power was weakening. Despite improvements in the economy, Schleicher was losing support from all parts of the political spectrum. In an attempt to shore up his support among farm labourers and the unemployed, he threatened to release a report implicating the misuse of public funds by a number of Junkers estate owners, with suggestions that Hindenburg's family was involved. On 22 January, von Papen paid one of his regular visits to the Hindenburg residence with the intention of persuading him that there was now an alternative to Schleicher. He laid out the details of his various meetings with Hitler and with the Ruhrlade, suggesting that a Nationalist/National Socialist pact would have more chance of achieving a majority in the Reichstag than Schleicher, whose policies were going down badly all round, particularly with heavy industry and the offended landowners. He hinted that the Reichswehr generals were also inclining towards Hitler, particularly now that the left-wing Strasser had been dismissed. Hindenburg may already have been inclined in the same direction, partly by his son Oskar who had, earlier that day, met and spoken in private with Hitler. No one can be certain of what was said, but some historians claim that Oskar's previous distaste for the Nazis had been replaced with his realization that they 'had' to be taken into government. It is speculation to suggest that this may have had something to do with the misused public funds. All the while, however, von Papen was keen to assure Hindenburg that he could keep Hitler under control.

HITLER BECOMES CHANCELLOR

Earlier that same day – another event, this one more public – had illustrated Hitler's greatest value to the people of Berlin and Germany in general: he offered strength and opposition to the Communist Party. Joseph Goebbels had organized a demonstration of 10,000 SA men in Bülowplatz, in front of the Communist Party headquarters. The Communists announced that a counter-demonstration would take place on the same day. The stage was set for a huge and violent street battle. At short notice, the government banned the Communist demonstration and offered the Nazis police protection. With police in place, armed with machine guns and armoured cars, Hitler arrived, and the marching began. The SA taunted the Reds in their own backyard. The event was seen as a huge propaganda success for the National Socialists.

Schleicher now realized that he had no chance of achieving a majority in the Reichstag so on 28 January he went, cap in hand, to Hindenburg demanding its dissolution and emergency powers to rule by decree under Article 48. Hindenburg refused, leaving Schleicher with no choice but to offer his resignation.

For two days, Schleicher, von Papen, Hitler and Hindenburg continued their political deliberations, each with their own advisers. Berlin was alive with rumours and counter-rumours. Messages with offers and demands were relayed from one to another. By the evening of 29 January, both Schleicher and von Papen had offered Hitler the chancellorship. Hitler weighed his options, rejecting Schleicher because he was too strong and choosing von Papen because of his weakness. The following morning, Hitler was summoned by the president and appointed chancellor in a brief ceremony. In accepting the post, Hitler made a brief speech in which he swore to 'carry out his obligations without party interests and for the good of the whole nation'. He also agreed to 'uphold the Constitution, respect the rights of the President and, after the next election, to return to normal parliamentary rule'. Hindenburg replied, saying, 'And now, gentlemen, forwards with God.'[10]

Von Papen was then delighted to introduce his hand-picked cabinet. There were only three National Socialists on the list: Hitler, Wilhelm Frick as minister of the interior, and Göring as minister without portfolio. The others were made up of right-wing conservatives, such as Alfred Hugenberg, Franz Seldte of the Stahlhelm and the aristocratic General von Blomberg. Of course, as vice-chancellor and minister president of Prussia, von Papen felt that he was the power behind the throne. 'Within two months we will have pushed Hitler so far in the corner that he'll squeak,'[11] he boasted to a political colleague.

Of course, Hitler had other ideas.

Chapter 7

Masters of Germany

Later that day, Goebbels wrote in his diary, 'Hitler is Reich Chancellor. Just like a fairy tale.'[1] Indeed, it was extraordinary that a lowly Austrian lance corporal from the Bavarian army had taken a political party with a half a dozen members and a few pfennigs in a rusty tin box into power in just over a decade. It was a great political triumph for himself and for the Nazi Party. However, Hitler had not really seized power; rather it had been given to him by others, all of them united in their dissatisfaction with democracy and the failure of capitalism in Germany in the 1920s and early 1930s.

Everyone wanted a piece of Hitler because they believed that having him as chancellor would be to their advantage. Conservatives, like von Papen, and members of the former aristocratic ruling class wanted an end to Weimar and a return to authoritarian government. Some dreamed of a return to the good old days, perhaps even the return of a descendant of the Kaiser. The army wanted him to carry out his promise to tear up the Versailles Treaty and end its restrictions. Big business had come round to the idea that Hitler's admiration of free enterprise and his dislike of communism and the trade unions would lead to rising profits. The middle classes wanted their jobs back, safe streets and food on the table, and the rural population wanted to see an end to the decadence of Weimar and for Hitler to make good on his promise for 'Work and Bread'.

On the evening of Hitler's appointment and in the days that followed, Goebbels had hastily organized the staging of a number of victory parades in Berlin and other cities. The event in Berlin was particularly spectacular as hundreds of uniformed, goose-stepping, jackbooted SA, SS and Stahlhelm soldiers marched under the Brandenburg Gate and through the city's government

Chapter 7

quarter carrying banners, flags and flaming torches. The 'Horst Wessel Song' and other Nazi songs rang out, accompanied by various marching bands. Some 60,000 civilians, many waving red and white swastika flags, joined in the celebrations as the 'river of light' flowed through the streets, watched by Hitler and Hindenburg from different windows along Wilhelmstrasse. To add drama, Goebbels had arranged for commentary on the event to be broadcast on state radio in cities across the country. Later that evening, there were disturbances following the parades, with black, red and gold flags – the symbol of the hated Weimar Republic – burned and violent street fights with communists.

For the marchers and some of the onlookers – particularly the young – the feeling was ecstatic. Melita Maschmann, a 15-year-old Berliner taken to watch the parade by her sceptical parents, expressed the feeling. She said, 'I longed to hurl myself into this current, to be submerged and borne along by the current.'[2] They saw it as an awakening, a 'national uprising', the beginning of a new era, a new regime that would restore the natural flow of German history. For others there was less reason for optimism. Between May 1928 and November 1932, the Reichstag had been dissolved four times and not one of the country's political parties had plucked up the courage to take on the challenge of government. Others still had more serious reservations. In his campaign for power, Hitler had not hidden his intentions. His enemies had reason to fear for their lives: Marxism would be eradicated, and the Jews would be dealt with. The army would be restored to its former glory, the Versailles Treaty would be rejected and *Lebensraum* would be found in the east. Many were afraid, alarmed even at the rhetoric and the violence and prejudices of the new regime. The Impressionist painter Max Liebermann, a Berliner by birth but with Jewish heritage, said of the parade going past his house in Pariser Platz, 'I couldn't even begin to eat as much as I'd like to be able to throw up.'[3] It is also rumoured that on the evening of Hitler's appointment, Erich Ludendorff, who had played his part in the Beer Hall Putsch, sent a telegram to Hindenburg in which he said, 'I solemnly prophesy that this accursed man will cast our Reich into the abyss and bring our nation to inconceivable misery. Future generations will damn you in your grave for what you have done.'[4]

THE MEETING, 20 FEBRUARY 1933

In reality, of course, Hitler – though he was head of the Reich government – was not really yet 'in charge'. There were only three National Socialists in the new cabinet, which was dominated by conservatives. As intended, Hitler dissolved the Reichstag and called for new elections in early March. Goebbels was thrilled. 'Now it will be easy,' he wrote in his diary on 3 February, 'to carry the fight, for we can call on all resources of the State. Radio and press are at our disposal. We shall stage a masterpiece of propaganda.'[5] However, as state assets were not allowed to be used for election purposes, to stage Goebbels' masterpiece they needed money.

On 16 February, on the instructions of Hjalmar Schacht, invitations were sent by telegram to Germany's wealthiest and most influential businessmen. They were invited to attend a fundraising meeting with Hitler at Hermann Göring's house, the official residence of the new Reichstag president. At 6 pm on 20 February, two dozen suited, booted and elegantly dressed gentlemen arrived for the meeting in a fleet of cars. The guest list included many of the Nazi Party's regular contributors: Friedrich Flick, Albert Vögler, Emil Kirdorf and various executives from I.G. Farben and the potash giant Wintershall. New faces included Gustav Krupp von Bohlen, chairman of the Krupp steel empire; cloth, battery and arms manufacturer Günther Quandt; automobile manufacturer Wilhelm von Opel; Bavarian banker Baron August von Finck; and Kurt Schmitt, CEO of the insurance giant Allianz. The guests were welcomed by Göring and Walther Funk, before the new chancellor arrived with Otto Wagener. Master of ceremonies was Hjalmar Schacht.

The businessmen were expecting a briefing on Hitler's future economic policies; what they got was 'a piece of Nazi political theatre'.[6] After shaking hands with his guests, Hitler spoke at length, outlining his political views, the importance of private enterprise, the threat of communism, the end of elections and democracy and his plans for rearmament. 'Now we stand before the last election,' he concluded, 'regardless of the outcome, there will be no retreat'.[7] Krupp responded enthusiastically on behalf of the industrialists 'for having given us such a clear picture' of Hitler's ideas. Hitler then gave the floor to Göring and left the room. Göring got straight to the point. He promised stability, a favourable climate for business, but at the cost of 'financial sacrifices' needed for the coalition to win the upcoming election, 'surely ... the last one for the next ten years, probably even for the next hundred years'.[8] Schacht then got down to business, suggesting that the National Socialists and the DVNP coalition needed a campaign fund of 3 million Reichsmarks (about $20 million today). After a brief discussion between the various businessmen, the money was pledged there and then. It may seem astonishing now, but it was 'nothing more for the Krupps, Opels, and Siemenses than a perfectly ordinary business transaction, your basic fund-raising'.[9] For these canny businessmen it was an investment in the future, and it was their companies that would proceed to power Germany into the forefront of the European economy: BASF, Bayer, Agfa, Opel, I.G. Farben, Siemens, Allianz, Telefunken.

Evidence given during the Nuremberg trials in 1945–6 reveals the breakdown of the contributors to this huge fund and underlines further (see Chapter 6) that it included money coming from the USA and, probably, from Britain. The largest contributors were Krupp, who is said to have pledged 1 million Reichsmarks, and I.G. Farben, which committed itself for almost half the money. Much of it came from the company's US subsidiary and must have been approved by the board, which included Edsel Ford, of the Ford Motor Company, directors of the Federal Reserve Bank of New York including Paul Warburg, the Standard Oil Company and even members of Franklin D. Roosevelt's Georgia Warm Springs Foundation. There is also evidence of American money making up part of the contributions from AEG (German General Electric) and from Fritz Thyssen, who were both closely associated with Wall Street financiers. British involvement centred around the private bank Delbrück Schickler, through which the donations found their way to Hjalmar Schacht for distribution. The bank was a subsidiary of Metallgesellschaft, a huge non-ferrous metal company, whose principal shareholders were I.G. Farben and the British Metal Corporation (BMC). BMC directors Walter Gardner and Oliver Lyttelton had made handsome profits mining non-ferrous metals, such as copper, zinc, lead and nickel, and exporting them to Germany, and were keen to continue doing business with Germany during Hitler's proposed rearmament process.

Gustav Krupp had really been impressed with Hitler's address, particularly in his promises to curb the power of the trade unions and in his ideas of rearmament. For surety, he held a meeting with a group of important army officers and was pleased to hear that they supported Hitler. A few days later, Hitler's RM400,000 tax debt and a substantial bill at the Hotel Kaiserhof had been paid off. Having been sceptical of Hitler for so long, Krupp's opinion had radically changed. On 1 April, Krupp agreed a deal with the new chancellor that if Hitler supported Krupp as the 'head' of German industry, then he would ensure Hitler received financial backing.

NAZI TERROR BEGINS

Following Hitler's appointment as Reich Chancellor, between February and June 1933 the Nazis launched a campaign of terror across Germany. SA and SS troops meted out shockingly ferocious violence, particularly against their political rivals the Communist and Social Democrat parties but also including Catholics, Nationalists, liberals and conservatives. There were serious beatings, torture and deaths across the country. These were calculated acts, which according to Richard Bessel were 'used deliberately and openly to intimidate opposition and potential opposition. It was used to create a public sphere permeated by violence and it provided a ready reminder of what might be in store for anyone who stepped out of line.'[10] It is also clear these actions were intended to provoke a reaction. According to a note in Goebbels' diary, the Nazis were desperate for a Red or Socialist revolution to 'burst into flames' in order to suppress it and secure the complete power they craved.

But with no evidence of a revolution from either the communists or the socialists, the Nazis stoked these flames for themselves. Around 9 pm on the evening of 27 February, people walking near the Reichstag heard the sound of breaking glass and almost immediately smoke and flames were seen billowing around the building's gilded cupola. Hundreds of firefighters worked to quell the fire. Göring was there first, exclaiming, 'This is the beginning of the

Chapter 7

According to an Exchange Berlin telegram sent by Reuter on the night, the Reichstag fire was 'started by documents which were set alight in six different places' simultaneously. Although clearly not the work of a 'half-demented, half-blind Dutchman', the Nazis used the incident for a huge power grab.

Communist revolution! ... Every Communist must be shot where he is found ... Every Communist deputy must this very night be strung up.'[11] 'This is a God-given signal,' Hitler said to von Papen when they arrived at the scene. 'If this fire, as I believe, is the work of the Communists, then we must crush out this murderous pest with an iron fist.'[12] Neither had any evidence of their assertions. Almost immediately, the police arrested a half-demented, half-blind Dutch Communist, Marinus van der Lubbe, who was found, semi-naked, at the rear of the building. He had flammable materials and firelighters with him and they blamed him for starting the blaze. It was a handy coincidence for the Nazis that this itinerant Dutch arsonist had been overheard in one of the city's bars boasting about setting fire to public buildings. He had been picked up by the SA and 'encouraged' to set fire to the Reichstag. However, he was not capable of setting such a huge blaze on his own.

Although the real truth of what happened was never discovered, even at Nuremberg, according to William Shirer, 'the idea for the fire almost certainly originated with Goebbels and Göring'.[13] In addition, Rudolf Diels, who had recently been appointed head of the Gestapo, revealed at the post-war trial that, 'Göring knew exactly how the fire was to be started' and had ordered him 'to prepare, prior to the fire, a list of people who were to be arrested immediately after it'.[14] Shirer's explanation of the story is that the Reichstag building was linked to Göring's Presidential Palace via an underground passage, built to carry the central heating system. It was used that night by a group of stormtroopers carrying petrol and self-igniting chemicals, which they scattered in several places around the building. They returned to Göring's house, and van der Lubbe was sent in alone. The fire, which burned for two hours before being brought under control, gutted the interior of the building.

The following day, Hitler took full advantage of the incident by declaring a state of emergency and persuading President Hindenburg to invoke Article 48 of the Weimar Constitution and rule by decree to 'ensure public safety and order'. They drafted a document, later known as the Reichstag Fire Decree, which abolished freedom of speech, assembly, privacy and the press, legalized phone tapping and interception of correspondence, and suspended the autonomy of federated states, like Bavaria.[15] The legal idea of habeas corpus was suspended, allowing suspected terrorists or revolutionaries to be arrested and detained without charge. Hindenburg signed the decree that, in effect, allowed the Nazis to do anything they wanted. That night the SA carried out mass arrests, using their carefully prepared lists of Communist leaders and Reichstag deputies, Social Democrats, leading left-wing intellectuals and trade union leaders. In all, some 4,000 were seized, a number of whom were candidates standing in the upcoming elections. They were brought to SA barracks, beaten, tortured and detained.

THE LAST DEMOCRATIC ELECTION FOR 16 YEARS

Having devastated the Communists, the Nazis turned their attentions to other political opponents in the week before the federal elections. Brown-shirted stormtroopers carried out acts of aggression and violence in towns and cities across Germany, with the intention of showing everyone who was in charge. Sunday 5 March, election day, was memorable for its menacing atmosphere. Goebbels had worked his magic once more: Nazi posters, black, white and red flags and banners with swastikas were in evidence throughout the country, with little evidence of the opposition. Radio loudspeakers played Hitler's recent speeches. Transport was laid on to take voters to the polling stations. Railway stations and bus terminals were guarded by police and armed stormtroopers walked the streets looking for anyone campaigning for the 'other' parties.

Despite the intimidation, in the last democratic election for 16 years, the National Socialists failed to get a majority. With just over 17 million votes, they had secured 288 out of 647 seats with 44 per cent of the total vote. The Social Democrats came second with 120 seats and the Catholic Centre Party third with 93. The Communists polled almost 5 million votes and took 81 seats, but von Papen's Nationalist Party were hugely disappointed with just over 3 million votes and 52 seats. The results showed that two-thirds of the voters, who gave their support to the Nazis, the Nationalists and the Communists, were opposed to Weimar democracy. In practical terms, the National Socialist/Nationalist coalition gave the government a small majority, which enabled it to carry on governing. However, it was not enough for Hitler's stated purpose of amending the constitution of the Reichstag. He needed a two-thirds majority to pass an Enabling Act, which would mean turning over its constitutional functions to Hitler and therefore giving him full power.

For a week after the election the brownshirts, now over a million strong, carried on their campaign of violence across Germany, beating up and even killing their political opponents, looting party offices, and stealing assets and funds while claiming protection under the emergency Reichstag Fire Decree. In a hugely symbolic gesture, they also raised the swastika on official state government buildings everywhere, intimidating local officials through sheer force of numbers. On 20 March Heinrich Himmler, Reich Leader of the SS, announced the opening of a 'concentration camp' at Dachau, just outside Munich. It was initially intended to intern Hitler's political opponents, namely Communists, Social Democrats and other dissidents. Stories of the horrible conditions and sadistic cruelty of the camp guards spread quickly, as intended, and served as a warning to anyone thinking of resisting the new Nazi regime. Other camps opened around the country in the following days and arrests followed quickly; some 35,000 people were said to have been incarcerated by the end of April.

GOEBBELS' PROPAGANDA PLAY

By that time, Germany had become a dictatorship with 'the appearance, however threadbare, of legal and political legitimation'.[16] On 21 March, the first day of spring and the anniversary of the day in 1871 when Bismarck opened the inaugural Reichstag at the start of the German Empire, Joseph Goebbels organized the 'Day of Potsdam', a ceremony to mark the state opening of the newly elected Reichstag. Because of the damage to the original building, the ceremony took place at the Protestant Garrison Church at Potsdam, where Frederick William I and his son Frederick II were buried. The venue, the symbolic centre of the Prussian monarchy, was chosen by the Nazis as a sop to worried conservatives and traditionalists over their actions since Hitler's appointment as chancellor. For von Papen and Hindenburg, who still had the

Chapter 7

In a gesture intended to show the alleged unity of the nation and the continuity of the Third Reich, Prussia and the German Empire, Hitler bows deferentially as he shakes hands with Reich President Paul von Hindenburg, who is dressed in the uniform of an imperial field marshal.

power to get rid of the chancellor and replace him with someone else, things were not going as they had planned. Goebbels' ceremony was intended to demonstrate the unity of the old and the new Germany.

Hindenburg, dressed in his Prussian field marshal uniform, received the frock-coated new chancellor and they marched slowly down the aisle, pausing to bow at the empty seat of Kaiser Wilhelm II before coming to a stop in front of the altar. The president then said a few words, giving his blessing to the new government. Hitler's reply was filled with praise for the older man, who appeared to be moved by the ceremony. As Goebbels' camera bulbs, microphones and film cameras flashed, whirred and clicked, Hitler bowed low to Hindenburg and clasped his hand, showing deep humility towards a man whose political power he intended to rob 'before the week was up'.[17] It was a brilliantly orchestrated 'propaganda play', photographed and filmed for everyone to see. Following the service, Hindenburg reviewed a huge parade of paramilitaries and the army. Similar parades were held in the country's major cities. Events in Potsdam were broadcast throughout Germany on the radio and on public loudspeakers. The celebrations ended after dark with torchlit processions. Hitler attended a performance of Richard Wagner's opera *Die Meistersinger von Nürnberg* at the Berlin State Opera House.

PEACE OR WAR?

Two days later, the Kroll Opera House in Berlin's Königsplatz, named as the temporary home of the Reichstag, hosted its first session of the new government. There was no secret as to the main business of the day as Hitler proposed the Enabling Act, which would allow him, as chancellor, and his cabinet to enact laws, including those that altered the constitution, without the approval of the Reichstag or the president – thus establishing the conditions for dictatorial rule. The streets around the opera house were filled with stormtroopers, yelling and screaming in the faces of the deputies as they arrived for the session. The inside of the chamber too was filled with SA and SS men, lining the walls and blocking the exits. The walls were festooned with swastikas and other Nazi banners. The atmosphere was febrile and menacing – the Nazis' month-long campaign of street violence had done its job.

The bill, which required a two-thirds quorum and a two-thirds majority to pass, was not assured. However, the Nazis had done their homework. The Nationalists were in favour. The Social Democrats and the Communists were not. However, none of the 81 Communist deputies was present – many of them were in Dachau while others were on the run – and 26 Social Democrat deputies were absent for fear of their lives. However, more votes were needed to ensure the bill's passage and Hitler had been in discussions with the Catholic Centre Party, who held 73 seats and were split on the issue at hand. Some feared the consequences of voting in favour of the Act; others feared the opposite. Party chairman, Prelate Ludwig Kaas, asked Hitler for guarantees of the party's survival and the new chancellor responded positively, without signing a letter of agreement.

On the day, Hitler opened proceedings. His speech included all his normal tropes, against Versailles, Weimar and the communists. He emphasized the importance of Christianity in German culture, promised to protect the interests of the churches and outlined a number of future Nazi policies including *Lebensraum*, *Gleichschaltung* ('co-ordination', meaning the process of the Nazis taking complete control of the country), the eradication of Marxism, judicial reform and the rearmament of the Reichswehr. Addressing concerns about potential 'unchecked authority' of the Enabling Act, he said that the Reichstag would not be dissolved.[18] He pointed to the calm condition of the country's streets and the disciplined and bloodless nature of the Nazi Party's actions. Before commending the Act to the deputies, he added a sting in the tail of his words if the Act was rejected: 'The Government is just as determined as it is prepared to accept a notice of rejection and thus a declaration of resistance. May you, Gentlemen, now choose for yourselves between peace or war!'[19]

Other party leaders spoke in reply to the chancellor but only one spoke against the Act – Otto Wels, chairman of the Social Democrats. In fear for his life, he was said to have carried a cyanide capsule in his waist pocket as he spoke. He argued that the Act would destroy 'the basic principles of humanity and justice, freedom and socialism ... ideas which are eternal and indestructible'.[20] He sat down amidst the mocking laughter of the Nazi deputies and a harsh rebuttal from Hitler. The voting figures were 444 in favour of adopting the bill and 97 against. The result of this vote actually meant that the Reichstag was no longer active in German politics; the cabinet rarely met and within three months all political parties expect the Nazi Party were banned or pressured into dissolving themselves. By then, Germany was a one-party totalitarian state.

FUNDS BEGIN TO FLOW

Although, as historian Henry Ashby Turner has proved, there had been no great flow of money from Germany's big businesses until the meeting in February 1933, it now seemed that the dam had finally burst. Of course, money had been given for leverage should the Nazis come to power, and that had occurred.

Before Hitler's appointment as chancellor and the takeover of political power in Germany by so-called 'legal means', it had not been in anyone's interests to be known to give money to Hitler; it was certainly not in his interests to be accused of being a 'capitalist puppet'. But those days were gone. As chancellor, Hitler received an initial combined salary and expenses of RM47,200 per year. Added to this was the *Adolf Hitler Spende*, officially known as the Adolf Hitler Donation of the German Economy and supposedly intended 'to support the SA, the SS, Hitler Youth and political organization of the Nazi party'.[21] Following the meeting of industrialists at Göring's house on 20 February, Gustav Krupp had agreed to oversee such a fund and took up his role in April. His reasons for agreeing were not as 'intended' but were aimed at securing favours for big business from the new government. Nonetheless, his colleagues in German industry raised at least RM30 million in 1933, although estimates as to the actual amounts raised that year and the following years vary wildly. In reality, the money donated in 1933 and 1934 was allocated as party funds. By 1935, however, it had become part of Hitler's personal fortune.

Other money began to flow freely into Hitler's bank accounts, too. Royalties for his book *Mein Kampf*, which sold over a million copies in 1933, was RM861,146. In May 1933, Goebbels had banned any unauthorized use of Hitler's name or image on commercial products. In 1923, Hitler had agreed to make his friend from Munich, Heinrich Hoffmann, his personal photographer. This meant that no one else was allowed to photograph him.

Hitler found Hoffmann funny and admired his knowledge of painting and his easy social manner. In turn, Hoffmann encouraged Hitler's passion for collecting art and introduced him to a young employee of his, Eva Braun, who would, of course, later become his mistress and then his wife. When Hitler became chancellor, Hoffmann was able to take full advantage of his favoured position in Hitler's entourage. He started two private companies: one the publisher of National Socialist photographs and the other as publisher of photo-propaganda books. His photos were published as postage stamps, postcards, posters and picture books, eventually making him a millionaire. Hitler too profited greatly from the royalties of the reproduction of his image taken by

Chapter 7

Hoffmann. Books, such as *The Hitler Nobody Knows* (1933) and *Jugend um Hitler* (1934) had huge sales, and both made a fortune from royalties.

Hoffmann was a canny businessman: he made use of copies of some of Hitler's own paintings, then he made deals with Postal Minister Ohnesorge for a copyright image of the Führer to be used on postage stamps as well as special 'collectors' stamps, available at all post offices in Germany and in occupied territories, which sold millions annually. Income from these various sources went into a Cultural Fund, set up in 1937. The fund's average annual income is estimated to have been between RM25–RM35 million. Like the *Adolf Hitler Spende*, this was Hitler's money, and it was he who decided how to spend it.

As former NSDAP business manager and by now general manager of the Nazi publishing house Eher Verlag, Max Amann was beginning to turn Hitler's personal finances around with the increasing sales of *Mein Kampf*. As early as January 1933, the Nazis made moves on other publishers too. One was the Jewish-owned Ullstein publishers, one of the largest producers of newspapers, periodicals and books. By using anti-Semitic threats to staff members, subscribers and advertisers, despite a company reorganization that included the appointment of a non-Jewish manager, the company was forced to sell the business, valued at RM60 million, for RM6 million.[22] This process of 'Aryanization', the Nazi term for the seizure of property from Jews and its transfer to non-Jews, was soon to become a central part of a campaign of forced expulsion of Jews from economic life in Nazi Germany. Hitler's personal intervention in the acquisition, which saw it in the hands of Amann rather than the official Nazi Head of Press Joseph Goebbels, prompted Frederick T. Birchall of the *New York Times* to speculate that there was 'little doubt that the [subsequent] profits went to the Führer himself'.[23]

Hitler's tax return for 1933, the last he ever submitted, claimed his income as RM1,232,335, the majority of which came from sales of his book. But back in 1933, his payable tax, after allowances, was given as RM297,005. Hitler had no intention of paying taxes and announced that since the majority of his income came from his work as a writer, he would donate his salary as chancellor to charity in the hope that this 'magnanimous' gesture would find favour with the Munich State Finance Office. His plan worked over the course of time; having not paid tax in 1933 or 1934, confirmation that he was tax-exempt was issued in early 1935, shortly before he resumed receiving his salary, which by then had risen to RM60,000 a year.

TRICKERY

The National Socialist Party itself was also shrugging off its money worries and began with what William Shirer described as 'an elaborate piece of trickery.'[24] The new government declared 1 May 1933 as a national holiday, the 'Day of National Labour' – as was traditional in Europe. The move was welcomed by the working classes across the country though many of them were 'forced to attend' having been threatened with dismissal if they did not. Trade union leaders were flown to Berlin to take part in what Goebbels hoped would be the 'greatest mass demonstration Germany had ever seen' at Tempelhof airfield.[25] Hitler ended his speech to the crowd of up to a million people amid a sea of Nazi flags with the motto, 'Honour work and respect the worker!' The following day, trade union offices across the country were raided by SA and SS troops, furniture, equipment and funds were smashed or looted, the leaders were beaten and then arrested, and the unions were dissolved. The once powerful trade union movement disappeared almost overnight. Its funds were transferred to the *Deutsche Arbeitsfront* (DAF), the national labour organization of the Nazi Party. These funds were considerable. The unions had 4 million members and an annual turnover of RM184 million, and had invested their dues and strike funds in banks, newspapers, workers' hostels, shops, other businesses and property. All assets were now under the control of Head of the DAF Robert Ley and money is said to have flowed freely from him to party headquarters. In addition, the party was receiving generous state subsidies, said to be in the region of RM5.96 million in 1935 and RM88.56 million in 1940.[26]

Following the complete dissolution of the trade unions and the planned closing down of all other political parties, Goebbels' diary entry for 3 May 1933 records with triumph, 'The revolution goes on ... We are the masters of Germany'.[27]

Chapter 7

From the sweaty, sticky-floored beer halls of Munich to the estimated million-strong crowds that attended the Nuremberg rallies to hear him, Hitler's speeches played a major part in his rise from a lowly army corporal to Chancellor of Germany.

Chapter 8

The Big Guns Arrive

German rearmament after World War I had begun almost immediately after the guns fell silent. However, because of the terms of the Versailles Treaty, which imposed stringent restrictions on post-war German armed forces aimed at rendering them incapable of offensive action and starting another war, it remained 'small, secret and informal' for a number of years.[1] This was despite the Social Democratic Chancellor Hermann Müller passing laws approving the 'illegal' actions and financing them.

Although political factions in Germany were bitterly divided in the 1920s amid the fallout of the German Revolution, there were strands of thinking that united the German people, primarily the unjust terms of the Versailles Treaty. They all recognized the need to reinvent the armed forces, and most particularly the Reichswehr, to protect the country's borders. Though in violation of the terms of the treaty, the Weimar government therefore tolerated the training and equipping of the police force and paramilitary groups, such as the *Freikorps*, the Stahlhelm, the SA and the SS, maintaining them as an official reserve for the regular army. Funds, often coming from the army and sanctioned by its commander, Hans von Seeckt, were used to set up armament plants overseas – in the Netherlands, for example, where they also hid stocks of existing weapons. There was also money for R&D in military technology, such as tanks, rocketry and aeroplanes – with the aim of designing, developing and testing new weapons, rather than producing and storing them in large quantities.

In addition, German industrialists acquired or started foreign subsidiary companies to develop and manufacture weaponry on foreign soil. For example, Krupp acquired Swedish arms manufacturer Bofors as well as setting up

Chapter 8

Head of the Reichswehr 1920–26, General Hans von Seeckt's political skills were responsible for the success of German military rearmament in the 1920s and 1930s despite restrictions imposed by the Treaty of Versailles.

Siderius in the Netherlands, which produced artillery. Rheinmetall bought the Swiss company Solothurn, which was involved in the production of anti-aircraft guns. But perhaps the most successful relationship in this clandestine rearming was between Germany and the Soviet Union, the two outcasts of Versailles. Two treaties, signed at Rapallo in Italy in 1922 and at Berlin in 1926, set up extensive economic interactions between the two countries. This included secret military co-operation. For the Soviets, this meant access to German military expertise in terms of training and technology; for the Germans, this led to the setting up of a flying school, a chemical weapons plant, a tank school and two tank factories. The Russians also hosted Reichswehr battlefield manoeuvres – all far away from the beady eyes of the Allied Control Commission, which had been set up to ensure that the Versailles clauses were upheld. This brilliant strategic collaboration, initiated primarily by General von Seeckt, played a pivotal role in rebuilding Germany's military power.

MILITARY BUSINESS

Hitler lost no time in telling his military leaders that rearmament was his top priority. In fact, on 2 February, three days after his appointment as chancellor, he had addressed army and navy leaders at the home of the army commander-in-chief, General von Hammerstein. He outlined his true domestic and international political agenda, which was to establish a dictatorship for the purpose of waging war. He also underlined his opinion that the armed forces were the most important socialist institution of the state and should remain unpolitical and impartial. He announced his intention to reintroduce national service and that there was to be no fusion of army and SA.[2] In March, Hitler appointed his old friend Dr Schacht as president of the Reichsbank to help arrange the financing of rearmament and on 4 April created the Reich Defence Council to start a new and secret rearmament programme. Well aware that he could not have come to power without the support of the army and that their continued support would be crucial when Hindenburg, by then 86 years old and in poor health, died, Hitler then passed a new Army Law that abolished the jurisdiction of the civil courts over the military and handed over these responsibilities to the officer corps. His campaign to retain the support of the military was welcomed by the generals and admirals it was aimed at.

Some radical members of the Nazi Party had different ideas. In June, Ernst Röhm, chief of the SA, which was by now a force of some 2 million men, made a speech vowing to continue what he called 'the second revolution'. Having destroyed the left-wing parties, he wanted to mete out the same treatment for the right wing: 'big business and finance, the aristocracy, the Junker landlords and the Prussian generals, who kept a tight rein over the Army'.[3] Goebbels was in support of this thinking, but Hitler was not. For the chancellor, appeasement and order were necessary until he had consolidated his position. Hitler had always regarded the SA as a political force; for Rohm they were a military force, the future revolutionary army, a people's army ready to fight on the streets. Hitler did not agree: the Reichswehr had helped him all along and he needed their backing. The SA, for Hitler, was more like a mob.

On 6 July, Hitler spoke to the SA and SS leaders, forcefully making the point that a second revolution would 'lead only to chaos'. The enmity dragged on as 1933 turned to 1934, when Hitler publicly thanked Röhm for his work and made him, along with Rudolph Hess, the deputy leader of the party, which temporarily restored relations. But disillusionment and frustration were rife among the rank-and-file stormtroopers who had believed that their work would mean more money and better jobs.

Chapter 8

PREACHING PEACE, MEANING WAR

Rearmament continued at a hugely increased rate as Hitler rose to power in the early 1930s, helped by Germany's weak and isolated position in Europe. The scale of the project had been exposed in 1931 by German journalist Carl von Ossietzky, which had brought condemnation and suspicion from the country's neighbours and led to diplomatic isolation. Similarly alerted to their country's military weakness, the vast majority of German people were in favour of getting rid of the shackles of Versailles and restoring the nation's great status. Hitler's response was to preach peace. On 17 May 1933, he spoke to the Reichstag in answer to the words of President Roosevelt delivered in an address the previous day. The US president had proposed that the major European nations should agree to the abolition of all their weapons of war – bombers, tanks and heavy artillery – to disarm for peace. Hitler thanked the president for his proposal and pledged that German was ready 'to disband her entire military establishment and destroy the small amount of arms remaining to her, if the neighbouring countries will do the same'.[4] He went on to claim that Germany did not want war and had no wish to 'Germanize' other peoples. He also repudiated the terms of the Treaty of Versailles, blamed reparations for Germany's economic crisis and ended his speech with the threat that if Germany was not allowed equality in terms of its armed forces and the same armaments as its neighbours, then it would withdraw from the Disarmament Conference and the League of Nations.

Hitler's words of peace were greeted with relief across the world, in government circles, news bureaus and newspaper columns. Roosevelt's secretary was quoted as saying that, 'The President was enthusiastic at Hitler's acceptance of his proposals'.[5] But when the various Allied nations insisted that it would take them eight years to bring their armament stocks down to Germany's level, Hitler followed through on his plan to disengage from both the Conference and the League. Though his actions were risky, involving possible sanctions, an armed attack or even invasion, they were a calculated risk, and they paid dividends. There were no sanctions and no invasion. He announced that the decision to leave Geneva was to be put to the German people in a plebiscite, in which 96 per cent of Germans turned out and 95 per cent voted in favour of leaving (of course, there were rumours of a fix). Despite this, it was clear that Hitler had the support of the German people, which was strengthened when he stopped reparation payments completely.

MEFO BILLS

Behind the scenes, Dr Schacht had been hard at work on rearmament funding with the minister of defence, General von Blomberg. Blomberg was practical and willing to work within the RM700–800 million set to be available each year, but Hitler was impatient and demanded that billions rather than millions should be allocated to the project. Sums like these were not available from taxation or public loans, though income from these sources was also used for the purpose. Hjalmar Schacht came up with a plan, which was both effective and easy to conceal. He founded a dummy company, Metallurgische Forschungsgesellschaft (Mefo for short), with notional capital of RM1 million. The company was outside of the government and had no real operations, except as a vehicle for the exchange of its Mefo promissory notes from the government as payment for delivered armaments. In exchange, the drawer could present his Mefo bills at any German bank, which would then rediscount the bills at the Reichsbank. The system allowed the government to lower its legal loan interest rates and take on bigger debts with the Reichsbank, then prohibited under existing statutes, and benefitted the manufacturers with a new influx of money to spend. This form of money was ideal, as it was not recorded in the books, left no paper trail and did not raise inflation levels. Amounts are not exact, but it is assumed that billions of these bills were issued.

The system of disguised discounting was soon able to 'guarantee to the Reichswehr the fantastic sum of RM35 billion over an eight-year period'.[6] The bills, guaranteed for five years from issue, would start to come due in 1939 and eventually lead to Schacht's resignation from the bank. By then, however, rearmament was all but complete.

In the meantime, Hitler's decision to leave the Geneva Conference sent the message that Nazi Germany intended to rearm in defiance of both Versailles and Roosevelt's suggested disarmament agreement. After a slow start, now with almost unlimited funding, the pace of rearmament increased exponentially.

KRUPP AND THYSSEN

Of course, Hitler was not a socialist, nor was he an economist. However, he had power, a pact with the Reichswehr leadership and the support of Gustav Krupp and other leading industrialists garnered at the meeting at Hermann Göring's house in February 1933. He proceeded to put other measures in place to enable the rearmament issue to proceed quickly. He put his nationalist coalition partner, Hugenberg, in charge of agrarian policy. The landowners' main organization, the Reich Agrarian League (*Reichslandbund*), had been strongly pro-Nazi before Hitler became chancellor, but farmers needed help to defend property on which they owed rent, often to industrialist landowners, to pay higher import duties to help sales, and support for grain prices. In

Arms manufacturer Gustav Krupp and industrialist Fritz Thyssen both profited hugely from their association with the National Socialists. Thyssen played a key role in funding the Nazi movement while Krupp, initially sceptical about Hitler, changed his mind when the Nazis seized power in 1933.

order to soothe tensions between the landowners and the industrialists, which had existed since the 1890s, Hitler had destroyed the trade unions, so cutting the price of labour. The adoption of a work-creation plan and the Mefo-bills method of funding set up by Schacht allowed the rearmament programme to gather pace.

Leading the charge to rearm was Krupp AG, the largest company in Europe at the beginning of the 20th century and Germany's leading armament manufacturer in both world wars. Led by Gustav Krupp, the company had huge holdings. Within Germany, it held a controlling interest in 110 companies, which worked out of 87 industrial complexes. It also had interests in 142 other German complexes.[7] Abroad, Krupp had interests in a hundred or so other companies, ore pits, coal mines, hotels, banks and a cement works.

During the 1920s and 1930s, Krupp had been set against Hitler but was swayed by his anti-trade union opinions. Krupp's ruthlessness in pursuit of profit made him reconsider his position. Having given generously to the Nazi cause, he made good on his promise to help rearm Germany in the build-up to World War II. He built and delivered warships, submarines, Tiger tanks, trucks, locomotives, howitzers, held guns, anti-tank and anti-aircraft guns, and munitions.

Of course, it is easy to argue that Krupp was simply a German firm fulfilling orders for the German government. Just standard business practice. But it was later recorded that the firm had employed 55,000 displaced persons, 18,000 prisoners of war (POWs) and 6,000 inmates from concentration camps, who were leased as part of the Nazi 'Extermination through Work' programme. They were overworked and underfed, paid little and treated like animals. Hundreds of young women in the company's employ had their heads shaved in the shape of a cross and were worked to death. There were many other German companies in a similar position but whose actions were not so naked in their financial ambitions.

One of Germany's wealthiest men during the Weimar era, Fritz Thyssen took over his father's steel and iron empire in 1926 and created United Steel Works two years later. The company employed 200,000 people and controlled more than 75 per cent of Germany's iron ore reserves. He was an early supporter of the Nazis, providing them with funds – including for the purchase in 1930 of the Palais Barlow in Munich, which was converted into the headquarters of the NSDAP and known as the 'Brown House' – and growing rich providing them with war materials and arranging contacts with other leading industrialists, which ultimately helped fuel their rise to power. Much of the money involved was handled through a Thyssen-controlled bank in the Netherlands, which, in turn, had connections in Wall Street. However, Thyssen eventually lost faith in the Nazis, alarmed at their violence and their increasing anti-Semitism and anti-Catholicism, and fled the country in 1939, before being arrested in France and spending time in the concentration camp system. Thyssen was liberated from Dachau by the Allies in May 1945. Rearrested in 1948, he was tried as a supporter of the Nazi Party. He did not deny this and accepted responsibility for the mistreatment of Jews in his workforce, while denying the employment of slave labour. He agreed to pay RM500,000 in compensation and was acquitted of all other charges.

SIEMENS

In the 1930s, Siemens was Germany's leading industrial manufacturing conglomerate specializing in war-related electronic equipment. Founded in Berlin in 1847, the company suffered badly during World War I and the depression that followed. During the 1930s, Siemens supported the Hitler regime in exchange for lucrative contracts to build electronic switches for the military. As the new government began rearming, the company experienced massive growth, with revenues increasing continuously from 1934 onwards and reaching a peak during World War II. During the pre-war years the company further profited through the Nazi Aryanization Programme, which expropriated Jewish businesses and properties, then resold them at below-value prices to approved companies, such as Siemens.

As the Nazis' demands for armaments increased, German workers were being taken from the factories and drafted into the military, so manufacturers turned to slave workers to meet the ensuing labour shortfall. From 1940 onwards, Siemens relied increasingly on slave labour from countries occupied by Germany, exploiting some 80,000 prisoners of war, Jews, Gypsies and other inmates from concentration camps. Siemens was a leading participant in the Nazis' extermination programme and ran factories nearby and even inside concentration camps, such as Auschwitz, Buchenwald, Mauthausen, Ravensbrück, Sachsenhausen and others. In Auschwitz, thousands of prisoners worked in a Siemens factory that supplied the camp with electricity. During the final years of the war, the company ran some 400 plants manufacturing and supplying the camps with electrical parts.

The factories were created and run by the SS, which, under Heinrich Himmler's command, was responsible for crimes against humanity. Siemens' general director, Rudolf Bingel, was a personal friend of Himmler and made full use of his connections to ensure that the company did well under the Nazis. Working conditions inside the camps were appalling, with no heat, no light, no water or sewage facilities and no protection from the rain. The six working days a week were 10–12 hours long with no pay, in fear of being beaten, executed or sent to the gas chambers. Food, when it came, was in the form of stale bread, washed down with coffee made from acorns. Female slave workers were forced to undertake the dangerous, often deadly work of making electrical circuit boards for V-1 and V-2 rockets. They were subjected to all types of exploitation, with the ever-present threat of death if they objected. Female slave workers were also employed in construction, yoked together in teams like animals to pull giant rollers to pave camps' streets.

In 1945, Hermann von Siemens, head of the company, was charged with war crimes and appeared at Nuremberg. The charges were later dropped, and he was reinstated by the Allies to assist in the rebuilding of Germany as a bulwark against the Soviet Union. Company representatives were unapologetic, claiming that they had complied with the Nazis 'out of fear' and had dealt 'admirably with the Jewish Question', unaware perhaps that they were using Nazi terminology to make the point.[8] They even claimed that they had received thank-you letters from some of the company's former slave labourers. More recent events, however, have reawakened the company's

Chapter 8

Nazi past. In 1998, under threat of lawsuits issued by US lawyers on behalf of former slave labourers, Siemens agreed to set up a $12 million fund in compensation. This was in addition to $4.3 million it had paid to the Jewish Claims Conference in 1961.

However, whether or not the company has learned its lessons was tested in 2002, when public opinion forced the company to abandon its plan to register the trademark 'Zyklon' for a new line of products including gas ovens, the same name as the poison gas – Zyklon-B – used to exterminate prisoners in Nazi death camps such as Majdanek and Auschwitz!

COMPLICITY

Countless other arms manufacturers, such as Hugo Schneider Aktiengesellschaft Metallwarenfabrik (HASAG) and Walther and Zeiss Ikon, were involved in the exploitation and murder of slave labour in a similar manner and some on a massive scale. Companies from other industries also took advantage of the Nazi regime in a wide range of sectors: iron and steel production, mines and quarries, construction, design and production of ships and submarines, airships and aeroplanes, fuel production, tyre production, electrical equipment, pharmaceuticals, data provision, stone-works, production of uniforms, radio technology, wireless telegraphy and so on. Less obvious spheres of business were also required by the Nazis: banking and finance, insurance, food production – including by companies like Dr. Oetker, Bahlsen and Maggi – the organization of the Aryanization scheme, the transport of prisoners to concentration camps, the renting out of slave labour, the construction of crematoriums for the extermination camps and the manufacture of the ovens to be used inside (see pp. 185–86).

It is important to note that by 1932, links between the world of big business in Germany and the Nazi Party were extensive: over 50 per cent of the companies listed on Berlin's stock exchange had ties to the party and they experienced a boom in stock value when Hitler became chancellor the following year. The stories of these companies are many and varied. What bound them together was perhaps simply their intention to survive, or to play their part in the reconstruction of Germany. For others, it was simply a way of maximizing profits whatever the costs.

Other notable German companies, not mentioned elsewhere in this book but with strong links to the NSDAP, whose stories could have been told include (but are not limited to): Adidas, Deutsche Luft Hansa, Dornier, the Flick family, Heinkel, Hoechst, Messerschmidt, Miele, Mittelwerk, Opta Radio, Reichswerke Hermann Göring Raxwerke, Rheinmetall-Borsig, Hermann Röchling, Shell plc, Valentin, Carl Zeiss AG and Zeppelin.

BOSCH

Bosch started life in 1886 as a supplier of magnetos for gas and then automobile engines. A few years later, these had become standard ignition devices using a spark plug. As road traffic grew, so did the company, its automotive and other products and its factory sites, which were spreading across the world by the 1930s.

Founder, Robert Bosch, was a liberal man and a pacifist. He was also a progressive employer, introducing an eight-hour day for his workers as early as 1906. In 1926, in his home town of Stuttgart, he became a founding member of the *Verein zur Abwehr des Antisemitismus*, an organization similar to the Anti-Defamation League, dedicated to fighting anti-Semitism. Despite being vehemently anti-Hitler, the company became deeply involved in the war economy, employing thousands of forced labourers, POWs and female concentration camp prisoners, many from Warsaw. They were used in the production of electrical equipment for tanks, tractors and trucks, often in conditions of secrecy. Many lived and worked in 'inhumane conditions' while others were 'brutally abused'.

In recent years, the company has confirmed that from 1933 Bosch was 'entangled with the rearmament' of the Third Reich. The spokesperson also admitted that it employed about 20,000 slave labourers and had direct contracts with the Nazi Party. But it also helped to rescue Jewish associates and support the resistance movement, providing money to help Jews emigrate and hiring them in an effort to help them avoid persecution.

Chapter 8

In a twist of irony, when Robert Bosch died in 1942, the Nazis afforded him a state funeral. Two years later, the *Bosch-Kreis* (Bosch Circle), a small group of the company's senior executives, which had included Robert Bosch, were involved in the 20 July plot, the failed attempt to assassinate Hitler.

CARS FOR ALL

Hitler had a long-standing obsession with cars, which he used as propaganda during his campaigns for power. In early 1933, he had made a speech to members of the industry in Berlin in which he described car manufacture as the most important industry of the future. In a follow-up to the event, the *Völkischer Beobachter* published an article in which it extolled the virtues of car ownership in the form of a *Volksauto* or *Volkswagen*, a car for the people, available for RM1,000 (around $140 at the time) – an idea that Hitler had been advancing privately. Hitler engaged the services of Ferdinand Porsche to design the car. The 'strength through joy' car was first displayed at the Berlin Motor Show in 1939, shortly before the start of World War II that instantly halted production. Alongside the Volkswagen, in 1934 Hitler ordered the construction, using state funds, of 1,000 km (620 miles) of Autobahn every year, to be built using an workforce of 600,000 unemployed. Strikes, sickness, hunger and misery saw the project slow down and then stop when the war began. Despite the propaganda campaign, it is a myth that the Nazis were the creators of the German Autobahn.

Hitler's speech in Berlin had been a tonic for the German automobile industry with production and sales increasing immediately. Mercedes, which had produced the first combustion engine-powered car in 1896 and established a reputation for producing cars for millionaires early the following decade, benefitted from the patronage of Nazi, Italian Fascist and Japanese officials, including Hitler, Göring, Mussolini and Hirohito, during the 1930s. The Führer drove a 770 model with a bulletproof windscreen. From 1937, Mercedes turned its attentions to military products, including aircraft, tanks and submarines. Using some 60,000 or so forced labourers, the company also produced barrels for Mauser 98k rifles, the gold-standard choice of the Reichswehr.

The Big Guns Arrive

Although the Volkswagen has Hitler to thank for its existence, the first 'Beetle', as it was renamed to distance it from the Nazi period, did not roll off the assembly line at the factory in Wolfsberg, until 1945. The one millionth arrived 10 years later, becoming a symbol of the German economic miracle of the post-war years.

In 1988, following a lengthy study of its wartime activities commissioned by the company, the by-then-named Daimler-Benz company agreed to pay $12 million compensation to the victims of its forced work programmes. It was a similar story of opportunism, exploitation and cruelty for the other major German automobile makers, including Adler, Audi, BMW, Opel, Porsche and Puch, who drew on slaves from Mauthausen, Dachau, Papenburg, Sachsenhausen, Natzweiler-Struthof and Buchenwald camps among others, many of whom were worked to death on a starvation diet and punishing schedules.

Chapter 8

FOREIGN INVESTMENT OPPORTUNITIES

Of course, it wasn't just German companies that were involved in the exploitation of slave labour (see also Chapter 4). Both the Dawes and Young Plans had pumped billions into the German economy in the 1920s. These loans, which when combined provided 70 per cent of Germany's income, were 'officially' designed to help Germany pay its First World War reparations, but, in fact, also ensured 'favourable conditions for US investment' by stabilizing the German Mark and also restoring the country's lucrative military-industrial potential.[9] It was an incredible investment opportunity and during the 1930s American money from companies like Standard Oil, DuPont, General Electric, telecom company ITT, General Motors and Ford Motors began to flow into Germany. It found its way into the coffers of German companies such as pharmaceutical giant I.G. Farben, radio and electrical suppliers AEF and Siemens, the aircraft manufacturer Focke-Wulf, and automobile manufacturers Opel and Volkswagen. Many American companies, such as Ford-Werke, General Motors, Kodak AG and Coca-Cola, set up subsidiary companies in Germany, building factories to supply local interests, meaning that many of the companies involved in Germany's burgeoning war machine were under the financial control of American investors.

Money had been a constant issue for the NSDAP since its foundation and, towards the end of 1932, the party's lack of funds and, in particular, Hitler's own personal debts, were seen by his supporters at home and abroad as endangering his campaign to take power. Ten days after Hitler's meeting with von Papen at Kurt Baron von Schröder's house in Cologne, on 14 January 1933 Hitler was invited to a meeting at von Schröder's bank in Berlin (it was Hitler's bank). Present at the meeting were the Dulles brothers, John Foster and Allen W., of the New York law firm, Sullivan & Cromwell, who represented the bank, von Schröder and Montagu Norman, governor of the bank of England. Although little information on the discussions had that day exists, a secret agreement was reached to secure funding for the Nazi Party going forward.

Following Hitler's appointment as chancellor, the financial relationships between the new government and Britain, the USA and other European countries became 'extremely benevolent'.[10] Soon after becoming chancellor, Hitler refused to carry on paying reparations. There were few objections from either Britain or France. In fact, Hjalmar Schacht visited the USA in May 1933 having secured new loans of $1 billon from Wall Street. The following month, he returned from a meeting with Norman in London with another $2 million in loans and with significant reductions on other, older loans. Perhaps the worst example of naked financial greed was that of Standard Oil. In 1934, the company bought 2,954 sq km (730,000 acres) of land and built refineries to supply the Nazis with oil. In addition, US aeroplane firms Pratt & Whitney, Douglas and the Bendix Corporation supplied the latest equipment and know-how to Germany to help rebuild its air force – it is said that the Junker-87 dive-bomber was built using purely American technology. Total American investments in the German economy are estimated to have been $475 million.

DID THEY JUMP OR WERE THEY PUSHED?

Naturally, businesses in other European companies were attracted by these opportunities, some even by the Nazis' anti-Semitic views. French beauty company L'Oréal, for instance, thrived under the Third Reich. Its founder, Eugène Schueller, was a noted anti-Semite and collaborated with the Nazis and the Vichy government during their occupation of France. His business interests included contracts to supply huge quantities of paint to the Germany Navy, making him fabulously rich. After the war, he was accused of collaboration and arrested but charges were never brought against him. In fact, the occupying Nazi regime saw immense value in the French fashion industry and a number of other famous fashion houses were keen to embrace the opportunities it offered. These included Chanel, Cristóbal Balenciaga, Louis Vuitton, Christian Dior and Hugo Boss, who designed and manufactured uniforms for the SA, the SS and the Hitler Youth.

The Nazis were keen to take advantage of companies and factories in all of their occupied territories. In France and the Netherlands, they requisitioned the national railway companies, SNCF and NS Reizigers, to transport Jews,

Chapter 8

Gypsies and other Holocaust victims to the extermination camps. In Poland, they forced local labour to construct the crematoriums in Auschwitz. After annexing Czechoslovakia in 1938, the Nazis took over the Škoda Works in Pilsen. They stopped manufacturing cars and returned to the conglomerate's original task of manufacturing weapons. The highly skilled workforce were experts in tank building and produced the Panzer 35(t) and the Panzer 38(t), which were used extensively by the Wehrmacht in the invasions of Poland, France and the Soviet Union.

After the war, companies from inside and outside Germany acted in different ways in the face of accusations or revelations of their collusion. Some admitted it and carried on in the face of the criticism; others paid money to their victims or families in compensation. Some commissioned historians to produce reports on the connections; others denied their involvement or said they had no choice. Did they jump or were they pushed? Perhaps the most honest reason came from Ingvar Kamprad, founder of the Swedish company IKEA. Although the story of his involvement was first revealed some 50 years after the war, as a 17-year-old Kamprad had been a member of the Swedish Nazi Party – which had close ties with its German cousin and was represented by a swastika symbol. He had some sort of official position in the organization and was active in member recruitment. In an interview he gave to *Forbes* magazine in 2000, Kamprad said, 'Perhaps even you did something in your youth that you now know was stupid. Why did I not reveal this past foolishness myself? Simple. I was afraid it would hurt my business.'[11] Kamprad died in 2018. His three sons, all billionaires, inherited part of the IKEA empire and are among those whose family members had Nazi ties.

Other notable American and European companies, not mentioned elsewhere in this book but with strong links to the NSDAP, whose stories could have been listed, include (but are not limited to): Alcoa, Associated Press, Baccarat, Bank of Canada, Chase National Bank, Crédit Suisse, Gillette, IBM, IT&T, JAB Holdings (Krispy Kreme, Insomnia Cookies and Pret a Manger), MGM, Österreichische Saurerwerke, Singer, Universale

Hoch- und Tiefbau, United Fruit, Universal Pictures, Westinghouse and Woolworths.

Chapter 9

Blitzkrieg!

For the National Socialists, the number one enemy of the *Volk* was 'the Jew'. Anti-Semitic activities, which had been a central element of the NSDAP's racial movement since its inception, aimed at excluding Jews from the *Volksgemeinschaft* ('national community'), began in Berlin on 1 April 1933 with a boycott of Jewish-owned businesses. Though the boycott was 'officially' only supposed to last one day, in towns and villages across the country, local party members and SA groups took the opportunity to continue the campaign as they saw fit, exposing boycott-breakers in the local papers and even using physical violence on Jewish shop and business owners.

At various points in the early 1930s, the German media and the Reichsbank had estimated that the combined wealth of German Jews (in 1933 this was 0.77 per cent of the German population[1]) could have been up to RM20 billion (20 per cent of national wealth). When the Nazis took power, these estimates were raised. Retrospective statistics, compiled this century, put the figure at somewhere between RM8–16 billion in 1933, RM5 billion in 1934 and RM4.4 in 1935. It was Nazi propaganda at work. In addition, a raft of new, racist laws banning Jews from public service, the civil service, farming and teaching, and banning them from publishing newspapers and magazines further drove the process of excluding Jews from German economic life. In 1934, they were banned from the stock exchanges. Some fled the country and state agencies plundered what they left behind as Jewish shops, dwellings and businesses were quickly 'Aryanized' and sold off to German people for a fraction of their value. They also levied a tax on the Aryan buyers of the businesses and on Jews leaving the country who had to pay a Reich flight tax and other compulsory payments before they were allowed to flee, taking what little they had left with them.

TARGETING THE ENEMIES OF THE STATE

The campaign of terror unleashed on the Nazis' enemies was overseen by a series of institutions with their headquarters in central Berlin: the Secret State Police (Gestapo), the State Police, the Security Service (SD), the Political Police, the SS and the SA. In the early days of the new regime, the German people were happy to accept and even support Nazi terror and the removal of certain personal freedoms, believing the propaganda that supported it claiming that their country was heading for a better future without 'enemies of the state and of the people'.[2] The people felt safe, knowing that the Gestapo and the new concentration camps were only interested in communists or socialists, Jews, homosexuals, Gypsies and other undesirables. For those who had doubts about supporting the ruthless and powerful new regime, the Blood Purge of 30 June 1934 was convincing. This operation, planned and carried out by Hitler, Himmler's SS and Göring's special police, included the murders of Ernst Röhm, Gregor Strasser, hundreds of other SA leaders and other enemies of the party, including General von Schleicher, Gustav von Kahr and Father Bernhard Stempfle, who allegedly knew too much about the suicide of Geli Raubal.[3]

Fear of operations like this, later dubbed 'Night of the Long Knives', guaranteed people's willingness to point the finger of denunciation at others: those who colluded with Jews, associated with foreign workers or listened to foreign radio, for example. This did much to consolidate National Socialist rule. In 1935, the campaign against Jews was rapidly accelerated by the 'Nuremberg Laws', which classified Jews as second-class citizens, forbade marriages between Jews and Aryans and criminalized sexual relations between the two 'races'. The sign *Juden unerwünscht* ('Jews not welcome') had become a common sight outside shops, hotels and beer gardens throughout the country. Having already been removed from German economic life, these laws were intended to exclude them from the social life of the community, with the ultimate aim of expelling Jews from Germany.

Blitzkrieg!

The process of Aryanization increased widely following the passing of these laws, from which both the German state and its people materially profited from freed-up jobs, homes, furniture, companies and property.

OLYMPIC-SIZED ILLUSION

By 1936, Germany appeared to be in a good place for its Aryan citizens. Hitler was gradually freeing the country from the restrictions of Versailles and rearming vigorously. Unemployment figures were on the way down, welfare payments were reduced and tax revenue increased. There were a few complaints about personal freedom, workers' rights, the food supply

Leni Riefenstahl (on the ground, centre) directing the filming of American runner Archie Williams who had just won the gold medal in the 400-metre 'dash' at the Berlin Olympics for her award-winning film Olympia *(1938).*

Chapter 9

and Jewish persecution but they were easy to ignore since the people were getting what they wanted: stability. That summer, Berlin hosted the Olympic Games, which attracted thousands of foreign visitors to Germany. The tourist business, already in full flow, brought in huge amounts of badly needed foreign currency. The Games' organizers and the locals put on a good show and visitors were impressed by what they saw. It was a propaganda triumph for Hitler, who had a new 100,000-seat track-and-field stadium built for the athletics as well as a number of other, smaller venues. The Games were the first to be televised, while radio broadcasts reached 41 other countries. Filmmaker Leni Riefenstahl was commissioned to film the Games and the subsequent movie, *Olympia* (1938), which pioneered many of the techniques still used in film and TV coverage of sports events, and won the Best Film award at the Venice Film Festival in that year. After the Games, foreigners returned home 'greatly impressed' by what they had seen – a far cry from what they had expected from the news reports they had been reading at home.

For Jews at this time, of course, the story was somewhat different. The laws against them (at least 2,000 anti-Semitic laws and regulations were passed between 1933 and 1945) had been increasingly stringent, and by now at least half of the Jewish population of Germany had been deprived of any means of livelihood. Casual violence and public humiliation of Jews accused of racial defilement and even murder had become commonplace. There were regular articles and photographs in local papers denouncing German citizens who 'bought from Jews'. Many Jews were not able to buy food, milk for their children or drugs and medicine. Following the events on the night of 9–10 November 1938, matters grew much more serious.

Two weeks earlier, on 28 October, 17,000 Polish Jews living in Germany were arrested and interned in 'relocation camps' intended for deportation. On hearing the news of his family's arrest, a 17-year-old student living in Paris, Herschel Grynszpan, went to the German embassy and shot Ernst vom Rath. When arrested, Grynszpan said, 'Being a Jew is not a crime. I am not a dog. I have a right to live and the Jewish people have a right to exist on earth.'[4] Hitler immediately charged Joseph Goebbels with a response.

Blitzkrieg!

After dark on 9 November, a pogrom saw violence unleashed against Jews all over Germany. Mobs made up of SA and SS troops and members of the Hitler Youth as well as civilians attacked Jews in the streets, in their homes, at work and even at their places of worship. Over 900 synagogues were burned to the ground, blown up and torn down. Businesses were destroyed, schools and cemeteries were vandalized. Non-Aryans were threatened and beaten up, well over a hundred Jews were murdered and 30,000 Jewish men were arrested and deported to concentration camps in Dachau, Buchenwald and Sachsenhausen. The broken glass that littered the streets outside the burned-out shops and synagogues earned the event the name *Kristallnacht* ('Night of Broken Glass').

The interior of the Fasanenstrasse synagogue in Charlottenburg, Berlin, on the morning of 10 November 1938, one of 1,400 synagogues damaged during Kristallnacht. The largest synagogue in the city, it was a symbol of Jewish integration in Germany and targeted specifically by Joseph Goebbels.

Further anti-Semitic rules followed: Jews were to be gathered together into ghettos and subjected to curfew, were not allowed to own guns, and had their driving licences suspended and their radios confiscated. German Jews were fined RM1 billion for vom Rath's death and for 'broken windows'. The Reich government then confiscated all insurance payouts to Jews whose businesses and homes were looted or destroyed that night, leaving the Jewish owners personally responsible for the cost of all repairs. When those guilty of perpetrating the violence of 9–10 November went unpunished, it marked a turning point in German racial policy. On 30 January 1939 Hitler gave a speech in which he explicitly threatened 'the annihilation of the Jewish race in Europe'.[5]

BUDGET CRISIS

Despite the appearance of good financial management, Nazi economic policy since 1933 had brought about a financial crisis by 1939. To get unemployment figures down and finance its huge rearmament plans, the government had borrowed enormous sums of money. Despite the rise in tax income, the savings on reduced welfare and Schacht's Mefo bills plan, the sums had not worked. Having spent at least RM45 billion on the military, in August 1939 the national debt stood at RM37.4 billion – three times more than the total state revenues for 1937. In 1939, the first year of World War II, the regime needed RM16.3 billion for civilian expenditure and RM20.5 billion for the military plus an additional RM3.3 billion for payment of past debts. State revenue that year was expected to be between RM17 and RM18 billion. Hitler, well aware of the country's parlous economic situation, had already ramped up exploitation of German Jews, turning in 1937 to a more systematic dispossession of their assets. Jews leaving the country were now relieved of any currency, stocks, stamps, jewellery, gold, silver, precious stones, artworks and antiques before they were allowed to leave. When they had left, their businesses and homes were Aryanized. After the *Anschluss* (annexation) of Austria in March 1938, Austrian Jews were subjected to the same treatment. With Germany's financial situation worsening by the day,

Hitler's plans for the further expansion, dispossession and exploitation of Jews and others in countries to the east, with Czechoslovakia and Poland first, became more urgent.

In April, after receiving a demand from the *Wehrmacht* for RM11 billion for their 1939 budget, the Nazis dug deeper into Jewish pockets. A government edict was issued, requiring all Jews to declare any assets in excess of RM5,000. That summer, it was estimated that German and Austrian Jews 'possessed wealth worth around RM8 billion' over and above the RM5,000 limit.[6] Jews were then forced to exchange most of their assets for government stocks and bonds. Following *Kristallnacht* and the subsequent atonement payment of RM1 billion imposed by the government on the German Jewish community, the alarm was raised by the Reichsbank, who feared that in order to raise the money Jews would clearly have to sell off their government bonds. The government immediately stepped in and prohibited Jews from selling their bonds. The long-winded plan worked and state revenues for 1938–9 increased by 6 per cent. Adding in income from Jewish emigration tax and other anti-Semitic measures of more than RM5 million and RM1.5 million from Aryanization, the uplift was more like 9 per cent. News of the country's rebounding economy went down well with the German public.

ON A WAR FOOTING

But the public did not know everything. As early as 1934 Hjalmar Schacht had admitted to the American ambassador that Hitler and his party were absolutely committed to war. In December 1936, in preparation for this intended conflict, Hitler asked Minister-President Generaloberst Hermann Göring to draw up a secret and ambitious Four-Year Plan to reorganize the German economy for war. Plans were to reorganize agriculture, commerce and industry from a military viewpoint and make Germany completely self-sufficient in strategic war materials, such as rubber, gasoline and steel.

Such military activity is usually financed by a rise in taxes but the Nazis, keen to maintain the support of the German public, wanted to avoid this. The Third Reich's plans for the wartime economy exempted 70 per cent of the population from a 50 per cent tax rise, a further 26 per cent incurred some charges, and only the wealthiest 4 per cent paid the full amount. A suspension of overtime, night-time, Sunday and holiday pay was imposed at the start of the war but reinstated shortly afterwards. Tax rises on beer, spirits and tobacco were also introduced but in a sensitive manner, with 20 per cent as the top rate and less for drinkers in beer-loving regions. Tax on wine was not increased so as not to damage the wine-making industry.

In 1939, the German political leadership had decided that it had three viable sources of income for the war effort to come. Firstly, it was fully prepared to tax the rich and, in particular, businesses that were involved in rearmament, whose production was increasingly geared to the needs of the military. Secondly, it was prepared to fully exploit the economies and the resources of the countries that Germany was shortly to occupy. Thirdly, it was to continue with its policies of expropriating the assets of German Jews and of those living in what the Nazis had come to call Greater Germany.

In November 1941, the government issued an additional ordinance of the Reich Citizenship Law. Outstanding government debts to Jewish institutions or individuals were erased. In one stroke, the assets of German Jews, many of which had already been converted into government bonds, were officially expropriated. Civil servants were asked to leave as little evidence of this action as possible. Debt cancellations were to be entered 'without recording the name of the individual Jew who had given the securities in payment'.[7]

Wiping out old debts without compensation was ideal for a budgetary policy guided by the idea that no more than 50 per cent of what was needed for the war should be acquired on credit. Now, new lines of credit could be opened. Revenues in Germany alone from this form of stealing were estimated to be somewhere around RM2 billion.[8]

SHAME, GUILT AND SADISM

The historian William Shirer was living in Vienna during the Anschluss in March 1938. On the morning of 12 March, the German Army invaded; no one stopped it and not a shot was fired. Germans and Austrians were

Blitzkrieg!

Anti-Semitic violence and humiliation began across Austria immediately after the Anschluss. So-called 'scrubbing parties, were organized in Vienna in which the city's Jews were forced to scrub the streets while being mocked by jeering crowds.

enthusiastic about it. However, Shirer gives a vivid account of the treatment Jews could expect from the invading army. Headed up by Reinhard Heydrich and administered with ruthless efficiency by Adolf Eichmann, the Office of Jewish Emigration was 'set up' to issue permits for Jews to leave the country. In reality, as soon as German troops arrived in Austria, they began a campaign of sadistic cruelty to dehumanize and shame Jewish men and women. Taken off the street, groups of Jews were made to clean public latrines and SA and SS barracks toilets while being jeered at by stormtroopers and members of the public. Thousands of others were rounded up, arrested and jailed with their possessions confiscated. Rather than transporting Jews from Austria to the concentration camps in Germany, they ordered the construction of a camp at Mauthausen on the Danube. During the seven years of its existence, some 90,000 people died there in appalling conditions. This number included over 35,000 officially listed executions.

The so-called 'peaceful' annexation of Austria was a major success for Hitler, and his ambitions for a further conquest turned towards Czechoslovakia, 'the most modern, developed and industrialized economy in Eastern Europe'.[9] The provinces of Bohemia, Moravia and Silesia had once been the heart of the Austrian Empire and produced the majority of its army's arms, in particular at the Škoda Works. He was also aware that in the war that was coming, the German people would have need of food. The fact that Czechoslovakia had advanced agricultural production and food-processing industries made it clear that Hitler's interests in this new conquest were largely economic. Planning for the invasion, code-named 'Case Green', which had first been drawn up in 1937, was put back on the table in April the following year.

CZECHOSLOVAKIA 'DESTROYED'

Alarmed at the 'noises' of a German move on Czechoslovakia, the British, the French and the Russians were on the alert, fearing the possibility of a new European war. Prime Minister Chamberlain and President Daladier were involved in diplomatic discussions. Hitler was at pains to conceal his plans, believing that his military was not yet ready for war. As a pretext, he insisted that his concerns were merely for the 3 million ethnic Germans living in the Sudetenland, a province in northern Czechoslovakia. There had been 'rumours', obviously untrue, that the Czech government had been abusing and committing 'atrocities' on its German subjects. Tension built further in May, when Czech President Beneš ordered a partial mobilization. Hitler was furious and deeply humiliated that his plan had been revealed and at the support given to the Czechs by London, Paris and Moscow.

Hitler had made no secret of his dislike of this country carved out of the Hapsburg Empire and included Czechs, Slovaks, Hungarians, Russians and Germans. In the deliberate provocation of a country created by the hated peace treaties signed at the end of World War I, on the evening of 12 September 1938, Hitler's closing speech of that year's Nuremberg Rally was broadcast over the radio. In the speech he demanded that the Czech authorities give 'justice' to the Sudeten Germans. If they did not return the land on which the German population lived to Germany, then a European war would follow. The following day, in another planned move, the Nazi-supporting Sudeten German Party *Freikorps* took to the streets in protest at their treatment. A wave of violence followed, against Jews, Czechs and other anti-fascists. Martial law was declared but the unrest continued, with riots, shoot-outs and several hundred dead and wounded. In haste, and after much shuttle diplomacy, the Munich Agreement, about which the Czechs were not consulted, was signed by Nazi Germany, Britain, France and Italy on 30 September 1938. This agreed to German annexation of the Sudetenland in exchange for a pledge of peace from Hitler. Because of the collapse of the Beneš government, Hitler was also granted *de facto* control over the rest of Czechoslovakia, giving the Nazis access to coal, iron, steel and other commodities. But he did not get what he really wanted ... war.

Within six months, Hitler had broken the agreement and invaded and occupied the remainder of Czechoslovakia. On 14 March 1939, with Hitler's blessing, Slovakia declared its independence. The following day, Hitler met with Czech President Emil Hácha and secured free passage for his troops across Czech borders. By the end of that day, German soldiers had occupied Bohemia and Moravia – in which the Czech armaments industry was sited. The area was declared a German protectorate. By evening, Hitler was in Prague. By the end of the year, Czechoslovakia had ceased to exist.

THE THERESIENSTADT GHETTO

The Nazi occupation of Bohemia and Moravia followed a similar pattern to its actions in Germany and Austria in terms of its treatment of the 118,000 or so Jews who lived in the Protectorate. Jewish rights and freedoms began to be limited, there was street violence, and synagogues were attacked and burned. There were riots in Brno in which several Jews were beaten and murdered. Jewish doctors and lawyers were banned, as were any Jews in positions of leadership in industry and other businesses. Local fascist groups

Chapter 9

tried to take advantage of the situation for themselves, but the Nazi authorities clamped down on this immediately. They wanted Jewish assets and property for themselves. Emigration was initially encouraged, for huge fees and the cost of leaving all property to the Reich. But this became more difficult as the number of states willing to take in Jewish emigrants decreased rapidly. To deal with this problem, Reinhard Heydrich ordered the creation of the Theresienstadt Ghetto, north of Prague. It served as a ghetto-labour camp at first, in which conditions were so bad that tens of thousands of people died mostly from disease or starvation, then as a transit camp for Czech Jews who were sent on to concentration camps in the east and the death camps at Auschwitz, Majdanek and Treblinka. Of the approximately 140,000 Jews sent to Theresienstadt, some 90,000 were deported and roughly 33,000 died in the camp itself.

WAR AND TERROR!

At dawn on 1 September 1939, Germany invaded Poland in an unprovoked attack. Deploying 1.5 million men, 2,000 tanks and 400 fighter planes supporting about 900 bombers, they attacked from the north and the south. The invading force employed blitzkrieg ('lightning war') tactics, using overwhelming force using air attacks, followed by the advance of fast-moving armoured units who would secure positions for mechanized infantry. Britain and France declared war on Germany two days later. On 17 September, the Soviet Union invaded Poland from the east. The Polish government fled the country the same day and on 28 September, Poland officially surrendered. In October, the Nazis organized a part of German-occupied Poland, including East Prussia and the cities of Danzig, Warsaw, Krakow, Radom and Lublin, into an administrative area called the General Government, under the Nazi Party lawyer Hans Frank. In the east, the Warthegau was overseen by a German civilian government.

Jews made up some 10 per cent – more than 3.3 million people – of the population of Poland, so the invasion brought increasing numbers of them under Nazi control. In the first few days of the invasion, it was clear that Nazi anti-Jewish policies had escalated in their ruthlessness. On 5 September in

The majority of the Jewish population of Leszno in Poland were massacred by the Einsatzgruppe VI *during the German invasion in 1939, including 20 members of the Polish Gymnastic Society, a local teacher and a lawyer who were lined up against a wall and shot on Saturday 21 October.*

Piotrków, for example, German troops encountered a group of unarmed Jews hiding with their rabbi, and shot them. The following day, they set fire to houses in the Jewish quarter and shot those trying to escape the flames. They stole what they wanted from the houses, stripping them of everything – furniture, clothes, linen and carpets. They would invite local Poles to join in the looting.

Poland was the first stop in Hitler's plan of Germany's geographic expansion. It also became a testing ground for National Socialist 'racial' and population policy, a model for the *Lebensraum* for the Aryan master race he intended to impose throughout Eastern Europe. In a move planned before the invasion by Heinrich Himmler and Reinhard Heydrich, task forces made up of the Security Service, the Gestapo and the police were to instigate a clear-out of Jews, intelligentsia, the priesthood and the aristocracy. The SS began a campaign of arrests, deportations and murders. During the blitzkrieg phase of the invasion, newly formed *Einsatzgruppen* (mobile killing units) had been ordered to follow behind the front-line troops, root out and kill any of those listed in the *Sonderfahndungsbuch Polen* (Special Prosecution Book). The list, compiled by the Gestapo, contained the names of over 60,000 prominent Polish and Jewish citizens. But their orders were also intended to spread fear and terror in the population. Jews were humiliated and killed at will. In Będzin, Jewish homes and businesses were wrecked, orthodox Jews had their beards and earlocks cut off and 29 hostages were executed in the main square. Flamethrowers were used to set light to the city's synagogue and those fleeing the building were shot. There were similar scenes in Katowice, Krzeszowice, Dulowa and Trzebina. In Dynów and Przemyśl, Jews over the age of 14 were rounded up, taken to a nearby forest, forced to dig their own mass grave, and shot.

Those Jews who survived had few, if any, choices. Hitler wanted Poland cleared of Jews and Poles, to assist in the Germanization of the occupied territories. Many were forced to flee east; others were organized into ghettos and became slave labour. Various anti-Jewish laws were soon issued. By the end of 1939, all Jews in Poland aged over ten had to wear yellow stars on their sleeves, and shops had to display signs on their windows to indicate that they were Jewish. Jewish homes, belongings and businesses became German property. Occupied Poland was home to over a thousand ghettos, the biggest of which were in Warsaw and Lodz, and hundreds of forced labour camps. Conditions inside both were deliberately harsh, in the knowledge that many of the inhabitants would die.

EXPLOITATION AT HOME AND ABROAD

The economic advantages of using forced labour are obvious: workers are cheap (if they are paid at all), can be made to work long hours, have no rights, can be made to undertake dangerous work without safeguards and can be used to offset labour shortages. But the Nazis went a lot further. Although there are no reliable figures as to how many forced labourers the Nazis used during the war, the figure is generally believed to be between 8 and 12 million. Before deportation, from Poland and Russia, the workers were required to turn over their assets to a local administrator. Money raised from the sale of these assets was paid to the German treasury, which would, in theory, pay it back when the workers returned home. In exchange, forced labourers deported to Nazi Germany were paid, although their wages were between 15 and 40 per cent lower than those of their fellow German workers. However, their wages were also subject to state regulation and the Reich 'appropriated 60 to 70 per cent of them' by imposing 'general administrative revenues'.[10] This scheme is estimated to have added RM500 million to the Reich tax income between 1941 and 1945, taking some of the burden off German taxpayers.

Another huge source of income for the Nazis during these years, as already mentioned, was Aryanization. It took place in Germany itself and in many of the countries occupied by German forces. In Germany, Jewish-owned assets were first nationalized and then privatized and sold on, meaning that the revenue raised from the sale of businesses, houses, flats and other assets went to state treasuries and the German war chest.

The German authorities learned quickly in the domestic sphere. Legal measures for plundering Jewish assets, in particular property, were essential for controlling the process of its seizure, a matter swiftly dealt with by issuing *Rechtssicherheit*, secure legal titles to businesses or real estate. The economics of the Aryanization issue were dealt with by means of financial bureaucracy. It was essential to the German authorities that the process of war had to pay for itself; no one wanted the increasingly impoverished Jewish population to become a burden to the state. Money made from the proceeds of Aryanization was therefore used to pay the costs.

A similar principle was used in the occupied territories, where matters were subject to local laws and therefore more complicated. For this reason, local officials were employed by the Reich authorities to control the process, organize ownership and sales, and deposit the proceeds in local *Reichskommissariat* bank accounts. In turn, this money was used locally to pay the costs of occupation, the building of camps, for example in the

Chapter 9

Netherlands and Serbia, or war compensation claims. Historian Götz Aly describes this as 'essentially a gigantic, trans-European trafficking operation in stolen goods'.[11]

This kind of economic discrimination played a big part in the effectiveness of Nazi anti-Semitism. Already burdened by Nazi propaganda that exaggerated claims of Jewish wealth, with their businesses and property confiscated and their subsequent ever-diminishing means, the chances for Jewish families to flee by emigration were severely reduced, as was their physical and mental ability to resist repression.

CONCENTRATION CAMPS

Soon after Hitler's appointment as chancellor in January 1933, the Nazis had built a series of camps in which their alleged political opponents could be 'concentrated'. Established on a local level where they were deemed necessary, these camps were gradually disbanded; only Dachau, set up in 1933, remained in operation. They were soon replaced by a more centralized camp system, headed up by Reichsführer Heinrich Himmler and under the control of the SS. These new camps, organized in order to provide slave labour for the German war effort, were overseen by the *Inspektion der Konzentrationslager* (IKL), a department of the SS Economic-Administrative Main Office.

Standing outside the laws of the German state, based on the authorization of Hitler as Führer, people could be incarcerated indefinitely, without committing a crime and without charges simply because the authorities deemed them a danger – politically or racially – to German society. In the camps, 'unofficial' cruelty and death were constant and intended. Jews, social democrats, communists, liberals, Freemasons, Jehovah's Witnesses, clergy who opposed the Nazis, members of national oppositions, non-Germans (after Germany had occupied other countries), Roma, Sinti and gay men were all included in the list of 'persons of danger' to the Reich.

Hard work had long been regarded in Germany as a sign of proper social habits and personal discipline on which social 'order' was dependent. Nazi propaganda used these ideas, labelling the people in the camps as criminals and subversives who needed to be educated in social discipline. So, prisoners were put to work, without equipment, clothing, nourishment or rest in pointless, back-breaking labour that produced nothing. However, as war approached and labour shortages began to bite, this army of forced labourers were reassigned, at first to SS-owned or -operated businesses, and then to produce construction materials for new Reich settlements to be built in Eastern Europe.

Despite the fact that historians cannot ascertain exactly when the Nazis planned their 'Final Solution to the Jewish Problem', the invasion of the Soviet Union in June 1941 certainly marked a new level of their plan to exterminate European Jewry. Although the Nazis had built a number of major concentration camps before the war, Sachsenhausen, Buchenwald, Flossenbürg and Ravensbrück were all inside German borders. Camps were built in Austria, France and Poland. Auschwitz I was in use by 1940. The invasion, which represented a huge escalation of the war, saw a subsequent expansion of prisoners: foreign forced labourers, foreign political opponents, resistance fighters and POWs. The numbers were overwhelming. In an effort to deal with the problem, Himmler authorized his *Einsatzgruppen* units to kill all Jews without restriction, resulting in the swift murders of whole Jewish communities. Hitler came under pressure from key figures in the Nazi hierarchy to clear space in the Greater German Reich and the Protectorate for new prisoners to arrive. To make room in the Minsk Ghetto, German soldiers and local collaborators transported some 25,000 inhabitants to a local ravine and shot them. There were similar stories in all the ghettos of the Greater German Reich.

A solution was needed, quickly.

Chapter 10

Annihilation

By the end of 1939, German troops had murdered about 7,000 Polish Jews, while the Gestapo and SS units had searched for and killed some 60,000 members of the Polish intelligentsia. In January 1940, Hitler authorized the systematic killing of unwanted groups of people by signing off the so-called 'euthanasia' programme, which would eventually see approximately 70,000 sick and disabled people, deemed as 'life unworthy of life', murdered, often by using gas, in specially appointed facilities in Germany. It was a badly kept secret, despite efforts to make it so in order to avoid unrest among local citizens. There were worries among many Germans that other Nazi murder campaigns would be organized, but these were pushed aside because it was evident that non-Jews were not in imminent danger.

However, Nazi intentions were made clearer during the German invasion of the Soviet Union in June 1941, which marked the beginning of the Nazis' 'war of extermination'. Operation Barbarossa, as it was code-named, was according to Nazi ideology intended to eradicate communism and provide *Lebensraum* for German citizens. It was to be a racial war between German 'Aryans' and subhuman Slavs and Jews. The Eastern Front saw huge battles, bitter fighting, horrific atrocities and an enormous number of casualties as German forces swept through the Baltic republics, Byelorussia, Ukraine and on to the Soviet Union. By late July, however, the Reichswehr's advance had stalled and morale at home was low, made worse by food shortages. The Nazis were quick to blame the Jews for draining the food supply. Himmler visited the troops on the front line and encouraged them to complete the annihilation of the Jews.

By October, they had taken Smolensk and Kharkov and laid siege to Sevastopol and Leningrad. Millions of Soviet soldiers were isolated and taken prisoner. During the early months of the invasion the mass killings of Jews were commonplace. In Odessa, for example, at the end of October 1941, over 20,000 Jews were shot, hanged or burned alive by Romanian troops from the Axis forces and German *Einsatzgruppen*, in reprisal for an explosion at the occupying commandant's office. The bomb had been put there by retreating Russian soldiers, but the blame was put on Jews. A further massacre of 5,000 Jews, who assembled by order in the nearby village of Dalnyk, followed a day later. The following month, all Jews remaining in the city were required to register with the Romanian authorities, who were then able to identify the businesses and properties of their future victims. By December, 55,000 Jews had been sent to a concentration camp in Bogdanovka; by 15 January 1942, they had all been shot. The remaining Jewish population of the city – perhaps 35,000–40,000 – were then sent to a newly created ghetto. Appalling conditions and no shelter in the Ukrainian winter led to mass mortality from hypothermia. It is estimated that around a thousand Jews survived what is regarded by some as the beginning of the Holocaust.

BRUTAL VIOLENCE UNLEASHED

The ruthlessness of mass killings during the invasion of the Soviet-held territories increased. Lithuania, occupied by Soviet forces in June 1940 until they fled in the face of the invading German Army the following year, had already witnessed widespread anti-Jewish repression. As Reichswehr forces approached, pro-German Lithuanian mobs began to attack Jews who they accused of siding with the Soviets. The violence was particularly brutal in Kaunas, the capital of Lithuania and the centre of the country's Jewish community. Between 26 and 27 June, riots broke out in the city. These two days of brutal violence saw more than 800 Jews killed, including the public beheading of Rabbi Shraga Hurvitz. Events culminated in the massacre of more than 50 Jewish men, who were beaten, hosed and then murdered with iron bars while being watched by a large crowd outside Lietukis garage. During July and August, occupying German forces corralled the remaining Jews, some 30,000 people, in a ghetto in Kaunas. The ghetto was divided into the small ghetto and the large ghetto, separated by Paneriai Street and connected by a wooden bridge. Inmates deemed capable of hard work lived in the large ghetto and were given work permits and employed in the construction of a nearby airbase. On 26 September, almost 2,000 Jews, including women and children, were arrested on the pretext of attempting to assassinate the commander of the ghetto guards. They were taken to Fort IX, one of a series of 19th-century forts that once guarded the city, where they were all shot. On 4 October, the Nazi authorities transported the remaining 1,800 residents of the small ghetto to Fort IX, where they too were shot. The same day, the ghetto hospital was burned down with 60 people, including a doctor and a nurse, still inside.

Following the liquidation of the small ghetto, German police and soldiers began looting the large ghetto. Working in groups of three or four, they took whatever they wanted, shooting inmates every now and again to instil fear. Several weeks later, the German authorities promised that the looting would end if residents of the ghetto freely handed over their valuables, whether it was money, gold, jewellery, musical instruments, stamp collections and so on. Traumatized residents had no choice but to agree. On deadline day, they had handed in a huge number of possessions, valued at RM50 million.

By the end of 1941, only 40,000 of the 250,000 Jews living in Lithuania remained alive. By March 1942, German death squads and collaborators had murdered over 600,000 Jews in the occupied Soviet territories.

SICKENING INHUMANITY

On the battlefields, German soldiers were ordered to act with impunity. Having authorized the 'Commissar Order', in contravention of international law, the Nazis authorized the murder of the Red Army's 'political officers' and any prisoners of war their soldiers took. The Soviets had also not signed up to either the Hague or Geneva conventions on the treatment of POWs, and brutality in battle was outdone by the treatment of the millions of captured Red Army soldiers. Nazi justification for their treatment of

Chapter 10

The German invasion of the Soviet Union was a war of racial extermination waged without regard for the laws and customs of war. The conditions in which Soviet POWs were kept – overcrowded, often without shelter, adequate clothing and little or no food or water – were part of a deliberate policy for mass death.

Soviet POWs was their Bolshevism, their 'sub-humanity' and their part in the 'Jewish conspiracy', as Alfred Rosenberg's equation suggested: 'Russia=Bolshevism=Jewry.'[1]

Interned in makeshift camps, the POWs had little or no shelter, other than holes in the ground, inadequate clothing and hardly any food – perhaps 700 calories a day, comprising bread made from wood, sugar beet husks or straw flour and, when desperate, leaves and grass and even rotten meat and bones tossed to them through the barbed wire. If they did not die from starvation, then typhoid, dysentery and freezing cold winter nights would likely kill them. 'They could be shot for the slightest misdemeanour, or just out of mischief, for fun.'[2] When the numbers of POWs grew too large, the soldiers were forced to march hundreds of miles to occupied Poland or Germany. Those too injured or too tired to continue were shot on sight.

In truth, the mass killing of POWs was a deliberate policy to free the German Army of the costs of their care. In July 1941, in anticipation of the invasion, the Reich Security Main Office had issued a rule that any 'politically and racially intolerable elements' among the POWs should be transferred to the SS and killed – this included intellectuals, communists and Jews. As a result, mass killings took place in secure areas outside various concentration camps: some were starved, some were burned alive, others were shot in trenches. Estimates of the number of victims killed in this way by the end of the year range from 140,000 to half a million. In early 1945, it was estimated that of the 5.7 million Soviet soldiers captured by German forces, some 3.3 million (57 per cent) had been killed, making them the second largest group of victims of Nazi racial policy.[3]

WANNSEE

Towards the end of 1941, the 'Jewish Problem' was becoming more acute. Jewish emigration was stopped and deportations 'to the east', mainly to existing and crowded ghettos, began. Because of the huge numbers involved, these deportations were badly organized and haphazard. To bring some kind of clarity to the operation, in January 1942 leading Nazi officials met at Wannsee, near Berlin, to review the situation. Heydrich laid out his plan for dealing with the 11 million Jews remaining in Europe, putting them to work building roads in the east. Those unable to work would be subject to 'special treatment', a euphemism for mass murder. Although the method of murder was not decided, successful experiments in using gas for the purpose had been undertaken at Chelmno. Following the so-called Wannsee Conference, five new extermination camps were planned and built. By September that year, Chelmno, Belzec, Sobibór, Treblinka, Majdanek and Auschwitz-Birkenau, all located in occupied Poland, were in operation murdering the Jewish population of Europe.

The process of murder was developed and adapted as each new camp came into operation. The first deportation, from the Lodz Ghetto, took place

Chapter 10

In January 1942, thousands of Jews in the Lodz ghetto were sent by train to an unknown destination. Mostly the elderly and the young – they were considered 'unproductive' by the Germans. Their 'destination' was Chelmno, the first Nazi death camp, where 55,000 of them were murdered in the next five months.

four days before the Wannsee meeting. Around a thousand Jews were told to sell their belongings or pack them up and bring their suitcases, and exchange their Polish money for German Marks in preparation for 'resettlement'. They were given warm clothing and sausage and bread for the journey. A short freight train journey took them to Koło, where they were allowed to visit the synagogue. After transferring to a narrow-gauge track, they were dropped off at Powiercie and taken by truck to Chelmno. The deception continued as they received a warm welcome, the promise of work and food. They were then sent to undressing rooms, where they labelled and deposited their valuables for 'safekeeping' and stripped ready for the disinfection of their clothes and a shower.

At Chelmno, specially adapted trucks were used as killing sites. Between 50 and 70 Jews were shut in the back, then the doors were closed and sealed. One end of a tube was attached to the truck's exhaust pipe and the other was directed into the vehicle's interior. The engine was started, and carbon monoxide gas was pumped into the space where the victims were crowded, killing them by asphyxiation within 10 or 15 minutes. The truck then drove to the nearby Rzuchów forest, where the bodies were stripped of any jewellery and gold teeth and buried in mass graves. Anyone still alive at that point was shot by SS or police officials. The graves filled quickly, and the smell of decomposition began to emanate into the air. That summer, specially selected prisoner units, called *Sonderkommando*s, were ordered to dig up and burn the corpses. To maintain the veneer of secrecy, from then on, the bodies were incinerated in open-air ovens. By the end of the war, at least 172,000 people had been murdered at Chelmno.

DEATH CAMPS: THE 'FINAL SOLUTION'

During the course of World War II, the Nazis constructed some 44,000 camps and ghettos – in Germany and Nazi-controlled Europe – in which to incarcerate those they labelled as 'enemies of the state' who might be a threat to the survival of the regime. There were several types of camps: concentration camps, forced labour camps, transit camps, prisoner of war camps and killing centres. Although they varied in purpose and in the types of prisoners detained, all camps were administered as instruments of exploitation and control. There was no regard for health or life and tens of thousands of people were deliberately killed in each of the camps, whatever its purpose.

It was the death camps that represented the apex of Nazi intentions to implement the so-called Final Solution, which would see the annihilation of Jews from Europe. Following the guidelines set out at Wannsee, three camps were built near the eastern boundary of the General Government in order to accommodate the deportation and killing of 2 million Jews and some Gypsies who lived there. The operation was called Operation Reinhard. The camps were all built alongside railway lines for ease of transport. They were divided into an administrative section, accommodation blocks and gas chambers. At Belzec, as at Chełmno, in the first few weeks of its opening, new arrivals were told to remove their clothing and hand over their valuables, and then were gassed. Their bodies were buried in pits. As the operation grew more efficient, some Jews were kept alive to sort the confiscated property, remove gold teeth from the corpses and dig up the already buried bodies for cremation on open pyres in an effort to conceal evidence of the mass extermination of some 450,000 people.

It was a similar story at Sóbibor, though the operation was more efficient. Again, constructed on a rail line, the camp was camouflaged, and the gas chambers were built to resemble shower rooms. A selection process was introduced that separated those who would be killed immediately from those who would work at the camp for a few months before they too were gassed by carbon monoxide pumped into gas chambers. Victims arrived here from the General Government, as well as France, Germany, Austria, Czechoslovakia and the Netherlands. The camp was destroyed by the Nazis in October 1943, following an uprising by prisoners. Estimates suggest that between 170,000 and 250,000 people were killed at Sóbibor.

Following the closure of Sóbibor, its commandant, SS-Obersturmführer Franz Stangl, was moved to Treblinka. Constructed near the railway, this camp was situated in a heavily wooded, sparsely populated area in an attempt to conceal the huge scale of its undertaking. The short lives of the prisoners there mirrored those of the victims at Belzec and Sóbibor, though the process, eventually using 13 gas chambers, was more efficient still. In its eight months of operations, approximately 870,000 Jews and Gypsies from the General Government, Slovakia, Greece and Macedonia were murdered at Treblinka. Following its closure, the evidence of the murderous activities that took place there was so great that a campaign, called Operation 1005, was undertaken. This saw the camp torn down, and the ground ploughed over and turned into farmland.

MAJDANEK

On Heinrich Himmler's instruction, a concentration camp was established at Lublin in September 1941. It was to be built alongside the Lublin–

Annihilation

Lviv highway and near to the Lublin railway station in full view of local inhabitants. Its Polish name was Majdanek. Groundworks were done quickly by Polish/Jewish and Soviet POWs; specialist building works were done by some 35 local building firms. The camp was huge, covering over 2.4 sq km (600 acres). This was watched over by 18 observation towers and intended to house 250,000 prisoners, comprising 22 prisoner barracks, seven gas chambers, two crematoriums, storehouses, workshops, laundries and a tall brick chimney. Due to high demand, inmates started arriving well before the work was completed. In fact, the work was never completed.

During its years of operation, inmates from other camps and the ghettos of Warsaw and Bialystok were transported here, as were Jews from all parts of Europe. Conditions in the camp were terrible, and as many as 60 per cent of the camp's victims – men, women and children – died from disease, starvation, overwork and through floggings, hangings and beatings by sadistic camp guards. The gas chambers were fully operational, and many prisoners were killed using Zyklon-B gas, which is why Majdanek was declared a death camp. Shootings were common and thousands of Soviet POWs were executed. On 3 November 1943, as part of the so-called Operation *Erntefest* ('Harvest Festival'), about 18,000 Jews were shot in a single day while loud music was played to drown out the sounds. Corpses were initially buried but, as the number of victims increased, they were burned in furnaces.

Despite hurried attempts by German camp guards to cover up evidence of mass murder, inmates, corpses, skulls, bones and ashes were discovered by the Russian troops who arrived soon after the Germans abandoned the camp. Today, major sections of the camp are still standing. The original gas chambers and crematoriums are preserved in silent tribute to the camp's victims. Next to the gas chamber building stands a dome-shaped structure, inside which is a colossal pile of ashes taken from the furnaces. Although the numbers are disputed, estimates of the number of people murdered at Majdanek range from 120,000 to 360,000.

Chapter 10

'CAPITAL OF THE HOLOCAUST'

But the zenith of the Nazi death camps was Auschwitz, now referred to by some as the 'capital of the Holocaust'. It was here that the Nazis put into practice the most effective methods of exploiting the mass murder of European Jewry. When it opened in 1940, it was initially intended to be a detention centre for Polish political prisoners. However, following the implementation of the Final Solution, its potential for expansion, its position in the centre of all German-occupied countries and its close proximity to a network of railway lines prompted its development as a death camp.

It was situated on a former military base at Oświęcim near Krakow in southern Poland. At its peak, the camp consisted of three main camps. The main gate of Auschwitz I, the original camp, greeted its arrivals with the inscription *'Arbeit Macht Frei'* ('Work Makes You Free'). It housed between 15,000 and 20,000 prisoners. Auschwitz II was in the nearby village of

Personal possessions brought by deportees to the camps, such as Auschwitz, where they were murdered. They bear witness to the scale of the Nazi plunder of their victims and their owners' attempts to preserve humanity behind the barbed wire.

Birkenau, and was added to the camp in 1941 on the orders of Heinrich Himmler. The largest camp, it held 90,000 prisoners. It also housed a number of 'bathhouses', which contained sophisticated gas chambers with huge double oak doors and a crematorium with 15 furnaces inside. Dotted around the site were a further 40 or so subcamps, which served to house slave labourers. The largest of these, Buna-Monowitz, was known as Auschwitz III and housed some 10,000 prisoners.

THE KILLING

The prisoners, mostly European Jews, arrived on trains, which would stop at one of the three unloading platforms, known as ramps. Camp staff, alerted to the arrival of the 'Transports' by sirens, would assemble along the length of the ramp. When the boxcar padlocks were unlocked and the door opened, those inside were greeted with shouts and the barking of orders. 'Leave your suitcases and packages behind; just take your hand luggage!' The men, women and children who had survived the journey, often with little or no food and water, climbed stiffly down on to the ramp and were ordered to line up in front of the wagons.

As they lined up in two columns ready for selection, men and older boys in one column and women and younger children of both sexes in the other, the 'murmur of generators and the whirr of huge ventilators started up'[4] in order to raise the temperature in the red-brick ovens to the maximum level. Mercifully, the exhausted arrivals had little idea of the fate that awaited them at this point. Following a signal, the people were led up to a group of camp doctors and other functionaries, who asked for their names and occupations, looked them up and down and motioned that they go to the left or to the right. To the left went the women, children, the old, the sick and the exhausted; to the right went people who 'looked fit for work'.[5]

Tension and fear were palpable as the left-hand column, comprising some 3,000 people, was led along a gravel path and down a set of steps towards a huge concrete building. At the door was a sign in various languages informing them that this was a bathing and disinfection facility – it was reassurance

Chapter 10

Initially developed in the early 1920s as a cyanide-based pesticide, Zyklon B's uses included delousing clothes and fumigating ships, warehouses and trains. It's use in the mass murder of prisoners in Auschwitz and Majdanek was approved because it seen as a more 'humane' method of killing, not for the victims, but for the killers.

for some. Inside was a huge, brightly lit room with floor-to-ceiling columns. Around the walls and columns were wooden benches with numbered hooks above them. More signs and shouted orders told the new arrivals that they had to take their clothes off ahead of their shower. They had to tie their clothes and shoes up in bundles, hang them on the hooks and memorize the number for ease of collection after bathing. They were given ten minutes to prepare. The exhausted, beaten, helpless Jews, now relieved of their possessions, naked and ashamed, had no choice but to comply. A huge set of double doors at one end of the room was opened and the people stumbled into another, smaller, brightly lit chamber with nothing in it except four massive metal conduits with grates down their sides. The attendants, *Sonderkommando* and SS soldiers, left the room. They closed and sealed the doors and turned the light off.

Shortly afterwards, an ambulance arrived in the courtyard outside the shower building. It was marked with a red cross inside a white circle, the sign of the International Red Cross. An SS officer, accompanied by a member of its auxiliary health service, got out. The medical orderly carried four green canisters, also marked with a red cross. They climbed on to the roof of the concrete building, put on gas masks and removed the concrete cover of one of its four chimneys. One of the cans was opened and its contents of green pellets was poured down the shaft. The same act was repeated for the other three chimneys. The cans contained Zyklon-B gas. On contact with the air, the pellets began to vaporize and the gas flowed down into the crowded shower room. Within five minutes, 3,000 people had been murdered.

HELL ON EARTH

The clean-up was hellish but still efficient. Twenty minutes or so after the deadly gas had been released, extractor fans were turned on to remove any remaining traces of it. Lorries arrived outside, and the people's belongings were loaded and taken for real disinfecting and prepared for transportation to Germany. The corpses were sprayed with water to get rid of any pockets of gas and clear up the hideous detritus of the operation. Bodies were dragged by the wrists into a lift, which carried between 20 and 25 people at a time. Upstairs was the crematorium in which 15 furnaces were ready. Before incineration, the bodies were subject to the final humiliation. Their hair was shaved, any gold teeth were removed and tossed into a bucket of hydrochloric acid to dissolve any meat or bone left on the gold, and any gold or platinum rings or necklaces were collected and stored in a lockbox.

When ready, the bodies were loaded on to metal stretchers and tipped into the ovens one at a time. The bodies took about 20 minutes to incinerate. Auschwitz had four crematoriums, each with a daily output of 5,000 bodies. This meant that 20,000 people were murdered and reduced to ash each day. The ashes were then transported by lorry and dumped in the Vistula River.

For those prisoners who initially escaped the gas chambers – statistically about 20 per cent of those who arrived on the transports were deemed suitable for work and registered as prisoners – an undetermined number died from overwork, disease, insufficient nutrition or the daily struggle for survival in brutal living conditions. Arbitrary executions, torture and retribution happened daily in front of them. Of approximately 1.1 million Jews sent to Auschwitz, some 200,000 were chosen for slave labour, while about 900,000 were killed in the gas chambers.

THE SPOILS OF MURDER

By the time the death camps were at their peak, the robbing of prisoners had been organized into an efficient system. The figures were huge. For example, liberators at Majdanek discovered 820,000 pairs of men's, women's and juveniles' shoes with labels from shops in Paris, Vienna, Brussels, Trieste, Prague, Amsterdam and so on, packed and ready for shipment to Germany. Also found in a huge warehouse in Lublin were enormous quantities of underwear, dresses, suits, neckties, belts, bathrobes, pyjamas, children's toys, shaving brushes, scissors, knives and other household utensils. Items came from the Soviet Union, Poland, France, Greece, Italy, Norway, Denmark and elsewhere. In addition, money, valuables and gold were seized and sent to Berlin. Even the hair cut from their victims' heads was sold and used in the production of textiles and upholstery. In addition to the money raised, this added to the feelings of violation and dehumanization of Jewish victims and reduced any chance they had of fighting back or surviving an escape attempt. Although the figures are impossible to calculate, particularly in view of the fact that many items taken from the prisoners were put into the pockets of the camp guards who seized them, there is no doubt that the vast quantities of items stolen from Jews and others in the camps constituted an important source of revenue for Hitler's government.

Of course, it was not only the government that benefitted from the camps. Many German businesses, often local building companies, were involved in constructing myriad objects, including accommodation blocks, turrets, railway ramps, water supply systems, drainage ditches, model farms, huge factory halls, entire housing estates, offices and hospital blocks. Much of the heavy work was done by forced labourers who would be imprisoned there and would be overseen by SS troops. Of the Nazi leadership, Heinrich Himmler, appointed Reich Commissar for the Strengthening of the German Ethnic Stock in 1939, was most closely associated with the concentration camp system. Following Himmler's work in establishing the first camp, at Dachau in 1933, Hitler authorized him to establish a network of camps wherever they were necessary. As the system expanded, so did the demands of administration. Following the start of World War II and Himmler's decision to forbid the release of any concentration camp victims for the duration, camp matters were in the hands of the SS and the IKL. For the SS, the camps were a source of inexpensive labour for the war effort and for private businesses. As the labour shortage increased, so this became an even more lucrative business.

I.G. FARBEN

One private user of this slave labour was the chemical and pharmaceutical conglomerate I.G. Farben. Formed in 1925 by the merger of several chemical companies – Agfa, BASF, Bayer, Chemische Fabrik Griesheim-Elektron, Hoechst and Weiler-ter-Meer – Farben would become the largest corporation in Europe. Based in Frankfurt from 1931, the company had close ties with the liberal German People's Party in the 1920s and was spoken of as a Jewish company because it had a number of Jewish board members, managers and shareholders. However, the global depression at the end of the decade had a huge negative impact on the German chemical industry and, as the NSDAP began its rise to prominence, the company switched its allegiance. Gradually divesting itself of its Jewish employees, the company quickly became one of

Chapter 10

the Nazi Party's biggest financial backers – donating some RM4.5 million in total – and receiving favourable price guarantees and tax breaks following the Nazi takeover of the state in 1933.

With the Aryanization of the company complete, it invited Nazi sympathizers on to the board and its support of Hitler's policies became integral to the business. Included in Göring's Four-Year Plan of 1936, Farben became an essential component of the German war machine producing synthetic fuels and synthetic rubber tyres for use by military vehicles, as well as explosives. Working hand in hand with the Nazis, the company made huge profits and was able to buy competing companies and chemical factories in occupied territories, such as Czechoslovakia and Poland, on favourable terms.

In 1941, Farben wanted to extend its use of slave labour and negotiated an agreement with Himmler to oversee and pay for the construction of an I.G. Farben synthetic rubber plant at Monowitz near the Auschwitz concentration camp complex (it later became known as Auschwitz III). Its workforce, in 1943, was said to be about 30,000 strong. The SS charged Farben RM3 per day for unskilled workers, RM4 for skilled workers and RM1.50 for children. Life expectancy for Jewish workers in the so-called Buna Werke was three to four months. Those unfit for work were killed by lethal injection or gassed at Birkenau. By 1945, about 20,000 forced workers had died at the Monowitz plant.

Staff of the Bayer group at Farben were also involved in medical experiments at Auschwitz and at Mauthausen concentration camps. Prisoners were deliberately infected with typhoid, TB and other diseases in order to test the efficacy of drugs in development. Many of them died. In another experiment, Bayer paid RM150 per woman for 150 women, on whom they tested an anaesthetic. Despite the fact that they all died, the company sent a request for another delivery of women at the same price. Worst of all was Farben's connection with its subsidiary, Deutsche Gesellschaft für Schädlingsbekämpfung (Degesch), in which it had a 42.5 per cent stake. During the early years of the war Degesch was hugely profitable, in particular because of sales of the pesticide Zyklon, which was used in soldiers' barracks and concentration camps to fumigate clothing infested with lice (which carried typhus). From 1941, the first killings of human beings in the gas chambers of Auschwitz began in September, as described. Accordingly, sales of what was then known as Zyklon-B began to rise, as did Farben's profits. After the war, a number of Farben executives claimed at trial that they did not know about the gassings; others admitted that they had been told. However, survivors from the camp claimed that it was not possible for the former not to have known and that the killings and burnings were 'common knowledge' to everybody.

AN 'ORDINARY' COMPANY INVOLVED IN GENOCIDE

Unlike the so-called Operation Reinhard death camps at Belzec, Sóbibor and Treblinka, which were poorly built with fairly primitive facilities inadequate for efficient mass killing and the disposal of corpses, for the construction of the camps at Majdanek and Auschwitz, the SS brought in Topf and Sons to design and build state-of-the-art crematoriums, ovens and ventilation systems. This family-run company had been in business since 1878. In the 1930s, it employed over a thousand workers, producing crematory ovens for funeral homes. In 1939, they supplied portable ovens to the concentration camp at Buchenwald, which were capable of the disposal of a large number of prisoners who had died after an outbreak of disease. As a result, they were asked to supply ovens to Dachau, Mauthausen and Gusen.

In 1941, Topf sent the chief engineer, Kurt Prüfer, to discuss the building of a new crematorium at Birkenau. Conditions in Auschwitz were terrible and the extremely high mortality rates of prisoners required a modern and efficient system of disposal. As well as Prüfer, Kopf assigned three other engineers to the project: Gustav Braun as production manager; Karl Schulze, an engineer and installation expert; and Fritz Sander, a furnace expert. In July 1942, they were contracted to build four new crematoriums in addition to designing and constructing the shells of the buildings, damp-proofing, roofs, drainage, furnaces and chimneys. As Fritz Sander said during interrogation by Soviet officials in 1946, the 'new installations were to be built on the conveyor belt principle'.[6] To achieve this, the ovens had huge capacity, with between eight

Chapter 10

and 15 muffles (a muffle is the space into which the body goes) in each. The bodies were put on to inclined grates at the top of the oven, burning as they slowly slid down and ending up as ashes as the bottom, where they continued to provide heat to burn the new corpses loaded above. Although the ovens required at least two days to get up to the required temperature to work, this system resulted in an efficient and continuous-cremation furnace that required no extra fuel – a precious and expensive resource during wartime. At their peak, these crematoriums were in use 24 hours a day. In terms of keeping the operation of disposing of the thousands of corpses that arrived each day running, the ovens, the flues and the chimneys proved to be both resilient and economic. Topf and Sons were at the peak of their powers. So pleased were they with their work that Fritz Sander, with the approval of the company, applied for a patent for a four-storey crematorium that was supplied with bodies by conveyor belt, but the application was denied because their work was deemed top secret.

And yet according to them, Topf and Sons was an 'ordinary' German company. The company had fared badly during the depression but, as the economy took a turn for the better under Hitler's stewardship in 1935, the Topf brothers, Ludwig and Ernst-Wolfgang and their chief engineer, war veteran Kurt Prüfer got on the business bandwagon offered by the new regime and took the decision to join the Nazi Party. When questioned about his role in the construction of the crematoriums at Auschwitz, Karl Schultze said, 'I am a German and supported and am supporting the government in Germany and the laws of our government. Whoever opposes our laws is an enemy of the State, because our laws establish him as such. I did not act on personal initiative but as directed by Ludwig Topf.'[7] These words serve as a pertinent reminder of the roles played by many 'ordinary' people in the Nazi genocide.

Chapter 11

A Huge Criminal Gang

It is hard to look further than Thomas Kühne's assertion that from the start of the genocide, in 1941, 'the German nation established itself as a huge criminal gang'.[1] After 1933, the Nazis were keen to radicalize their idea of the *Volksgemeinschaft* in several ways. Firstly, they insisted that 'membership' was essential, dependent on racial purity and, in addition, ideological conformism. The final requirement, at first taught in what Kühne calls 'seemingly harmless ways' at Hitler Youth camping weekends and military barracks, was criminality. Camping games, such as getting up in the night and ambushing another tent with water bombs, had unspoken rules. All those in the attackers' tent had to take part; it was taken for granted that the soaked victims would not tell tales. Friendships were made like this, based on trust and leading to a feeling of security and comradeship between the insiders who conformed to these rules. Those who did not join in were, essentially, the 'enemy'. It would quickly become 'us versus them'. It was a short step from there to the *Freikorps* fighters and the SA thugs who were encouraged to 'do what they wanted', doling out brutal violence and murder, and who would loot, destroy and steal whenever they had the opportunity, but would do it together in the tradition of blood-brotherhood in which individual responsibility was dispensed with. The most brutal members and the killers were admired because they were necessary to constitute the 'us'. Criminality and street violence quickly became a cornerstone of the appeal of the Nazi Party, along with promising order, security, prestige and belonging to 'every Aryan German that was willing to conform to Nazi ideology'.[2]

HITLER'S SOCIALISM

This sense of togetherness and belonging was all part of Hitler's messaging from the outset. Of course, Hitler was not a socialist and had little real interest in Germany's workers. He only chose to add the words 'National Socialist' to the party's name in 1921 because he agreed that it would help the ultra-nationalist party appeal to the suffering lower-middle classes. From the moment he joined the party his sole focus was on achieving power at all costs, which meant courting popularity wherever he could find it. At that point, the party had no money but still needed a paramilitary arm to protect its members from rival parties. The *Sturmabteilung* (SA) was formed for this reason. The majority of its recruits, who were all volunteers, were men aged between 18 and 35. Many of them were former members of youth groups or other paramilitary groups such as the *Freikorps*. They were often unemployed, drifters, wanting to belong somewhere. Free food and lodging were provided and nights in the tavern were guaranteed, along with a uniform, a feeling of belonging and a structure for life. On top of that, the SA offered these fighting men a chance to indulge their aggression on the Jews or the communists, and if they were able to get away with the spoils, then there was nothing to stop them.

In return for their loyalty, the SA issued a scheme in which members bought the SA's own brand of cigarettes, with the profits going to any members seriously injured in their regular clashes with rival groups. Hitler was at pains to praise any SA members killed in action, describing them as martyrs. He would also give speeches at any of the funerals he could attend.

Examples of Hitler's determination to shore up support among the German people were most in evidence after 1933. The party's first campaign, against unemployment, was a success. However, as Richard Evans points out, 'Hitler's government was lucky in its timing'[3] because a number of programmes put in place under previous chancellors were starting to work by 1933. However, the creation of new businesses and public-works construction projects, such as road-building, were effective, as was a campaign to encourage women to stay at home and let men take their place at work. But Hitler's biggest success in terms of getting people back to work was to start a programme of rearmament, wherever possible far from the eyes of the world, because he did not know how it would react.

As a result of Hitler's 'job creation' scheme, in 1934 arms orders represented over half of Germany's iron and steel production, engineering projects and motor vehicles. Mauser and the Rhine Metal Company, who produced rifles, howitzers and machine guns, both increased their workforce. Krupps began large-scale tank production, and the navy ordered RM41 million worth of equipment and a further RM70 million worth of ships. The following year there were 72,000 workers employed in aircraft construction. As a result of demand, iron and steel, engineering, coal and mining companies increased their labour force and upped their production targets. With unemployment halved in this fashion between 1933 and the end of 1934, Nazi propaganda boasted that the 'battle for work' had been won. It was manna from heaven for millions of Germans.

KEEPING THE HOME FIRES BURNING

As war approached, economists began to suggest a system for its financing. As usual, it was based on broad tax increases. But the Nazi leadership were not in favour of this, insisting instead that the Nazi war machine was to be financed primarily by the people of the lands they were to conquer, and topped up by tax increases for German businesses and the country's wealthiest citizens. It was a policy borne out of the bitter memories of World War I, the experience of which was still in the memories of the German people and the Nazi leadership. During the 1914–18 conflict, the government made no provision for the women and children of the men fighting in the trenches. With the breadwinners gone, those left at home were provided with 'just enough to live on', but little else, and based on rules of compensation for soldiers' families during wartime that dated back to 1888. The results of these policies were traumatic: rising prices, currency devaluation, food shortages, starvation, outbreaks of TB and other diseases and post-war hyperinflation, all of which were hard to forget.

Most people were better off in 1939 than they had been in 1914, and the Nazis' Compensation for Military Deployment Law, published in August, made sure that current standards of living were taken into account when calculating family support payments. Payments were to be prompt and would include money to fulfil existing obligations, such as newspaper subscriptions, life insurance policies, instalment plans and mortgages.[4] The following year, Göring added further benefits, announcing that rents would be paid in full for the families of front-line soldiers. The response of the German population was overwhelmingly positive. After the victory over France, there were extra benefits. Tax exemptions were introduced on overtime, Sunday work, night work and holiday pay, and money would also be provided for insurance, coal, potatoes and other daily needs. Family payments were also tax-free. Stable prices, a freeze on rents and an exemption on asset seizure in case of debt, as well as an average income of 72.8 per cent of peacetime household income meant that families could live in comfort.[5]

SHOPPING ABROAD

On the front lines, the soldiers were financially well recompensed. In 1939, a regular monthly wage was around RM100. The money was transferred from families at home and paid in the native currency of the country where the soldiers were stationed. With food, coffee, cocoa, liqueurs, shoes, clothes and materials, soaps and perfumes still on the shelves of Europe, the millions of packages sent via the military mail to those left at home, where such items were no longer available, were welcome. Soldiers carried shopping lists from their loved ones at home and, on arriving in a new city, would 'storm' the shops in search of the items requested and returned home, on their frequent leave breaks, loaded down with suitcases, bags and packages stuffed with booty. In this way, and in the inevitable accompanying black marketeering, smuggling and looting of war, German soldiers were said to have cleared the shelves of Europe's shops.

In order to help the fight against inflation, front-line troops were encouraged to spend their wages where they were stationed. But some troops, particularly those on the Russian front, had little or no opportunity to buy anything, so they sent the money home. Various schemes were devised by the Reichsbank to prevent this happening. Firstly, troops from here were transported to Western Europe, in particular to France, for their rest and relaxation, where they were keen to spend their money in bars, restaurants and bordellos. The military ensured that the soldiers could easily exchange their roubles for francs in such a way that France paid for trips to the bordellos and the roubles found their way into the Reich's war chest.[6]

FISCAL CONTROL

The Nazi policy of exploiting the economies of countries occupied by Germany was a success but was not without its problems. The Reichsbank sent financial experts into the occupied territories, who often had to interfere in the running of their economies, for example, creating a new currency in Serbia and manipulating exchange rates and greatly overvaluing the Reichsmark in comparison with the French franc, the Italian lira and the Polish złoty. Each conquered territory was forced to pay a 'contribution for military protection'. It was charged annually and though nominally based on population quotes, was subject to the financial requirements of the Nazi war chest. The sums involved were large: the General Government in Poland, for instance, contributed 1.3 billion złotys in 1932 and 3 billion the following year. In addition, they received a monthly bill of 100 million złotys for the services of Reichswehr soldiers. In 1942, Denmark paid RM25 million, a figure raised to RM86 million for the first six months of 1944. In addition, in 1942 Denmark was forced to procure and supply thousands of cows, pigs and other foodstuffs and deliver them to the German Army headquarters in Norway. A significant proportion of this produce found its way to Germany itself. Germany's hunger for money knew no bounds and they also demanded an 'occupation cost' from their allies, Bulgaria, Slovakia and Romania.

When the war began, Germany was in a good financial position. The arms build-up meant healthy profits for German businesses, while mass employment meant money in people's pockets and healthy tax revenues for the government. However, as demand for military products increased, so the supply of goods for domestic consumption decreased and the scarcity of goods became a problem.

The major issue for the Reichsbank in all this financial skullduggery was to control inflation in Germany. By relieving the burden of huge tax rises on German citizens and passing this on to the governments of its occupied countries, and by the systematic looting and dispossession of Jews and other enemies of the state in Germany and elsewhere, the Nazi policy enabled the Reich to control inflation and cover 50 per cent of its running war costs, thus making a 'substantial improvement in balance of payments' for Germany at other people's expense.[7]

In 1943, military expenses increased exponentially. Due to scarcity, Germany was forced to increase its imports. A significant portion of these were paid for by the occupied countries' budgets, but the remainder was paid by notes of credit. By 1944, Germany owed some RM29 million. The then Reichsbank president, Walther Funk, described this foreign debt as 'an investment that will retain its value' and announced that these payments would be settled on the signing of peace treaties and then passed on to the occupied territories as 'occupation costs'.[8]

NAZI GOLD

Of all the items that the Nazis looted from their victims as they spread across Europe, the most important thing they were after was gold – and, in particular, monetary gold held by governments in central banks as part of their currency reserves. Of course, other items, such as fine art, jewellery, Oriental carpets, silverware, porcelain and glass stolen from individuals were useful too. These were all needed to help fund the German war effort.

By the time Britain declared war on Germany in September 1939, the Nazis had already looted 81 tonnes (90 tons) of gold from the Austrian central bank and deposited it in the Reichsbank. In addition, some 13.6 tonnes (15 tons) of gold and diamonds were stolen from the country's large Jewish community. Following the invasion of Czechoslovakia and the occupation of Danzig, the Nazis were said to have acquired about $97 million worth of gold. By pursuing this policy of the acquisition of gold, silver and valuables of all kinds during their military conquests, the Nazis were said to have looted between $545 and

A Huge Criminal Gang

$550 million by 1945. In order to meet their astonishing costs of occupation, arms production, armed forces, welfare payments etc., vast sums were needed. To avoid inflation, the Germans kept much of their gold hidden at home and in overseas banks in neutral countries, such as Portugal, Spain, Sweden, Norway and, in particular, Switzerland.[9]

In reality, Swiss 'neutrality' during World War II meant playing for both sides. During the early years of the Nazi Party, many Jews in Central and Eastern Europe had deposited their assets in Swiss accounts and safety deposit boxes in case the worst happened. In return, when Nazi persecution of the Jews began, the Swiss took steps to block the entry of Jews attempting to flee to the neutral country to which they had entrusted their money. Swiss banks were also seen by Nazi officials as the safest place for their money, which was often made up of valuables stolen from Jewish people. It is said that even the royalties that Hitler earned from *Mein Kampf* were kept in a Swiss bank account. The Nazis also chose to hide the gold reserves they plundered from other countries' central banks in Switzerland. Documents found in East German archives in the 1990s claim that Himmler arranged for a train loaded with hundreds of millions of dollars' worth of gold, jewellery and art to be sent to Switzerland in 1944 for deposit in the vaults of Swiss banks for safekeeping. It is also suggested that the US Legation in Bern advised Washington that in April 1945 the Swiss agreed to store 3,000 kg (6,600 lb) of gold, worth some $402 million.

Since the war ended, the Swiss banks have been reluctant to reveal the full details of their dealings with the Nazis. Many of the Jewish depositors perished in the death camps and their accounts, including money and personal effects, became dormant. Claimants, acting on behalf of dead family members, had few documents to verify their claims and the Swiss were not prepared to help. In the early 1960s, US and UK authorities and the World Jewish Congress made attempts to investigate but only a small fraction of the claims submitted were settled. Since then, further efforts have resulted in various pay-outs, which have been returned to the relevant central banks and individuals via the Allied Tripartite Gold Commission set up for the purpose. However, it is clear that only a fraction of the money has been returned to its owners by the Swiss banks.

Chapter 11

MERKERS MINE

Of course, Swiss banks were not the only place that the Nazis hid their looted treasures. As the fortunes of the German forces declined, in 1943 the Reichsbank began moving its gold reserves around the country for safety. In late 1944 and early 1945, the Allied bombing campaigns began to force the issue of the storage of production, materials and money underground. In February, the Reichsbank ordered its main currency reserves and a considerable quantity of foreign currency to be hidden in a potassium salt mine in the village of Merkers, near Gotha and some 320 km (200 miles) south-west of Berlin.

In March, General Patton's Third Army crossed the Rhine on its way to the heart of Germany. On 4 April, they took the village of Merkers and set up a command post to consolidate their holdings. They idly discussed rumours that there was Nazi gold hidden nearby but decided that they'd heard it all before. However, on the strength of the testimony of some displaced French women they encountered, the army decided to investigate the local Kaiseroda mine. At 10 am on 7 April, US officers and German mining officials entered the mine, took the lift some 650 m (2,130 ft) down and located the main vault, called Room No. 8, which was blocked by a brick wall and a steel door. The following day, they blew a hole in the wall. Inside, piled high, they found over 400 art masterpieces – including paintings by Manet, Rubens and Goya, Dürer's famous *Apocalypse* woodcuts of 1498, sculptures and ancient Egyptian papyri – and the bulk of the reserve from the German Central Bank. Those reserves included 8,000 bars of gold, 55 boxes of gold bullion, and hundreds of bales of foreign currency, a preliminary valuation of which indicated that the value of the gold, silver and currency alone was over $520 million. Much of this treasure had been plundered from the museums and central banks of occupied European countries. Their excitement was tempered with a grisly discovery that the SS had also used the mine to hoard gold and jewels taken from death camp inmates, including dental fillings, wedding rings, watches and other personal effects, all carefully sorted into containers. In the ensuing days, caches of stolen loot were found in other salt mines, in castles and in stately homes across Germany, Austria and Italy, which contained many of

In April 1945, in a vault approximately 23 metres wide and 45 metres long with a 4-metre-high ceiling hidden in the Merkers salt mine in central Germany, US Third Army officers and German mining officials found over 100 tons of Nazi gold bullion, silver, platinum, thousands of bags of domestic and foreign currency and 400 tons of artworks.

the world's greatest paintings, including works by Michelangelo, Jan van Eyck, Vermeer, Sandro Botticelli, Filippo Lippi and Giovanni Bellini.

By 1948, as much of the gold that could be identified was returned to the central banks from where it was stolen, and funds were available for restitution to individuals where possible. At a conference in London in 1997, several countries with claims on the remaining $60 million worth of the gold found at Merkers and still in the hands of the Tripartite Gold Commission agreed that the money should be donated to a Nazi Persecution Relief Fund to help Holocaust survivors and their families.

Chapter 11

RAUBKUNST

Despite his failure to secure a place at art school in his youth, Hitler had a genuine interest in art, dedicating passages of *Mein Kampf* to express his opinions on the subject. As early as 1925, he drew up plans for a German National Gallery in Berlin, of which he was to be director. His plan was to fill the gallery with his own collection of classical German art. Once appointed chancellor, Hitler commissioned the building of a gallery in Munich, called the *Haus der Kunst* ('House of Art'). It opened in 1937 to show a collection of Hitler-approved 'Nazi' art, which was not a success. When the exhibition closed, another one, called 'Degenerate Art', opened. Again organized by the Nazis but this time intended to show the paucity and decadence of works by modern artists from the schools of Cubism, Futurism and Dadaism, such as Georg Grosz, Paul Klee, Otto Dix, Pablo Picasso, Piet Mondrian, Marc Chagall and Wassily Kandinsky, these works had been seized from state collections all over Germany by means of *Raubkunst* ('art plunder'). The exhibition was a massive success, attracting over 2 million people in four months. When the exhibition closed, the art was sold off at an auction in Switzerland with the profits going into Nazi coffers. Some of the unsold artworks were burned in the courtyard of the Berlin Fire Department, an act of infamy similar to the Nazi's earlier well-known book burnings, but one that attracted art dealers who were prepared to spend their money on the remaining paintings and profit from the works themselves.

As already discussed, when they came to power, the Nazis began a systematic campaign to expropriate the property and assets of Jewish Germans – actions that continued in each territory they occupied when the war began in 1939. By this time, Hitler's plans for a European Art Museum had developed. As well as the museum in Berlin, he had plans to build a *Führermuseum* in Linz, the Austrian city of his birth. In 1940, the looting and requisition of art continued under the direction of the *Einsatzstab Reichsleiter Rosenberg* (ERR) under the control of Alfred Rosenberg and Hermann Göring. Stolen artworks were collected at the Museum Jeu de Paume in Paris before being offered to Hitler, taken by

A Huge Criminal Gang

Created and consecrated by Hitler, the Haus der Kunst in Munich was built to showcase the Führer's vision of great German art. A few days before its official opening, he visited the collection in the company of photographer Heinrich Hoffmann (right), President of the Reich Chamber of Fine Arts Adolf Ziegler (far left) and others.

Göring for his private collection, offered to other Nazi leaders or despatched for sale or for storage in Germany. Under the leadership of Rosenberg and Göring, it is estimated that the ERR seized over 20,000 art objects from German-occupied territories. Other looting organizations were formed and charged with procuring works for the *Führermuseum*, taking art from Holland, Belgium, France, Russia and North Africa. The art collections of prominent Jewish families, such as the Rothschilds and the Rosenbergs, were confiscated and kept in storage or sold. At the end of the war, the Third Reich had amassed a collection of hundreds of thousands of cultural objects. Despite meticulous planning and effort, Hitler's plans for his art museum in Linz were never realized.

CONTINGENCY PLANS

Even before the start of the war, the Allies were aware of Hitler's plans to loot Europe's museums and private art collections. Following the *Anschluss*, with war seemingly inevitable the director of the Louvre Museum in Paris, home to Leonardo da Vinci's *Mona Lisa* and other priceless works of art, decided to remove and hide the 3,600 paintings housed there. On 25 August 1939, the museum closed for three days for 'repairs'. In those three days, the art was coded, labelled, packaged, loaded into trucks and taken to the Château de Chambord in the Loire. The collection was then split up and sent to various other châteaux, museums and abbeys. At the end of the war, the items were safely returned to their home in Paris.

There was a similar story in Leningrad in the Soviet Union in June 1941, just after the announcement that Germany had invaded. Staff and volunteers were summoned to the Hermitage Museum in an attempt to pack up and despatch over a million artworks, which were to be sent on special trains to the city of Sverdlovsk (now Yekaterinburg) in the Urals. Two trains got through: the first with half a million of the museum's finest pieces carried in 22 goods wagons, the second with some 700,000 items from its reserve stock. A third train did not leave Leningrad because the Germans had cut off the rail routes.

THE 'MONUMENTS MEN'

In the face of this wholesale looting, in 1943 the Allies established the Monuments, Fine Arts and Archives programme (MFAA), popularly known as the 'Monuments Men'. This group of some 350 men and women, comprising museum curators and art historians, was formed to work with Allied troops to avoid the unnecessary destruction of cultural assets and to care for works of art that had been hidden from the invading German forces. Their tactics included using aerial photos to inform Allied airmen of important sites that they should avoid bombing. The list included, for example, Chartres Cathedral and the Santa Maria delle Grazie convent in Milan, home to Leonardo da Vinci's masterpiece *The Last Supper*, which he had painted on the refectory wall. In haste, before a huge Allied bombing mission of Milan in August 1943, the Monuments Men jury-rigged a scaffold of steel bars and sandbags around the wall to protect it. In the event, it was the only wall in the refectory still standing after the raid.

After the war, the MFAA were successful in tracking, locating and returning more than 5 million looted items, including works by Rembrandt, Vermeer, Botticelli, Manet and others, plus sculptures, tapestries, fine furnishings, books and manuscripts, scrolls, church bells, religious relics and even the stained glass the Nazis had stolen from the windows of a cathedral. Many of these items had been hidden in Nazi repositories in Germany and Austria.

Of course, *Raubkunst* was not confined to fine artworks. During the first months of Operation Barbarossa, the German invasion of the Soviet Union, which began in June 1941, they appropriated millions of tons of cereals, animal feed, potatoes, pigs, sheep and other meats, which were sent back to Germany. Also looted were home furnishings, ceramics, musical instruments, religious artefacts, books, documents and other cultural objects.

It has been estimated that the Nazis looted some 20 per cent of the art of Europe. Despite the efforts of the MFAA and the Roberts Commission to identify, recover and restitute these looted artworks, there are said to be as many as 100,000 still missing.

Chapter 12

The Nazi Rich List

On 2 May 1938, Hitler left Berlin on a train bound for Rome. His actions in reclaiming the Rhineland and the easy and triumphant seizure of Austria had prompted the 3.5 million Sudeten Germans to demand similar action in Czechoslovakia. But, aware of the possibility that France, Britain or the Soviet Union would resist German action to seize Czechoslovakia, Hitler needed the approbation of his only ally, Mussolini. Hitler's retinue, consisting of 500 'diplomats, generals, security agents, party leaders and journalists, all wearing uniforms of one type or another', travelled to the Italian capital in five trains.[1]

For Hitler, the importance of the journey was offset by intestinal pains and major concerns about his health. His physician, Dr Morell, had diagnosed fistulas and prescribed Mutaflor, which had eased the pain. But Hitler was preoccupied with worries that he had cancer. As a result, he spent the early part of the journey writing a will. Although the will was dated 2 May 1938, the document was first found by Red Army troops in the ruins of the Reich Chancellery in 1945 and hidden in the Soviet sector of Berlin until 1953.

The handwritten document requested that his body should lie in state in Munich in the Ehrentempel (Honour Temples), before his burial next to the Führerbau with the 16 party members who died in the Beer Hall Putsch. His entire fortune, including the Berghof (his house on the Obersalzberg) and his apartment in Munich, was to be left to the party apart from money and personal mementos for his mistress Eva Braun, his sisters Angela and Paula, his stepbrother Alois, sundry friends and various other members of his personal staff. He also appointed party treasurer Franz X. Schwarz as executor. In the event of Schwarz's death or inability to do so, Reichsleiter Martin Bormann would fulfil the role. Given that he wrote another will on the morning of 29 April 1945, the day before his suicide, this first will was deemed null and void. However, this did not stop claims, counter-claims and court cases over the various inheritances that dragged on until the 1960s and even later.

THE *ADOLF HITLER SPENDE*

The reason for all the wrangling over Hitler's wills is, of course, because he was rich ... fabulously rich. Exactly how a former vagrant, failed artist and lowly *Gefreiter* (Private) in World War I became so rich and exactly how rich is difficult to determine because there is little documentation. Added to that is the fact that much of his money came from donations, the sources of which were kept secret for the benefit of both the source and Hitler. The situation is further complicated because of Hitler's extensive art collection: his Personal Collection, which was financed from his personal funds, and the Linz Collection of paintings for show in the gallery he was to build in Linz – the city of his youth – many of which were obtained through looting.

When Hitler first joined the DAP in 1921 he became the party fundraiser and, in a sense, he did not stop his fundraising activities until he was appointed chancellor in 1933. Having had little use for money prior to joining, he started small-scale, cadging money for food and drink, stationery, pens, printing, renting rooms for meetings etc. His greatest success in accessing funds had come at the meeting at Göring's house on 20 February 1933, at which supporting German industrialists raised some RM3 million as a 'token of gratitude to the leader of the nation'.[2] This money, under the chairmanship of Gustav Krupp, at first said to be called the *National Treuhand* and to be used to fund the NSDAP, morphed into the *Adolf Hitler Spende*, which by 1935 had become 'Hitler's personal treasure chest'.[3] Estimates as to the amount of money raised from businesses in subsequent years in this way vary from RM1 million to RM1 billion! Hitler, whose grasp of economics was rudimentary, entrusted the management of the funds to his chief of staff Rudolf Hess, who in time passed the responsibility on to his deputy Martin Bormann.

Part of the Nazi propaganda campaign was the production of Nazi and, in particular, Hitler memorabilia. Using mass marketing and mass consumption, these items – often with an image of the Führer, appealed to a 'collectors' instinct', made money and depicted him as a powerful leader and heroic patriot.

The fund was further swelled by the organization of various unions for professionals, such as physicians, lawyers, teachers and those involved in cultural activities, film, radio, theatre, literature and so on. Membership was mandatory: 'no membership, no job'. Because the party controlled these labour organizations, a proportion of the dues collected were demanded by the *Adolf Hitler Spende*. As we have already seen, royalties from *Mein Kampf* continued to grow year on year, as did profits from his interests in Eher publishing. In addition, Chancellor Hitler's income from image rights, royalties on other books and postage stamps grew every year and from 1937 included sales in the occupied territories. Income from the post office was so significant that a 'cultural fund' was set up the manage the income from specially issued stamps featuring a portrait of the Führer. It is suggested that Hitler used this money to support artists, the purchase of paintings for the Linz gallery and to finance performing arts projects. In all this it is important to remember that from 1935, the German Chancellor Adolf Hitler was officially tax-exempt (see Chapter 7).

Chapter 12

PROPERTY PORTFOLIO

In 1945, Hitler owned a number of properties. In 1938, following the *Anschluss* and in a fit of nostalgia, Hitler bought the house in which he was born, at Braunau am Inn, and the family home in which he was brought up in Leonding, near Linz. He is said to have regarded both properties as places of pilgrimage. In 1929, he rented a second-floor apartment on Prinzregentenplatz in Munich. A year later, party funds were used to buy the nine-room property, which was redecorated to suit Hitler's growing political stature, and remained as his main home until he was named as chancellor in 1933. In 1938, he bought the entire four-storey building for RM175,000. The apartment was maintained but the rest of the building was used by security staff and other party workers. Hitler also owned a villa in Wasserburger Strasse in Munich, which he bought in 1936 for his girlfriend Eva Braun and where she lived with her sister Gretl. It is also thought that Hitler bought a 100 sq km (10,000-hectare) estate in Mecklenburg, part of Poland's Warthegau region following the German invasion in 1939. The actual ownership of the estate is difficult to determine, as it was apparently held in Martin Bormann's name. He administered the land and its properties, claiming that its purchase was to 'ensure Hitler's vegetable supplies', but it is believed that Hitler never visited.

THE BERGHOF

By far Hitler's most valuable asset, however, was the Berghof, his holiday home in the Obersalzberg of the Bavarian Alps near Berchtesgaden. His interest in this area stemmed from a visit he paid in the winter of 1922–3 to see his friend Dietrich Eckart, who was on holiday at the town's Platterhof Hotel. He was much taken with the breathtaking and monumental scenery of hills and mountains and the views across the lake into his native Austria. He returned to Berchtesgaden in 1926 on his release from Landsberg prison, where he stayed with colleagues at the Hotel Deutsches Haus to finish writing *Mein Kampf*. Two years later, he came again and rented a run-down, five- or six-room alpine-style chalet, Haus Wachenfeld, which sat 610 m (2,000 ft) up on the mountainside.

While mostly hidden from the public at large – with Nazi propaganda pushing the notion that Hitler was married to the nation rather than a woman – Hitler and Eva Braun's 15-year relationship was at its best at the Berghof, where she and her dogs were a constant presence when he asked her to move there in 1936.

He bought the property in 1933, installed his half-sister Angela Raubal as housekeeper, and immediately filled the house with bookshelves, busts and artwork. Although expansion of the property began immediately, plans were severely hampered by the arrival of crowds of Hitler's supporters, hoping for a glimpse of the Führer. At this point, it is thought that Hitler decided to make Haus Wachenfeld his official summer residence. Between 1935 and 1936 the house was refurbished and expanded by architect Alois Degano, with interiors designed by Gerdy Troost, under the supervision of Martin Bormann. Renamed the Berghof ('Mountain Court or Farm' in English), the new house was featured in an article in the November 1938 edition of *Homes & Gardens* magazine. The author was fulsome in his praise: 'The site commands the fairest views of all Europe […] The colour scheme throughout this bright airy chalet is light jade green. In outside rooms, like the sun-parlour, chairs and tables are of white, plaited cane […]

The curtains are of printed linen or fine damask in the softer shades [...] The guest bedrooms are hung with old engravings [...] [and] the Führer's own watercolour sketches'.[4] The centrepiece of the house was the great hall with a huge sprawling picture window with an open-air view of the snow-capped Untersberg mountain in Austria. According to legend, Charlemagne was sleeping in a cave of ice deep inside the Untersberg and waiting for the time he will be called back to save the Holy Roman Empire. It was not by chance that Hitler had his seat across from it.

In order to increase security and the Führer's privacy, Bormann bought 10,000 sq m (2.5 acres) of the accessible land on the mountainside. Local civilians were asked to sell the land. Some agreed readily; others did so only because they were compensated by the gift of houses belonging to deported Jewish families. Those who refused were intimidated into leaving or even deported to the prison at Dachau until they agreed to go. Their houses were demolished and replaced with new buildings. Homes were built here by Albert Speer, Martin Bormann and Hermann Göring. Other buildings went up, too: the Kehlsteinhaus lodge, known as the 'Eagle's Nest', was built on a rocky promontory nearby; barracks were built for the large contingent of SS troops that provided security; and a cinema, a school for young children, a bowling alley, accommodation for support staff, guest houses, tea houses, botanic gardens, underground bunkers and air-raid shelters were added. In addition, the local Hotel zum Türken was turned into quarters for the Reichssicherheitsdienst (RSD) security men who patrolled the compound. In all, the cost for the redevelopment was somewhere around RM980 million.

Though the Berghof began its life as Hitler's holiday home, the extensive renovations meant that it soon became a feature of Nazi propaganda, portraying its owner as 'a man of culture, dog lover and, good neighbour'.[5] Though it was not his real home, he was happy there. He moved Eva Braun here in 1936, though she continued to spend time in Munich, particularly when Hitler was away. At its peak, the Berghof complex served as the second centre of power of the Third Reich alongside its official capital in

Berlin. Hitler spent at least a third of his time here while in power. Important political discussions were had, negotiations were made, and decisions were taken at the house.

For all of these reasons, then, Adolf Hitler, of course, topped the Nazi Rich List.

THE NAZI RICH LIST

A list such as the one below is impossible to verify. Due to totalitarian censorship and the widespread use of the press for the ends of the state, data from the Third Reich is difficult to accept. In most cases, there is a limited paper trail; in others, there is nothing. For some of the leading Nazis there are details from their wills; others may not have even left wills. This list is included merely for the sake of interest and argument and has little veracity.

1 ADOLF HITLER: $5 BILLION–$6.5 BILLION

Having been poor and frugal in his early adult years, Hitler grew to love money both for the luxuries it bought him and the loyalties it ensured. Estimates of the real value of his estate vary wildly, from $1 billion to $40 billion! It is generally accepted, however, that on his death Hitler was the wealthiest man in Europe.

2 MARTIN BORMANN: $18 MILLION

Bormann was Hitler's private secretary and head of the Nazi Party Chancellery. Due to his proximity to the Führer, he enjoyed immense power, influence and anonymity – so much so that, by the end of World War II, he was the second most important Nazi leader. In his administration of Hitler's personal finances, he proved himself a master of intrigue, manipulation and political in-fighting, always expanding his personal power and wealth. In his management of the Berghof estate, he was able to manipulate Hitler into approval of his own schemes. He was sentenced to death *in absentia* at Nuremberg in 1946, but in 1998, genetic testing on remains found in West Berlin confirmed stories that he had died in May 1945, having committed suicide by cyanide capsule.

3 JOSEPH GOEBBELS: $12 MILLION

Goebbels drew salaries as Reich Minister of Propaganda, Defence Councillor, Gauleiter of Berlin, State Councillor and as a member of the Reichstag. He had business interests in film and radio, publishing houses and books and was founder and lead writer for the Nazi weekly *Das Reich*. He was also paid for his regular radio broadcasts. His property portfolio included a house in Wilhelmstrasse in Berlin, upgraded by the City, a luxury villa at Schwaben and a castle near Bernau. Goebbels was one of Hitler's right-hand men who completely controlled and regulated art and culture in Germany. Firmly anti-Semitic, he was one of the main architects of the Final Solution.

4 ALFRED ROSENBERG: $5 MILLION

One of the main promoters of key Nazi ideological beliefs, Rosenberg was appointed editor of the *Völkischer Beobachter* in 1923 and his book *The Myth of the Twentieth Century* outlined National Socialist racial theories. He served as head of the party's foreign affairs department and as Reich Minister for the Occupied Eastern Territories. He played a significant role in the mass murder of the Jewish people in the east, as well as the deportation of civilians to forced labour camps to support the German war effort. Rosenberg established and headed the organization *Einsatzstab Reichsleiter Rosenberg*, the mission of which was to loot cultural property from all over Europe, giving him ample opportunities for self-enrichment. Rosenberg was hanged for his crimes on 16 October 1946.

5 ALBERT SPEER: $1.5 MILLION

Hitler's chief architect (1933–45) and Minister of Armaments and War Production (1942–5), Speer came up with plans to rebuild the whole of Berlin as the new world capital Germania (which were not realized) and designed the setting for the triumphant Nuremberg Party Congress of 1934. As Minister of Armaments, he expanded the system of slave labour, using inmates of concentration camps to maintain the production of war materials. Sentenced to 20 years in Spandau prison at the Nuremberg trials, he was released in 1966, after which he began a career as a writer. Speer always portrayed himself as the 'good Nazi', for example, denying any responsibility for the Holocaust. Subsequent research has revealed his ability to reinvent the past. Speer's building work made him one of the wealthiest of the Nazi elite – a fortune that was maintained by several best-selling books.

6 ADOLF EICHMANN: $1.1 MILLION

From a strongly nationalist family, the young Eichmann was enrolled in the *Wandervogel* (German youth group) by his accountant father, where he was imbued with *völkisch* ideas. Working in the oil industry for his father, he sold oil products and kerosene, identifying sites and organizing the setting up of petrol stations. He joined the Austrian Nazi Party in 1932 and got a job with the SS, working at Dachau. He then transferred to the Security Service (SD), where he built up a reputation for dealing with Jewish issues. He had developed high-quality organizational skills and used them, initially, to accelerate Jewish emigration, accessing money from rich Jews to fund the movement of poor Jews. Disposal by emigration soon morphed into disposal by murder – a task he undertook in the same businesslike manner as he set up petrol stations.

7 ROBERT LEY: $1 MILLION

The day after May Day 1933, a national holiday to celebrate German workers, Hitler ordered the SA to destroy the trade union movement. A new union, the German Labour Front (DAF), replaced it. New laws meant an end to collective bargaining and a strike ban, meaning that workers no longer had any voice in management. Hitler appointed Robert Ley, a well-known alcoholic, as head of the DAF. It was soon labelled the 'most corrupt of all the major institutions of the Third Reich'.[6] With 25 million members each paying dues of 1.5 per cent of their wages, the DAF took in some $160 million each year. As well as receiving salaries as head of the DAF, Reich Organization Leader of the Party, Reichstag deputy and as a Prussian State Councillor, Ley received royalties from Labour Front pamphlets and books that officials were asked to buy for distribution to the members. It is fair to say that Ley became very rich through his labours.

8 HERMANN GÖRING: $800,000

Göring held various high-ranking positions within the Nazi Party, including commander-in-chief of the Luftwaffe. Despite his influential role, which granted him access to vast resources and wealth during the war, Göring's net worth significantly diminished over time. His fortune was largely acquired through bribery and corruption, the syphoning off of government funds, his involvement in art looting, and other illicit activities. However, following his capture and subsequent trial, many of his assets were confiscated or lost.

9 REINHARD HEYDRICH: $700,000

Aryan, blond-haired and blue-eyed, Himmler was quick to employ Heydrich in his newly formed SS in 1931. He rose quickly through the ranks. As head of the Security Service and later the Gestapo, Heydrich developed a reputation for machine-like efficiency and unflinching cruelty. He was the chief enforcer of Nazi terror in Germany and played a leading role in the Night of the Long Knives in 1934, *Kristallnacht* in 1938 and the creation of the Einsatzgruppen before the invasion of Poland. At the Wannsee Conference, he announced his multi-tiered plan for the extermination of European Jews: work camps, deportation and death. In 1941, he added Reich Protector of Bohemia-Moravia to his job titles, and attempted to Germanize Czechoslovakia to make *Lebensraum* for a larger Germany. On 27 May 1942, however, his car was stopped on a hairpin turn in V Holešovičkách Street in Prague and he sustained shrapnel wounds from a grenade thrown at the car. He died of sepsis a week later. In revenge, a thousand Jews were arrested and sent to the camps. The following day, the village of Lidice, which the Gestapo wrongly identified as having helped the assailants, was erased from the face of the Earth: all men over the age of 16 were shot dead, all the women were sent to Ravensbrück and most of the children were deported to Chelmno. The village itself was burned and razed to the ground.

10 HEINRICH HIMMLER: $0

Himmler was creative, intelligent and a brutal, sociopathic sadist. Head of the Gestapo, the SS and also the architect of the concentration and death camps, Heinrich Himmler is listed here because he was different from his fellow Nazi leaders in that he was not interested in personal wealth. He was frugal and did not steal; anything stolen because of his actions went directly into SS coffers. He had his salary but little else. He lived in state residences and liked the cars and state benefits but when wanting to buy a home for his pregnant mistress, he had to negotiate an interest-free loan from the SS. He rented Wewelsburg Castle in Westphalia as a retreat for members of the SS at a cost of RM1 per year. He planned to have it expanded into a palace complex, setting up a concentration camp in the grounds to house the building workers, and decorate it with the Bayeux Tapestry.

Himmler was obsessed with race and the superiority of the Aryans. In a notorious speech he gave at Posen (now Poznań) in 1943, he said: 'One principle must be absolute for the SS man: we must be honest, decent, loyal and comradely to members of our own blood and to no one else. What happens to the Russians, what happens to the Czechs, is a matter of utter indifference to me… Whether or not 10,000 Russian women collapse from exhaustion while digging a tank ditch interests me only in so far as the tank ditch is completed for Germany.'[7]

THE BUNKERS

In 1936, a subterranean air-raid shelter was built some 1.5 m (5 ft) underneath the cellar of the new Reich Chancellery. The *Vorbunker* ('upper bunker', as it became known) was fitted out with living quarters, dormitories, a conference area, a kitchen, bathrooms and storerooms. In 1936, the bunker's roof was strengthened with a 1.6 m (5.3 ft)-thick layer of concrete to support the weight of a new reception hall-cum-ballroom that was added to the old Reich Chancellery building next door. In the 1940s, the Allied bombing campaign of Berlin prompted the construction of another, deeper shelter. The *Führerbunker* was built 8.5 m (28 ft) under the old Reich Chancellery garden. Completed in

Chapter 12

The rear of the Führerbunker in the garden behind the Reich Chancellery. The corpses of Hitler and Eva Braun were burned in a shell hole in from of the emergency exit (left). The conical structure (centre) served for ventilation and as a bomb shelter for the guards.

1943 at a cost of RM1.4 million, it was deep enough to withstand the biggest bombs the Allies were using. Entry to the *Führerbunker* was through the *Vorbunker*; the two were connected by a dog-leg staircase with gas-proof reinforced-steel doors at either end. Altogether, the bunkers contained about 30 rooms, with heating, water and electricity.

Following the failure of the Ardennes Offensive in January 1945, Hitler returned to Berlin in his private train, the *Führersonderzug*. A fleet of armoured Mercedes carried him and his staff through the bomb-damaged and deserted streets of the city, which confirmed the rapidly collapsing Third Reich. He continued to live – now with Eva Braun and his dog Blondi at his side – work and take meals in the Chancellery. Efforts were made to make the *Führerbunker* more comfortable, with carpets on the floor and art on the wall.

Hitler's staff were moved there in January. In February, Hitler moved to the bunker to sleep and in mid-March he shifted his headquarters underground. With military defeat now inevitable, the atmosphere inside was insufferable. The rooms throbbed 24 hours a day with the noise of aeration ventilators and the walls were damp because of the city's high groundwater level. Some of Hitler's staff described it as a 'fetid hole in the ground' and a 'concrete coffin'.[8]

THE BATTLE OF BERLIN

On 20 March Hitler left the bunker for the last time. Visibly shaking from Parkinson's disease, yellow-faced perhaps from jaundice and looking old and haggard, he presented medals to members of the Hitler Youth in the Chancellery garden. On 16 April, the Red Army commenced their operation to capture Berlin, with fierce fighting taking place on the Seelow Heights, the last significant German defences east of the city. Four days later, Hitler celebrated his 56th birthday. Various members of the Nazi leadership and his personal staff had assembled outside his room to congratulate him on his anniversary. Outside, they could hear the muffled sounds of Soviet artillery fire, which was now in range. Göring, Speer and others made their excuses and left as quickly as they could, anxious to leave the city before the roads were blocked.

On 22 April, the ever-faithful Joseph Goebbels and his family joined Hitler in the bunker. Hitler ordered SS-Obergruppenführer Felix Steiner's Panzer Corps to launch a counter-attack on Soviet forces north of the city. When he heard that the order had not been obeyed, Hitler's rage was such that after a screaming fit and complete mental collapse, he declared that the war was lost. After recovering himself, Hitler ordered his adjutant Julius Schaub to burn all the documents in his safes in the bunker and the Reich Chancellery. He also arranged for Schaub to access his safes in Munich and the Berghof and burn the documents in those too. Then Hitler ordered members of his personal staff to leave Berlin.

As the Soviet forces continued their advance and planned encirclement of the German capital, Hitler's last hope, a possible link-up of the 9th Army and General Wenck's 12th Army, did not happen. On 25 April, the Reich was

Chapter 12

On his last exit from the bunker, on 30 March 1945, Hitler shook hands and awarded medals to 20 members of the Hitler Youth, including 12-year-old Alfred Zech, given an Iron Cross, Second Class for bravery in the defence of Berlin.

cut in two as American and Soviet troops met at Torgau on the Elbe River. By 27 April, the city was completely surrounded and those in the bunker had lost radio communication with the outside world. They had to rely on the telephone network for news. By this time, Soviet troops had fought their way to Alexanderplatz in the centre of the city and were inching their way towards Potsdamer Platz, a few hundred yards from the bunkers.

On 28 April, two pieces of news were received at the *Führerbunker* that signalled the end was near. The first was that Mussolini and his wife Claretta Petacci had been executed by an Italian partisan. Their bodies were taken to Milan and hung upside down on a metal girder above a garage in one of the city's suburban squares. The second was that Heinrich Himmler had been attempting to hold peace negotiations with Western Allies. For Hitler, who always referred to Himmler as the 'most loyal of the faithful', this was the most shameful betrayal in all history. In another volcanic rage, he stripped his former colleague of all titles and powers. In addition, he summoned Himmler's representative in the bunker, Waffen-SS officer Hermann Fegelein – who was married to Eva Braun's sister Gretl – and ordered his execution. He was immediately taken to the Chancellery garden and shot. It is said that, at this point, abandoned by a trusted friend and determined not to share the same fate as Mussolini, Hitler decided to end his life. Eva Braun told him she would die alongside him.

THE END

In the night of 28–29 April, Hitler's 25-year-old secretary, Gertrude Junge (known as Traudl), knocked on the door of Hitler's study expecting to take tea with him, the other secretary Gerda Christian, and Hitler's cook Constanze Manziarly, as had become a nightly tradition. But instead, Hitler wanted her to take dictation. He began with his 'political testament', which Junge later described as the same 'explanations, accusations and demands that I, the German people and the whole world know already'.[9] He began to dictate his will moments later, in essence leaving his possessions, 'in so far as they are worth anything, to the party, or, if this no longer exists, to the State. If the State too is destroyed, there is no need for further instructions on my part'. He left his collection of paintings to the Linz gallery. He named Martin Bormann as executor, who was to ensure that his relatives, his wife's mother and his 'faithful fellow-workers of both sexes' were given 'anything which is of worth as a personal memento, or is necessary for maintaining their present standard of living'.[10] Junge typed up the documents, to which she was asked to add the names of the new government ministers, under Admiral Karl Dönitz, who would replace Hitler as Reich President. The documents were finished and signed at about 4 am with Goebbels and Bormann as witnesses for the party, Generals Burgdorf and Krebs for the army and Lieutenant Nicolaus von Below for the Luftwaffe.

Chapter 12

As Junge was typing, Hitler had summoned a loyal city administrator, Walter Wagner. He arrived around 1 am and Hitler asked him to officiate at a wedding ceremony in which he was to marry his long-term mistress, Eva Braun. Hitler was dressed in his usual uniform, Eva in a black silk taffeta dress. Formalities were brief: both declared that they were of pure Aryan descent and free from hereditary disease. Both gave their word-of-mouth assent to the union, and they were declared man and wife. Following the ceremony, the newlyweds shared the congratulations of Hitler's faithful secretaries, Gerda Christian and Gertrude Junge, Joseph Goebbels and others, and smiled and chatted while drinking champagne and thinking of happier times, before retiring.

The following day, with the sounds of Russian guns getting louder, an eyewitness reported that Hitler's SS bodyguards were feverishly destroying the last of Hitler's personal papers. Hitler's Alsatian dog Blondi was given a cyanide capsule, and Eva's dogs were shot by their keeper. In the afternoon, Hitler presented cyanide capsules to the rest of his staff, saying that he was sorry not to be giving them something more fitting and pointing out that if his generals had been as faithful to him as they had then the war might have had a different outcome. At around 2.30 on the morning of 30 April, Hitler emerged from his private quarters to say goodbye to his 30 or so staff and then retired to bed.

Later that morning, he received the regular military reports of the situation across Berlin. He sat down to lunch with his secretaries before ordering his adjutant to get hold of 200 litres (53 US gallons) of petrol. He went back to his quarters and emerged again with his new wife. Another farewell ceremony took place, this time with Martin Bormann, Joseph Goebbels and others. Eva embraced Junge and said, 'Take my fur coat as a memory. I always like well-dressed women.' Hitler then turned to address the little group for a final time. 'It is finished,' he said. 'Goodbye.'[11]

THE DEATH OF NAZISM

Hitler led Eva back into his study and closed the door at around 2.30 pm. Soon afterwards, a single shot was heard. A little while later, SS soldier Rochus

Misch and Hitler's valet Heinz Linge went into the room to see two bodies: Hitler's slumped on the table and Eva's with her knees drawn up lying next to him on the sofa. Eva had died from cyanide and Hitler had shot himself in the head. The two bodies were wrapped in blankets and carried upstairs to the Chancellery garden. They were laid side by side into a shallow shell crater, doused with litres and litres of petrol and then set alight. Watched by a crowd of SS men, Martin Bormann, Heinz Linge, Joseph Goebbels and a few others who raised their arms in a final Nazi salute, the bodies burned. As the afternoon wore on, more petrol was added to keep the pyre going, as was the bloodstained carpet from Hitler's study. By 6.30 pm the remains of the bodies were collected on a piece of canvas and were placed in a shallow grave, where they were discovered two days later by Soviet troops rummaging through the debris of the by-then destroyed Chancellery.

On the evening of 1 May, with Hitler's entourage mostly still in the bunker, the final act began. At about 8.40 pm, Magda Goebbels ordered Helmut Kunz, an SS dentist, to inject her children with morphine. Magda, who had intended to crush cyanide capsules in their mouths, found that she could not do it. Dr Stumpfegger, in the bunker as Hitler's personal surgeon, carried out the murder of daughters Helga (aged 12), Hildegard (aged 11), Holdine (aged eight), Hedwig (aged seven) and Heidrun (aged four) and son Helmut (aged nine) in the same fashion that their mother intended. Goebbels and his wife then went upstairs to the garden, where she took her cyanide tablets and he shot himself in the head. One of the bunker sentries was ordered to shoot him again just to make sure. The bodies were doused with petrol and set alight. However, there was not enough petrol remaining to completely incinerate the corpses, which were still recognizable the following day when the Soviet soldiers arrived and wanted confirmation of their identities.

With Hitler and Goebbels, the two most fanatical National Socialists, now dead, those remaining in the bunker made their attempts to escape the doomed city. Some did so successfully, but many did not. For Nazi Germany, the end came quickly. On 7 May, Colonel General Alfred Jodl, commander of the Wehrmacht, arrived in Reims, France, to sign the official instrument of surrender.

Afterword

When all was said and done, it is estimated that the Nazis spent some $270 billion on World War II. Adjusted for inflation to today's dollars, the war cost Germany over $4 trillion. If you were to add in the costs of the 14 other major players in the conflict, including the USA, Great Britain, France, the Soviet Union, Italy, Japan and so on, the total cost to the world came in at approximately $1,301 billion, more than $19 trillion in today's dollars. It remains the bloodiest, largest and most expensive war in human history.[1]

During its 12 years of existence, the success of Hitler's Third Reich depended wholly on finance and the economy. The major factors in the National Socialist Party's rise to power included dissatisfaction with the reparations imposed on Germany at Versailles, hyperinflation in the 1920s and the Wall Street Crash of 1929 – all grist to the Nazi propaganda machine mill. Once Hitler had secured his position as Führer, Germany quickly became a one-party state with the nation's finances under its control. In addition, monies came pouring into its coffers from executives of leading companies who, in exchange, stood to make millions from rearmament and the war economy. The National Socialist Party established a top-down command structure with leaders at every level, to which all 'Aryan' Germans were subject. The Nazi leaders – from the lowest- to the highest-ranking – comprised Thomas Kühne's 'huge criminal gang' that begged and stole from Germany and from its conquered territories with impunity.[2]

*

Of course, in war it is natural that a nation's companies and businesses get involved in the 'war effort'. Failing to do this would most likely lead to non-profitability and subsequent closure. In addition, the Nazi regime made it difficult for businesses not to support them, by unleashing a campaign of coercion and terror against its own citizens, in particular Jews, communists, Social Democrats, homosexuals, Gypsies, Sinti and supporters of the Catholic Centre Party. The campaign of violence and intimidation '… during the early months of 1933, was used deliberately and openly to intimidate opposition and potential opposition' and was enforced by some 2.5 million stormtroopers, who 'provided a ready reminder of what might be in store for anyone who stepped out of line'.[3] This level of intimidation, aimed mainly at the working classes, was accepted by the peasantry and the middle classes, partly because it was not directed at them. It was also hard for the ordinary German not to kowtow to the new regime because of their fear of the alternative – communism.

However, the finger of blame points clearly to the great majority of German businessmen, particularly the leaders of the larger companies, who were happy to vastly increase their profits by using forced and slave labour, the 'Aryanization' of Jewish property and the plundering of companies in Nazi-occupied Europe – irrespective of the immoral and murderous activities of the Nazi regime. Many of them were opportunists driven by greed, others by anti-Semitism, nationalism, patriotism and self-protection. Whatever the reason, however, in 1947 and 1948 dozens of executives of Krupp and Flick and board members of I.G. Farben were convicted of war crimes and crimes against humanity in the USA and imprisoned for their crimes. Interest in these prosecutions abated soon afterwards, however, as American attention turned towards the threat of Soviet communism.

But the past is not so easy to bury and discussions on the behaviour of German businesses during the Nazi regime have continued to this day. Some unscrupulous business leaders have been arrested, tried and imprisoned; others have been open and honest in admitting their guilt; still others have tried to defend themselves, claiming they had 'no choice' but to comply with the Nazi leaders. Since the unification of Germany in 1990, however, a new openness has developed and businesses including Krupp, Volkswagen, BMW, Daimler-Benz, Siemens, Deutsche Bank, Hugo Boss and others have admitted their Nazi ties and allowed researchers to study their archives. As a result of this loosening of

Afterword

the secrets, some surviving former forced or slave labourers or their families have brought lawsuits against various companies and, in some cases, received compensation – albeit rather meagre. The accompanying acrimony and the costs of such lawsuits have generally been unsatisfactory.

The situation has eased further in recent years, as companies have realized that admitting the truth of their Nazi past leads to good PR. Some companies, such as Volkswagen, have set up a 'foundation to pay former forced and slave labourers' compensation,[4] and there are a number of national compensation schemes in Germany, Austria, Switzerland, the Netherlands and France. In addition, even now, some 80 years after the war, investigations into the secrets of corporate complicity between German businesses and the Nazi regime are ongoing.

*

As the second quarter of the 21st century begins, the world is faced with other, new, perhaps even more serious crises than those that have gone before: climate change, financial inequality, inflation, food and water security, AI, pandemics, immigration, the rise of hatred and anti-Semitism, doubts about the effectiveness of democracy, and, of course, the inevitable current wars. Faced with these enormous and seemingly intractable problems we have come to something of a crossroads. While some people are celebrating the 80th anniversary of the liberation of Auschwitz and listening with solemn appreciation to the harrowing stories of the few remaining survivors, others are looking to populist right-wing politicians for easy answers to difficult problems. The echoes of the populism that brought Hitler to power in 1933 are growing louder, turned up by individuals, political parties and events in many parts of the world, a growing number of whom are using tactics and ideas taken directly from the Nazi playbook.

The rise of extreme right-wing politics is often accompanied by the scapegoating of immigrants, who are accused of 'poisoning the blood' of their own country or described as 'animals' or 'vermin' rather than human.

Afterword

In addition, the establishment of 'internment camps', crying 'fake news', the spreading of 'disinformation' and naked racism are all tactics that were used by the National Socialists in Germany a hundred years ago. The optics of these tactics today are worrying, and have prompted both an increase in the media's use of the word 'fascism' to describe a new style of authoritarian illiberal democracy, and discussion of a changing world order.

*

At this difficult point in world affairs, it is essential that we remember what happened in Germany in the 1930s when a mix of right-wing fascist ideology, populism, the scapegoating of minorities, money and power all combined in the hands of a charismatic leader ... with such disastrous consequences. In the words of 86-year-old Auschwitz survivor Tova Friedman, who spoke to assembled world leaders in front of the camp gates on 27 January 2025: 'We are here to proclaim that we can never, ever allow history to repeat itself.'[5]

Notes

Foreword

[1] James & Suzanne Pool: *Who Financed Hitler: The Secret Funding of Hitler's Rise to Power 1919–1933*, p. 6, M&J Raven, London, 1978.

[2] Adolf Hitler, *Mein Kampf*, Ralph Manheim Translation, 1999, p. 220, Internet Archive, archive.org

[3] Ibid, p. 221.

[4] Ibid, p. 222.

[5] Ibid, p. 222.

[6] 'Adolf Hitler's Last Birthday', Warfare History Network, April 2020, warfarehistorynetwork.com

[7] Tim Wickenden, 'A Tale of Two Boys', Slugado Press, 2021, timwickenden.com

[8] Ibid (see Adolf Hitler, note [2]), p. 369.

[9] Ibid (all quotes in para, see Adolf Hitler, note [2]), pp. 369–370.

Chapter 1: From Rags to Riches

[1] James & Suzanne Pool: *Who Financed Hitler: The Secret Funding of Hitler's Rise to Power 1919–1933*, p. 1, M&J Raven, London, 1978.

[2] Ibid, p. 8.

[3] Ian Kershaw, *Hitler 1889–1936: Hubris*, p. 138, Allen Lane, The Penguin Press, London, 1998.

[4] Adolf Hitler, *Mein Kampf*, Ralph Manheim Translation, 1999, pp. 59–62, Internet Archive, archive.org

[5] Spartacus Educational, 'On this day on 23rd March', spartacus-educational.com

[6] William Shirer, *The Rise and Fall of the Third Reich: A History of Nazi Germany*, p. 119, Baku State University, elibrary.bsu.edu.az

[7] Ibid (see James & Suzanne Pool, note [1]), p. 27.

[8] Ibid (see Adolf Hitler, note [4]), p. 496.

[9] Ibid (see Ian Kershaw, note [3]), p. 132.

[10] Ibid (see William Shirer, note [6]), p. 38.

[11] Ibid (see Adolf Hitler, note [4]), p. 505.

[12] Ibid (see James & Suzanne Pool, note [1]), p. 36.

[13] Ibid (see James & Suzanne Pool, note [1]), p. 39.

[14] Kurt G.W. Lüdecke, *I Knew Hitler: The Story of a Nazi Who Escaped the Blood Purge*, p. 23, Jarrolds, London, 1938, Internet Archive, archive.org

[15] Ibid (see James & Suzanne Pool, note [1]), p. 56.

[16] Richard J. Evans, *The Coming of the Third Reich*, Allen Lane, Penguin, London, 2003, p. 188.

[17] Ibid (see William Shirer, note [6]), p. 45.

Notes

Chapter 2: Respectability and Disgrace

[1] Ian Kershaw, *Hitler 1889–1936: Hubris*, Allen Lane, The Penguin Press, London, 1998, p. 192.

[2] Fritz Sternberg, *Capitalism and Socialism on Trial*, J. Day, New York, 1951, pp. 258–260. Internet Archive, archive.org

[3] James & Suzanne Pool, *Who Financed Hitler: The Secret Funding of Hitler's Rise to Power 1919–1933*, M&J Raven, London, 1978, p. 52.

[4] *Hitler's Table Talk, 1941–1944: His Private Conversations*, Trans. Norman Cameron and R.H. Stevens, Introduced and with a New Preface by H.R. Trevor-Roper, Enigma Books, New York City, p. 168. Internet Archive, ia601305.us.archive.org

[5] Ibid (see James and Suzanne Pool, note [3]), p. 71–72.

[6] Ibid, (see James and Suzanne Pool, note [3]), p. 72.

[7] Ibid, (see James and Suzanne Pool, note [3]), p. 69.

[8] Ibid (see Ian Kershaw, note [1]), p. 184.

[9] Kurt G.W. Lüdecke, *I Knew Hitler: The Story of a Nazi Who Escaped the Blood Purge*, p. 61, Jarrolds, London, 1938, Internet Archive, archive.org

[10] Ibid (see *Hitler's Table Talk*, note [4]), p. 281.

[11] (see Ian Kershaw, note [1]), p. 193.

[12] William Shirer, *The Rise and Fall of the Third Reich: A History of Nazi Germany*, p. 60, Baku State University, elibrary.bsu.edu.az

[13] Ibid (see *Hitler's Table Talk*, note [4]), p. 273.

[14] Ibid, p. 273.

[15] Ibid (see James and Suzanne Pool, note [3]), p. 75.

[16] Ibid (see William Shirer, note [12]), p. 63.

[17] Alan Bullock, *Hitler – A Study in Tyranny*, p. 83, Harper & Row, London, 1962.

[18] John Toland, *Adolf Hitler*, Wordsworth Editions, Ware, 1976, p. 130. Internet Archive, archive.org

[19] *Chicago Tribune*, '"Heinrich" Ford Idol of Bavaria Fascisti Chief', 7 March 1923, reddit.com

[20] Elisabetta Cassina Wolff, 'Both Mussolini's and Hitler's rise to power followed the rules of democracy', University of Oslo, Department of Archaeology, Conservation and History, 2022, hf.uio.no

[21] Ibid.

[22] Ibid (see Ian Kershaw, note [1]), p. 206.

[23] Ibid (see William Shirer, note [12]), p. 63.

Chapter 3: *Mein Kampf* and the Golden Years of Weimar

[1] James & Suzanne Pool, *Who Financed Hitler: The Secret Funding of Hitler's Rise to Power 1919–1933*, M&J Raven, London, 1978, p. 86.

Notes

[2] Albert Lee, *Henry Ford and the Jews*, Stein and Day, New York, 1980, pp. 13–14.

[3] Hasia Diner, *The Jews of the United States, 1654 to 2000*. Quoted in 'Ford's Anti-Semitism', The American Experience, pbs.org

[4] *Nuremberg Trial Proceedings, Vol. 14*, 23 May 1946, The Avalon Project, avalon.law.yale.edu

[5] Henry Ford, *The International Jew: The World's Foremost Problem*, ed. Gerald Smith, Los Angeles, 1964, p. 40

[6] Adolf Hitler, *Mein Kampf*, Ralph Manheim Translation, 1999, p. 56, Internet Archive, archive.org

[7] Edwin Gustav Pipp, *The Real Henry Ford*, p. 21, originally published in 1923, babel.hathitrust.org

[8] 'What started Mr Ford against the Jews?' *Pipp's Weekly*, 5 March 1921, pp. 2–3

[9] Max Wallace, *The American Axis, Henry Ford, Charles Lindbergh and the Rise of the Third Reich*, p. 65, St Martin's Press, New York, 2003.

[10] Ibid, pp. 67–68.

[11] Stefan Link, *'Rethinking the Ford-Nazi Connection'*, GHI Fellow in International Business History, Harvard University, 2010–11, zeithistorische-forschungen.de

[12] Gritschneder, *Bewährungsfrist*, citing comments made in 1988 by Alois Maria Ott, former Anstalts-Psychologe in Landsberg Prison (quoted in Ian Kershaw, *Hitler 1889–1936: Hubris*, Allen Lane, The Penguin Press, London, 1998, p. 214.

[13] Richard J. Evans, *The Coming of the Third Reich*, Allen Lane, Penguin, London, 2003, p. 195.

[14] Ellen Wexler, 'Before He Rose to Power, Adolf Hitler Staged a Coup and Went to Prison', *Smithsonian Magazine*, 8 November 2023, smithsonianmag.com

[15] David King, *The Trial of Adolf Hitler: The Beer Hall Putsch and the Rise of Nazi Germany*, Macmillan, London, 2017.

[16] Ibid (see Ellen Wexler, note [14]).

[17] William Shirer, *The Rise and Fall of the Third Reich: A History of Nazi Germany*, p. 72, Baku State University, elibrary.bsu.edu.az

[18] Ernst Hanfstaengl, *Hitler: The Missing Years*, Eyre and Spottiswoode, London, 1957, p. 96.

[19] Michael Haskew, 'Adolf Hitler's Time in Landsberg Prison', October 2010, warfarehistorynetwork.com

[20] Ibid (see Richard J. Evans, note [13]), p. 197.

[21] Ian Kershaw, *Hitler 1889–1936: Hubris*, Allen Lane, The Penguin Press, London, 1998, p. 240.

[22] Ibid (see Adolf Hitler, note [6]), p. 339.

[23] Ibid (see Ian Kershaw, note [21]), p. 243.

[24] Ibid (see Adolf Hitler, note [6]) p. 450.

[25] Ibid (see Richard J. Evans, note [13]), p. 198.

[26] Ibid (see Ian Kershaw, note [21]), p. 253.

[27] Pearl Buck, quoted in Adam Smith, 'Paper Money', *New York* magazine, mid-1960s, pbs.org

[28] Ibid (see William Shirer, note [17]), p. 104.

Chapter 4: Resurrection

[1] William Shirer, *The Rise and Fall of the Third Reich: A History of Nazi Germany*, p. 104, Baku State University, elibrary.bsu.edu.az

[2] Adolf Hitler, quoted in Peter Ross Range, 'How Adolf Hitler Turned a Year in Jail Into a Step Towards Power', *Time* magazine, 26 January 2016, time.com

[3] US Congress Senate Hearings, Kilgore Committee, *Elimination of German Resources for* War, 2 July 1945, p. 648, econoicsvoodoo.com

[4] Louis Snyder, quoted in 'The Bamberg Conference of 1926' by C.N. Trueman, History Learning Site, 8 January 2025, historylearningsite.co.uk

[5] Cris Whetton, *Hitler's Fortune*, Pen & Sword Military, Barnsley, South Yorkshire, 2004, p. 263.

[6] James & Suzanne Pool, *Who Financed Hitler: The Secret Funding of Hitler's Rise to Power 1919–1933*, M&J Raven, London, 1978, p. 138.

[7] Ian Kershaw, *Hitler 1889–1936: Hubris*, Allen Lane, The Penguin Press, London, 1998. p. 278.

[8] Uwe Klussmann, 'Conquering the Capital: The Ruthless Rise of the Nazis in Berlin', *Der Spiegel*, 29 November 2012, spiegel.de

[9] Richard J. Evans, *The Coming of the Third Reich*, Allen Lane, Penguin, London, 2003, p. 208.

[10] Andreas Jordan, 'Gelsenkirchen and Emil Kirdorf', Gelsen Center, Portal for Urban and Contemporary History, gelsenzentrum.de

[11] Munich Documentation Centre for the History of National Socialism (NS-Documentationszentrum München, NSDOKU), 'From the "Brown House" to the NSDOKU', nsdoku.de

[12] Dietrich Orlow, *The Nazi Party 1919–1945: A Complete History*, Enigma Books, New York, 2010, p. 131.

[13] Fritz Thyssen, *I Paid Hitler*, Hodder & Stoughton, London, 1941, p. 133, Internet Archive, ia800801.us.archive.org

[14] Carroll Quigley, Professor of IR at Georgetown University, quoted in Anthony Sutton, *Wall Street and the Rise of Hitler*, Clairview Books, London, 2010, p. 24.

[15] Carroll Quigley, *Tragedy and Hope*, The Macmillan Company, New York, 1966, p. 324, Internet Archive, archive.org

[16] US Congress Senate Hearings, Kilgore Committee, *Elimination of German Resources for War*, 2 July 1945, quoted in Antony Sutton, *Wall Street and the Rise of Hitler* (see note [14]), p. 1.

[17] James Steward Martin, *All Honourable Men*, Little Brown and Company, Boston, 1950, p. 70.

[18] Anthony Sutton, *Wall Street and the Rise of Hitler*, Clairview Books, London, 2010, p. 31.

Notes

Chapter 5: The Pendulum Swings

[1] William Shirer, *The Rise and Fall of the Third Reich: A History of Nazi Germany*, p. 136, Baku State University, elibrary.bsu.edu.az

[2] James & Suzanne Pool, *Who Financed Hitler: The Secret Funding of Hitler's Rise to Power 1919–1933*, p. 246, M&J Raven, London, 1978.

[3] Quoted in Ben Novak, 'The Problem with Hitler: The Man Nobody Knows', academia.com

[4] Cris Whetton, *Hitler's Fortune*, p. 198, Pen & Sword Military, Barnsley, South Yorkshire, 2004.

[5] Ian Kershaw, *Hitler 1889–1936: Hubris*, p. 307, Allen Lane, The Penguin Press, London, 1998.

[6] Ibid, p. 343.

[7] Ibid, p. 341.

[8] Otto Wagener, 'Hitler: Memoirs of a Confidant', Yale University Press, New Haven and London, 1978, Internet Archive, archive.org

[9] Richard J. Evans, *The Coming of the Third Reich*, Allen Lane, Penguin, London, 2003, p. 265.

[10] William Shirer, *The Rise and Fall of the Third Reich: A History of Nazi Germany*, p. 131, Baku State University, elibrary.bsu.edu.az

[11] Ibid, p. 132.

[12] Ibid, p. 140.

[13] Ibid, p. 142.

[14] Ibid, p. 143.

Chapter 6: Road to Power

[1] Richard J. Evans, *The Coming of the Third Reich*, p. 274, Allen Lane, Penguin, London, 2003.

[2] Larry Eugene Jones, 'Nationalists, Nazis, and the Assault against Weimar. Revisiting the Harzburg Rally of October 1931', Canisius University, Buffalo, New York, jstor.org/stable/27668122

[3] Heinrich Hoffmann, *Hitler was my Friend: The Memoirs of Hitler's Photographer*, pp. 64–65, Frontline Books, Pen & Sword, Barnsley, South Yorkshire.

[4] Fritz Thyssen, *I Paid Hitler*, p. 132, Hodder & Stoughton, London, 1941, p. 133, Internet Archive, ia800801.us.archive.org

[5] Otto Dietrich, *The Hitler I Knew: Memoirs of the Third Reich's Press Chief*, p. 141, Skyhorse Publishing, New York, 2014, Internet Archive, archive.org

[6] James & Suzanne Pool, *Who Financed Hitler: The Secret Funding of Hitler's Rise to Power 1919–1933*, p. 450, M&J Raven, London, 1978.

[7] William Shirer, *The Rise and Fall of the Third Reich: A History of Nazi Germany*, p. 177, Baku State University, elibrary.bsu.edu.az

[8] Ibid, p. 177.

[9] Ibid (see James & Suzanne Pool, note [6]), p. 466.

[10] (all three quotes in para) Ian Kershaw, *Hitler 1889–1936: Hubris*, p. 423, Allen Lane, The Penguin Press, London, 1998.

Notes

[11] Franz von Papen, quoted in 'The Rise of Hitler: Hitler Named Chancellor', The History Place, historyplace.com

Chapter 7: Masters of Germany

[1] Joseph Goebbels, *The Goebbels Diaries 1924–1941*, KG Saur Verlag, Ed. Elke Fröhlich, Munich, 1987.

[2] Melita Maschmann, *Account Rendered: A Dossier on My Former Self*, p. 11, Abelard-Schuman, London, New York, Toronto, 1964, Internet Archive, archive.org

[3] Max Liebermann, quoted in 'Hitler's Rise to Power', the Official Website of Berlin, berlin.de

[4] Ian Kershaw, *Hitler 1889–1936: Hubris*, p. 427, Allen Lane, The Penguin Press, London, 1998.

[5] Ibid (see Joseph Goebbels, note [1]).

[6] Cris Whetton, *Hitler's Fortune*, p. 293, Pen & Sword Military, Barnsley, South Yorkshire, 2004.

[7] William Shirer, *The Rise and Fall of the Third Reich: A History of Nazi Germany*, p. 190, Baku State University, elibrary.bsu.edu.az

[8] Ibid, p. 190.

[9] Eric Vuillard, *The Order of the Day*, Other Press, New York, 2018.

[10] Richard Bessel, 'The Nazi Capture of Power', *Journal of Contemporary History, 39*, April 2004, uksagepub.com

[11] Ibid (see William Shirer, note [7]), p. 192.

[12] Lorraine Boissoneault, 'The True Story of the Reichstag Fire and the Nazi Rise to Power', *Smithsonian Magazine*, 21 February 2017, smithsonianmag.com

[13] Ibid (see William Shirer, note [7]), p. 192–3.

[14] Ibid (quoted in William Shirer, note [7]), p. 193.

[15] Ibid (see Lorraine Boissoneault, note [12]).

[16] Richard J. Evans, *The Coming of the Third Reich*, p. 349, Allen Lane, Penguin, London, 2003.

[17] Ibid (see William Shirer, note [7]), p. 198.

[18] Adolf Hitler, '23 March 1933 Reichstag speech', Wikipedia, en.wikipedia.org

[19] Max Domarus, 'The Complete Hitler: A Digital Desktop Reference to His Speeches and Proclamations 1932–45' Volume 1. P. 285, Bolchazy-Carducci Publishers Inc, Wauconda, Illinois, 2007, Turkish Anti-Defamation Alliance, tadalliance.org

[20] Ibid (see William Shirer, note [7]), p. 199.

[21] Ibid (see Cris Whetton, note [6]), p. 346.

[22] Philip Slomovitz, 'Prof. Hale's "Captive Press in the Third Reich" Tells How Nazi's Made Shambles of Newspapers', *The Detroit Jewish News*, 24 July 1964, Michigan Daily Digital Archives, digital.bentley.umich.edu

Notes

[23] Frederick T. Birchall, Chief European Correspondent for *The New York Times*, in his introduction to Bella Fromm, *Blood and Banquets: A Berlin Social Diary*, Geoffrey Bles, London, 1949, p. 9.

[24] Ibid (see William Shirer, note [7]), p. 202.

[25] Ibid (see William Shirer, note [7]), p. 179.

[26] Ibid (see Cris Whetton, note [6]), p. 300.

[27] Ibid (see Joseph Goebbels, note [1]).

Chapter 8: Rearmament – The Big Guns Arrive

[1] 'German rearmament', Wikipedia, wikipedia.org

[2] Jeremy Noakes and Geoffrey Pridham, eds., *Nazism, 1919–1945, Vol. 3: Foreign Policy, War and Racial Extermination*, pp. 20–1, Exeter University Press, Exeter, Devon, UK, 2001 edition, Internet Archive, archive.org

[3] William Shirer, *The Rise and Fall of the Third Reich: A History of Nazi Germany*, p. 181, Baku State University, elibrary.bsu.edu.az

[4] Ibid, p. 210.

[5] Ibid, p. 210.

[6] Ian Kershaw, *Hitler 1889–1936: Hubris*, p. 445, Allen Lane, The Penguin Press, London, 1998.

[7] 'ThyssenKrupp AG', Britannica Money, britannica.com

[8] Michael J. Bazyler, *Nuremberg in America: Litigating the Holocaust in United States Courts*, 34 U. Rich, L. Rev 1, 2000, University of Richmond Law Review, scholarship.richmond.edu

[9] Frederic Eger, 'The Americans who Funded Hitler, Nazis, German economic miracle, and World War II', 2002, stoducu.com

[10] Ibid.

[11] Madeline Berg, 'More Than A Dozen European Billionaires–Linked to BMW, L'Oréal, Bosch–Have Families With Past Nazi Ties', *Forbes* magazine, 2019, forbes.com

Chapter 9: Blitzkrieg!

[1] Aaron O'Neill, 'Estimated share of German private capital owned by Jews 1937', statista.com

[2] Various, *Topography of Terror: A Documentation*, p. 61, Stiftung Topographie des Terrors, 2010.

[3] William Shirer, *The Rise and Fall of the Third Reich: A History of Nazi Germany*, p. 223, Baku State University, elibrary.bsu.edu.az

[4] 'Kristallnacht, Germany's "Night of Broken Glass"', American Experience, pbs.org

[5] Adolf Hitler, speech to Reichstag, 20 January 1939, 'Reichstag Speech, January 30 1939', United States Holocaust Memorial Museum, encyclopedia.ushmm.org

[6] Götz Aly, *Hitler's Beneficiaries: Plunder, Racial War, and the Nazi Welfare State*, ch. 2, Verso, London, New York, 2007.

[7] Ibid, ch. 7.

[8] Ibid, ch. 7.

[9] Daniel Miller, 'The Czech Republic', in Richard C. Frucht (ed.), *Eastern Europe: An Introduction to the People, Lands, and Culture*, ABC-CLIO, Santa Monica, pp. 203–283, 'Occupation of Czechoslovakia (1938–1945)', en.wikipedia.org

[10] Ibid (see Götz Aly, note [6]), ch. 6.

[11] Ibid (see Götz Aly, note [6]), ch. 7.

Chapter 10: Annihilation

[1] Richard J. Evans, *The Coming of the Third Reich*, p. 178, Allen Lane, Penguin, London, 2003.

[2] Crystal Rayle, 'Captives of Hell: The Treatment of Soviet Prisoners of War Captured by the Nazi Army 1941–1942, University of North Carolina at Greensboro, his.uncg.edu

[3] 'Nazi Persecution of Soviet Prisoners of War', United States Holocaust Memorial Museum, encyclopedia.ushmm.org

[4] Miklós Nyiszli, *I Was Doctor Mengele's Assistant: The Memoirs of an Auschwitz Physician*, p. 34, Frap Books, Kraków, 2010.

[5] Ibid, p. 34.

[6] 'The Technology of Mass Murder', Facing History and Ourselves, facinghistory.org

[7] 'Testimony of Crematorium Engineers', A Teacher's Guide to the Holocaust, quoted from the interrogation transcripts by Prof. Gerald Fleming from the University of Surrey, in a *New York Times* article, 18 July 1993, fcit.usf.edu

Chapter 11: A Huge Criminal Gang

[1] Thomas Kühne, 'Friendship into Comradeship. Gang Culture, Genocide, and Nation-Building in Germany 1914–1945', Clark University, Worcester, Massachusetts 2010, academia.com

[2] Ibid.

[3] Richard J. Evans, *The Third Reich in Power*, p. 329, Allen Lane, Penguin, London, 2006.

[4] Götz Aly, *Hitler's Beneficiaries: Plunder, Racial War, and the Nazi Welfare State*, ch. 2, Verso, London, New York, 2007.

[5] Ibid, ch. 2.

[6] Ibid, ch. 3.

[7] Ibid, ch. 3.

[8] Ibid, ch. 7.

[9] *History Notes, Nazi Gold: Information from the British Archives*, Issue 11, September 1996, Foreign and Commonwealth Office.

Chapter 12: The Nazi Rich List

[1] John Toland, *Adolf Hitler*, Wordsworth Editions, Ware, 1976, p. 460. Internet Archive, archive.org

[2] William Shirer, *The Rise and Fall of the Third Reich: A History of Nazi*

Notes

Germany, p. 190, Baku State University, elibrary.bsu.edu.az

[3] Cris Whetton, *Hitler's Fortune*, ch. 12, Pen & Sword Military, Barnsley, South Yorkshire, 2004.

[4] Ignatius Phayre, 'Hitler's Mountain Home', *Homes & Gardens*, 1938. This article was, in fact, fabricated by writer William Fitzgerald based on Nazi propaganda sources, using photographs taken by Heinrich Hoffmann. David S. Wyman Institute for Holocaust Studies, new.wymaninstitute.org

[5] Despina Stratigakos, 'Hitler at Home', *Places Journal*, 2015, quoted in 'Berghof (residence)', Wikipedia, en.wikipedia.org

[6] Richard Grunberger, *A Social History of the Third Reich*, Phoenix, London, 2005.

[7] Heinrich Himmler, 4 October 1943, quoted in 'Nuremberg Trials Project', Harvard Law School Library, Item No. 3941, nuremberg.law.harvard.edu

[8] Mark Felton, 'Hitler's Bunker: Then and Now', markfelton.co.uk

[9] Gertrude Junge, quoted in Greg Bradsher, 'Hitler's Final Words: His Political Testament, Personal Will, and Marriage Certificate: From the Bunker in Berlin to the National Archives', archives.gov

[10] Control Commission Intelligence Bureau, quoted in 'The Discovery of Hitler's Wills', 4.00 hours, 29 April 1945, pp. 4–5, eisenhowerlibrary.gov

[11] 'Hitler's Last Days', Security Service MI5, mi5.gov.uk

Afterword

[1] Figures taken from 'World War Two Financial Cost', Neera Sahni, Research Services Leader, City of Parramatta Research & Collections, historyandheritage.cityofparramatta.nsw.gov.au

[2] Thomas Kühne, 'Friendship into Comradeship. Gang Culture, Genocide, and Nation-Building in Germany 1914–1945', Clark University, Worcester, Massachusetts 2010, academia.com

[3] Richard J. Evans, 'Coercion and Consent in Nazi Germany', Raleigh Lecture on History, 24 May 2006, thebritishacademy.ac.uk

[4] S. Jonathan Wiesen, 'German Industry and the Third Reich', Anti-Defamation League, New York, 1 January 2000, adl.org

[5] Quoted in 'Eighty years after the liberation of Auschwitz…', Jon Henley, *The Guardian Weekly*, 31 January 2025.

Bibliography

BOOKS

Alan Bullock, *Hitler – A Study in Tyranny*, p. 83, Harper & Row, London, 1962.

Norman Cameron and R.H. Stevens (trans), *Hitler's Table Talk, 1941–1944: His Private Conversations*. Introduced and with a New Preface by H.R. Trevor-Roper, Enigma Books, New York City, Internet Archive, ia601305.us.archive.org

Hasia Diner, *The Jews of the United States*, 1654 to 2000. Quoted in 'Ford's Anti-Semitism', The American Experience, pbs.org

Richard J. Evans, *The Coming of the Third Reich*, Allen Lane, Penguin, London, 2003.

Henry Ford, *The International Jew: The World's Foremost Problem*, ed. Gerald Smith, Los Angeles, 1964.

Ernst Hanfstaengl, *Hitler: The Missing Years*, Eyre and Spottiswoode, London, 1957.

Adolf Hitler, *Mein Kampf*, Ralph Manheim Translation, 1999, Internet Archive, archive.org

'Adolf Hitler's Last Birthday', Warfare History Network, April 2020, warfarehistorynetwork.com

Ian Kershaw, *Hitler 1889–1936: Hubris*, Allen Lane, The Penguin Press, London, 1998.

David King, *The Trial of Adolf Hitler: The Beer Hall Putsch and the Rise of Nazi Germany*, Macmillan, London, 2017.

Albert Lee, *Henry Ford and the Jews*, Stein and Day, New York, 1980.

Kurt G.W. Lüdecke, *I Knew Hitler: The Story of a Nazi Who Escaped the Blood Purge*, Jarrolds, London, 1938, Internet Archive, archive.org

Bibliography

Nuremberg Trial Proceedings, Vol. 14, 23 May 1946, The Avalon Project, avalon.law.yale.edu

Edwin Gustav Pipp, *The Real Henry Ford*, p. 21, originally published in 1923, babel.hathitrust.org

James & Suzanne Pool: *Who Financed Hitler: The Secret Funding of Hitler's Rise to Power 1919–1933*, M&J Raven, London, 1978.

William Shirer, *The Rise and Fall of the Third Reich: A History of Nazi Germany*, Baku State University, elibrary.bsu.edu.az

Spartacus Educational, 'On this day on 23rd March', spartacus-educational.com

Fritz Sternberg, *Capitalism and Socialism on Trial*, J. Day, New York, 1951. Internet Archive, archive.org

John Toland, *Adolf Hitler*, Wordsworth Editions, Ware, 1976, p. 130. Internet Archive, archive.org

Max Wallace, *The American Axis, Henry Ford, Charles Lindbergh and the Rise of the Third Reich*, p. 65, St Martin's Press, New York, 2003.

Tim Wickenden, 'A Tale of Two Boys', Slugado Press, 2021, timwickenden.com

OTHER SOURCES

Chicago Tribune, '"Heinrich" Ford Idol of Bavaria Fascisti Chief', 7 March 1923, reddit.com

'What started Mr Ford against the Jews?' *Pipp's Weekly*, 5 March 1921, pp. 2–3

Stefan Link, 'Rethinking the Ford-Nazi Connection', GHI Fellow in International Business History, Harvard University, 2010–11, zeithistorische-forschungen.de

Bibliography

Elisabetta Cassina Wolff, 'Both Mussolini's and Hitler's rise to power followed the rules of democracy', University of Oslo, Department of Archaeology, Conservation and History, 2022, hf.uio.no

Ellen Wexler, 'Before He Rose to Power, Adolf Hitler Staged a Coup and Went to Prison', Smithsonian Magazine, 8 November 2023, smithsonianmag.com

Index

Adolf Hitler Spende 129, 130, 202–3
AEF 146
Amann, Max 22–3, 25, 54, 56, 58, 66, 130
Arenberg, Prince of 31
Auf gut Deutsch 15
August Wilhelm of Prussia, Prince 94
Auschwitz death camp 178–82, 184–6, 221
Austria 156–7, 159–60

Bechstein, Carl and Helene 18, 31
Beer Hall Putsch 44–6
Below, Nicolaus von 215
Belzec death camp 176
Beneš, Edvard 160
Berghof, The 204–7
Bierbaumer, Käthe 22
Bingel, Rudolf 141
Birchall, Frederick T. 130
Biskupsky, Vasily 32, 50
Blomberg, General von 115
Bormann, Martin 201–2, 204, 205, 206, 207, 215, 216, 217
Borsig, Ernst von 27, 48
Bosch 143–4
Bosch, Robert 144
Brasol, Boris 50
Braun, Angela 201
Braun, Eva 129, 201, 204, 206, 212, 216–17
Bruan, Gretl 204, 215
Braun, Paula 201

Braun, Gustav 185
Bruckmann, Elsa 31, 54
Bruckmann family 16, 26, 66, 72
Brüning, Heinrich 81, 83, 96, 99, 101, 106–7
Buchrucker, Major 41
Buck, Pearl 61
Bund Oberland 35, 39, 44, 48, 75
Burgdorf, General 215
Buttmann, Rudolph 66

Cameron, Bill 50
Chamberlain, Houston Stewart 22
Chamberlain, Neville 160
Christian, Gerda 215, 216
Cuno, Wilhelm 40, 98
Czechoslovakia 160–2, 193

Daladier, Édouard 160
Das Reich 208
Dawes, Charles 78
Dawes Plan 60–1, 64, 77–8, 146
Degano, Alois 205
Denmark 191
Der Stürmer 27
Deutsche Kampfbund 39–40, 45–6
Deutscher Volkswille 27
Dickel, Otto 24, 27
Diehen, August 98, 103
Dietrich, Joseph 90
Dietrich, Otto 105
Dinger, Artur 66

Dönitz, Karl 215
Drexler, Anton 7, 8, 13, 21, 22, 25, 66
DSP 23
Duesterberg, Theodor 105
Düsseldorf Industry Club 102

Eagle's Nest 206
Ebert, Friedrich 17, 67
Eckart, Dietrich 15–16, 18, 21, 22, 23, 25, 50, 204
Eher Verlag 21, 54, 56, 130, 203
Ehrhardt, Hermann 17, 20
Eichmann, Adolf 209
Einsatzgruppen 163, 167, 170, 210
Einsatzstab Reichsleiter Rosenberg (ERR) 196, 198, 208
Enabling Act 127–8
Epp, Ritter von 21
Erzberger, Matthias 20
Esser, Hermann 40, 52, 56, 66, 67, 70
Evans, Richard 53, 188

Feder, Gottfried 66
Fegelein, Hermann 215
Finck, August von 119
Fitz-Gerald, William 206
Flick, Friedrich 76, 92, 119
Ford, Edsel 120
Ford, Henry 41, 43, 48–51, 66
Foster, John 146

235

Index

Frank, Hans 24, 57, 96
Frank, Richard 35
Freikorps 13, 17, 20, 21, 46, 188
Frick, Frederick 104
Frick, Wilhelm 66, 115
Friedman, Tova 222
Führerbunker 211–13
Führermuseum 196, 198
Funk, Walther 97, 102, 103, 104, 113, 119, 192
Funk, Wilhelm 26

Gansser, Emil 23, 33
Gardner, Walter 120
German Big Business and the Rise of Hitler (Turner) 87
German-Racial Defence and Defiance League 18
German Workers' Community (DWG) 24
German Workers' Party 7–8, 9–10, 14
Gestapo 123, 152, 163, 169, 210, 211
Gobineau, Arthur de 22
Goebbels, Joseph 68, 70, 71, 72–3, 84, 85, 94, 112, 114, 117, 118, 121, 123, 124, 129, 130, 131, 135, 208, 213, 215, 216, 217
Goebbels, Magda 217
Göring, Hermann 32–3, 38, 45, 46, 72, 76–7, 91, 94, 97, 98, 104, 119, 120, 121, 123, 190, 196, 202, 206, 210, 213
Grandel, Gottfried 21
Grynszpan, Herschel 154
Gürtner, Franz 53

Hailer, Fritz 51
Hale, William Bayard 26, 41
Hammerstein, General von 134
Hanfstaengl, Ernst 'Putzi' 16, 25, 26, 31, 41, 46, 52, 54, 56, 66
Harrer, Karl 13
Harzburg rally 100–1
Haus Wachenfeld 204, 205
Havenstein, Rudolf 60
Heidrich, Reinhard 173
Heim, Heinrich 35
Held, Heinrich 65
Hermitage Museum 198
Hess, Rudolph 25, 56, 72, 76–7, 104, 135, 202
Heydrich, Reinhard 162, 163, 210
Hill, Frank 51
Himmler, Heinrich 95, 125, 141, 163, 166, 167, 176, 183, 211, 214–15
Hindenburg, Oskar 113
Hindenburg, President 83, 96, 99, 100, 101, 105, 110, 113, 114, 118, 123, 124, 125–7, 135
Hitler, Adolf
  joins German Workers' Party 7–8, 11
  last days of 8–9
  builds up German Workers' Party 9–10, 14
  oratory skills 14–16
  support from social elite of Munich 16–17
  creation of Nazi Party 16–17
  start of political career 18–19
  and formation of SA 20, 21
  fund-raising 23–4, 31–3, 86, 87
  sees off party revolt 24–5
  and Ruhr occupation 29–30
  growing influence 34–5
  and Nazi first rallies 36–7, 38–9
  and Deutsche Kampfbund 39–40
  foreign interest in 41, 43
  and Mussolini 43–4
  and Beer Hall Putsch 44–6
  and Erich Ludendorff 47–8
  and Henry Ford 49–51
  on trial 52–4
  in prison 54, 56
  writing of *Mein Kampf* 56–8, 204
  sales of *Mein Kampf* 58
  during the 'golden years' 61, 63, 64
  reasserts power over Nazi Party 65–71
  appeals to industrialists 74–5, 86–7, 91–2, 97–8, 101–4, 119–21
  and Fritz Thyssen 75–7
  on election campaigns 83–5
  popularity of 87–8
  self-belief 88–90
  and Geli Raubal 94–6
  at trial of army officers (1930) 96–7
  and Brüning government 99–100
  at Harzburg rally 100–1

236

Index

stands in 1932
  Presidential election
  104–5
and von Papen
  government 106–7,
  109
and Schleicher
  government 111–12
becomes Chancellor
  114–15, 117–18
and Reichstag fire 123
at opening of new
  Reichstag 126–7
and Enabling Act 127–8
growth of personal
  wealth 128–31, 207
and Adolf Hitler Spende
  129, 130, 202–3
rearmament plans 134–5,
  136, 137, 158, 188–9
view of the SA 135, 188
interest in cars 144
and Night of the Long
  Knives 152
orders *Kristallnacht* 154
and annexation of
  Czechoslovakia 160,
  161
interest in art 196, 202
death of 201–2, 217
property portfolio 204–7
last days in Berlin
  212–17
Hitler Youth 71, 88, 187
Hitler's Fortune (Whetton)
  32, 86
Hoffman, Heinrich 16, 40,
  52, 58, 65, 90, 102,
  129–30, 206
Holocaust, The 166–7,
  169–86

Hugenberg, Alfred 99,
  100–1, 104, 112, 115
Hurvitz, Shraga 170

I Paid Hitler (Thyssen) 77,
  103
I.G. Farben 78, 103, 119,
  120, 146, 183–5, 220
Illustrierter Beobachter 58
IKEA 148
International Jew, The
  (Ford) 49

Jacobsen, Lars 50–1
Jodl, Alfred 217
Junge, Gertrude (Traudl)
  215

Kaas, Ludwig 127
Kahr, Gustav Ritter von 20,
  24, 37, 44–5, 52, 65, 152
Kämpfer Verlag 92
Kamprad, Ingvar 148
Kantzow, Carin von 32–3
Kapp putsch 17, 18
Kapp, Wolfgang 17, 18
Kaufmann, Karl 70, 71
Keppler Circle 102–3
Keppler, Wilhelm 102
Kershaw, Ian 34, 37, 57,
  58, 88
Kiep, Louis 103
King, Richard 53
Kirdorf, Emil 67, 74–5, 77,
  97, 104, 119
Klintzich, Johann 21
Krebs, General 215
Kriebel, Oberstleutnant 39,
  44
Kristallnacht ('Night of
  Broken Glass') 155, 210

Krupp AG 66, 119, 120,
  133–4, 139, 189, 220
Krupp, Gustav 119, 121,
  129, 138, 139, 202
Kuhlo, Dr 35
Kühne, Thomas 187
Kunz, Helmut 217
Kunze, Dora 22

Landsberg prison 52, 54, 56
Lehmann, Julius F. 32
Ley, Robert 112, 131,
  209–10
Liebermann, Max 118
Liebold, Ernest G. 51
Linge, Heinz 217
Lithuania 170–1
L'Oréal 147
Lossow, General von 24, 37,
  38, 39, 40, 44, 45, 52
Lubbe, Marinus van der 123
Lüdecke, Kurt 26, 50, 52
Ludendorff, Erich 17, 33,
  39, 45–6, 47–8, 66, 67,
  75, 118
Ludwig Ferdinand of
  Bavaria, Prince 39
Lüttwitz, Walther 17
Lyttleton, Oliver 120

Majdanek death camp
  176–7, 185
Manziarly, Constanze 215
Martin, James Stewart 79
Maschmann, Melita 118
Maurice, Emil 95
Mauser 189
Mayr, Karl 18, 33
Mein Kampf
  on joining the German
  Workers' Party 7, 8, 11

Index

on building up German
  Workers' Party 9–10
on SA 21
writing of 56–8, 204
sales of 58, 86, 130, 193,
  203
on art 196
Mercedes 144–5
Merkers mine 194–5
Misch, Rochus 216–17
Monuments, Fine Arts
  and Archives programme
  (MFAA) 199
Morell, Dr 201
Müller, Hermann 133
Mussolini, Benito 43–4,
  201, 214
'My Political Awakening'
  (Drexler) 7, 8
*Myth of the Twentieth
  Century, The*
  (Rosenburg) 208

Nazi Party
  creation of 16–17
  and *Völkischer
    Beobachter* 21, 22
  funding for 23–4,
    25–7, 31–3, 35, 85–7,
    97–8, 101–4, 112–13,
    146
  first rally 36–7
  temporarily banned 52,
    54
  Hitler reasserts power
    over 65–71
  reorganization of 72–3
  resurgence in support 73,
    83–5, 87–8, 97, 108–9
  new headquarters 75–6
  ideological differences in
    94, 94

and 1932 elections 109
and 1933 election 124–5
Neithardt, Georg 53–4
Nevins, Allan 51
Nietzsche, Friedrich 22
Night of the Long Knives
  152, 210
Norman, Montagu 146, 147
Noske, Gustav 17
NS-Briefe 68

Olympia (film) 154
Olympic Games (1936)
  154
Opel, Wilhelm von 119
Ossietzky, Carl von 136

Papen, Franz von 106–8,
  109–10, 112–14, 115,
  123, 124, 125–6, 146
Petacci, Claretta 214
Pfeffer, Franz 70, 71, 89, 94
Pfordten, Theodor von der
  44
Pietsch, Albert 67
Pipp, Edwin 50, 51
Pittinger, Otto 34, 35
Poincaré Raymond 29
Poland 162–4, 173–5, 191
Pool, James and Suzanne
  50, 67–8
Porsche, Ferdinand 144
Prüfer, Kurt 185, 186

Quandt, Günther 119
Quigley, Carroll 78

Rath, Ernst vom 154–6
Rathenau, Walther 21
Raubal, Angela 205
Raubal, Geli 94–6, 152
Raubkunst 196–9

Rechtssicherheit 165
Reichsbank 60, 78, 91, 98,
  135, 137, 151, 157,
  190–1, 192, 194
Reichstag fire 121–3
Reichstag Fire Decree
  123–4
Reinhard, Fredrich 102
Reventlow, Ernst 23, 47
Reynolds, Rothay 41
Rhine Metal Company 189
Riefenstahl, Leni 153, 154
'Road to Resurgence, The'
  (Hitler) 74–5
Röhm, Ernst 13, 20, 35, 37,
  38, 39, 45, 66, 94, 97,
  135, 152
Romanov, Cyril 32
Romanov, Victoria 32
Roosevelt, Franklin D. 136
Rosenberg, Alfred 15, 22,
  25, 66, 196, 208
Rossbach, Gerhard 52
Rostberg, August 98, 103

SA
  formation of 20–1, 188
  and Beer Hall Putsch 44,
    45
  bans on 52, 105
  in street brawls 90–1,
    107, 121
  reorganization under
    Röhm 94
  growth of 104
  and Reichstag Fire
    Decree 124
  and 1933 election 124,
    125
Sander, Franz 185, 186

238

Index

Schacht, Hjalmar 60, 78, 91, 94, 98, 100, 101, 102, 119, 120, 135, 137, 139, 147, 156, 157
Schäffer, Councillor 38
Scheubner-Richter, Max Erwin von 26–7, 32, 44, 45–6
Schirach, Baldur von 49, 87–8
Schleicher, Kurt von 96, 97, 99, 106, 107, 109, 110–13, 114, 152
Schmitt, Kurt 119
Schnitzler, Georg von 97–8
Schröder, Admiral 23
Schröder, Kurt von 67, 102, 112, 113, 146
Schueller, Eugène 147
Schultze, Walter 46
Schulze, Karl 185, 186
Schwarz, Franz 85, 86, 201
Seeckt, Hans von 38, 40, 41, 100
Seidlitz, Georg von 16
Seidlitz, Gertrud von 16, 26, 31
Seisser, Hans von 44, 45, 52
Seldte, Franz 115
Shirer, William 16, 22, 27, 54, 83, 95, 112, 123, 131
Siemens 140–2, 146
Siemans, Hermann von 141
Škoda Works 148
Snyder, Louis 67
Sóbibor death camp 176
Soviet Union 169–74, 198, 199
Speer, Albert 206, 208–9, 213

SS
    first public appearance of 71
    Hitler as leader of 94
    bans on 105
    in street brawls 121
    and Night of the Long Knives 152
    in Poland 164
    and concentration camps 166
    and the Holocaust 169, 175, 181, 183, 184, 185
    and Merkers mine 194–5
Stangl, Franz 176
Stempfle, Bernhard 152
Stennes, Walter 23, 94
Stinnes, Hugo 47, 86
Strasser, Gregor 56, 66, 67, 68, 69, 70, 71, 72, 110, 111–12, 152
Strasser, Otto 92, 94
Strauss, Emil von 91, 104
Streicher, Julius 27, 56, 66
Stresemann, Gustav 40–1, 59–60
Stumpfegger, Dr 217
Sutton, Anthony 103
Swiss banks 193–4

Thälmann, Ernst 105
Theresienstadt Ghetto 162
Thule Society 11, 13, 18, 22, 24, 32, 72
Thyssen, Fritz 27, 47–8, 67, 75–7, 94, 97, 100, 102, 103, 120, 139–40
Topf, Ludwig 186
Topf and Sons 185–6
Troost, Gerdy 205

Truman-Smith, Captain 41
Turner, Henry Ashby 87, 128

United Steel Works 48, 76, 78, 97, 139–40

Vogler, Albert 67, 78, 97, 103, 119
Völkischer Beobachter 13, 21–3, 25–6, 32, 33, 34, 54, 56, 58, 87, 208
Volkswagen 144, 221

Wagemann Circle 103
Wagnemann, Ernst 103
Wagener, Otto 91, 94, 119
Wagner, Richard 31
Wagner, Siegfried 31, 66
Wagner, Walter 216
Wagner, Winifred 31, 66, 95
Wall Street Crash 79–81
Wall Street and the Rise of Hitler (Sutton) 103
Wannsee Conference 173
Warburg, Max 104
Warburg, Philip 120
Wartenburg, Yorck von 23
Wels, Otto 128
Whetton, Cris 32, 86
Who Financed Hitler (Pool & Pool) 50
Wolff, Elisabetta 43
Wolff, Otto 98
Wolfgang Ernst 186
Wolfgang Ludwig 186

Young, Owen 78
Young Plan 78, 101, 104, 146

239

Picture Credits

Alamy
12, 19, 34, 36, 69, 108, 132, 159, 163, 172

Auschwitz Museum
180

Getty
42, 59, 80, 89, 91, 102, 102, 111, 134, 138, 145, 153, 174, 178, 195, 197, 203, 214

Public domain
53, 55, 62, 63, 76, 93, 95, 102, 106, 106, 110, 122, 126, 138, 154, 205, 212